Conservation Refugees

Conservation Refugees

The Hundred-Year Conflict between Global
Conservation and Native Peoples

Mark Dowie

The MIT Press
Cambridge, Massachusetts
London, England

For information about special quantity discounts, please e-mail special_sales@ mitpress.mit.edu

This book was set in Sabon by SNP Best-set Typesetter Ltd., Hong Kong. Printed on recycled paper and bound in the United States of America.

Library of Congress Cataloging-in-Publication Data

Dowie, Mark.
Conservation Refugees : the hundred-year conflict between global conservation and native peoples / Mark Dowie.
   p.   cm.
Includes bibliographical references and index.
ISBN 978-0-262-01261-4 (hardcover : alk. paper)
1. Indigenous peoples—Ecology. 2. Conservation of natural resources—International cooperation. I. Title.
GF50.D69   2009
333.72—dc22

                                                                2008032743

10 9 8 7 6 5 4 3 2 1

To Blake and Madeleine

Contents

Preface

The challenge is not to preserve "the wild" but peoples' relationships with the wild.
—Bill Adams, Cambridge University

What you are about to read is a good guy vs. good guy story. The major contestants, transnational conservation and the worldwide movement of indigenous peoples, share a goal that is vital to all of us—a healthy and diverse biota. Both contestants are communities of integrity led by some of the most admirable, dedicated people in modern civilization. Both care deeply for the planet and together are capable of preserving more biological diversity than any other two institutions. Yet sadly, they have been terribly at odds with one another over the past century or more, violently so at times, due mostly to conflicting views of nature, radically different definitions of "wilderness," and profound misunderstandings of each other's perspectives on science and culture. The observed arrogance of transnational conservation is a confounding factor; so is the unfortunate but quite understandable tendency of native people to conflate conservation with other imperial forces. The result of this century-old conflict is thousands of unmanageable protected areas, and an intractable debate over who holds the key to successful conservation in the most biologically rich areas of the world.

Not everyone on either side of this issue will agree with the assertion that this is a good guy/good guy story. One peer reviewer said that it was instead "a story about a hegemonic form of nature protection in a post-colonial context and its effects on formerly colonized peoples . . . [and] about the complex struggles and interactions that take place in this context." That is also true. But as imperious as some post-colonial conservation leaders have been, their larger mission has been to protect endangered wildlife and biological diversity. Thus they should not be assigned the same "bad guy" status as "extractive corporados" and others who push native people around and compromise ecosystems in their avaricious quest for resources and profit.

I wrote this book with the hope that as conservationists and native people converge uneasily they can come to agreement that they both own the interdependent causes of biodiversity conservation and cultural survival, that they need each other badly, and that together they can create a new conservation paradigm that honors and respects the lifeways of people who have been living sustainably for generations on what can only be fairly regarded as their native land. And it is my hope that native people will blend their ancient traditional knowledge systems with the comparatively new sciences of ecology and conservation biology, in search of new and better ways to preserve the diversity of species that is not only vital to their own security but also to all life on Earth. At this point, as the entire planet seems poised to tip into ecological chaos, with almost forty thousand plant and animal species facing extinction[1] and 60 percent of the ecosystem services that support life on Earth failing,[2] there may be no other way.

A Word about Terms

ill'-a-hee: earth, ground, land, country, place, or world.
—Chinook

Conservation: con·ser·va·tion n. 1. the preservation, management, and care of natural and cultural resources. 2. the keeping or protecting of something from change, loss, or damage.[1]

Until the latter part of the twentieth century, conservation tended to focus on the protection of so-called flagship species (also known as "charismatic megafauna")—lions, tigers, elephants, rhinos, pandas, and polar bears—and their particular habitats. However, the emerging science of conservation biology gradually forced organized conservation into a new strategy that called for the protection of biological diversity wherever it thrived. Unless I state otherwise, assume the latter meaning.

Western and *Northern* I use interchangeably to describe people, organizations, values, sciences, ideas, or institutions that are based either in Europe or North America.

Racism In the spirit of show-don't-tell, I do not use the word anywhere in this book. I really didn't need to. The incidents I describe speak for themselves, as does the fact that close to 100 percent of the people who have been evicted from homelands in the interest of conservation have been people of color. The unspoken (and rarely written) rationale for this policy is a certainty that European and American (i.e., *Northern*) science-based conservationists naturally understand the tenets of conservation, while primitive aboriginals do not. I should also make it clear at the outset that I do not consider any Northern conservation leaders to be racist, or believe that racist outcomes are always the result of racist intentions.

Imperial   I have been chastised, and will be again, for using this term to describe transnational conservation at any stage of its history. I fully admit that applying it to contemporary conservation leadership is much less appropriate than it was a century or even two decades ago. But what else to call half a dozen northern hemispheric organizations, with combined assets equal to the GNP of many countries, and strong ties to neoliberal industries and institutions, whose representatives travel about the world imposing a conservation paradigm that all too often deprives native people of their land and livelihoods?

Indigenous   This is the tough one. The central issue for indigenous peoples is recognition, and recognition depends partly on the definition of indigeneity. There is no legal definition of indigenous peoples, partly because there is no legal recognition of the word *peoples*.

Some Africans say that all black Africans are indigenous to Africa, so there is no point in differentiating between Batwa and Bantu, Basarwa and Tswana. The government of Botswana in fact has officially declared that all of its citizens are indigenous—from the ancient Basarwa Bushmen who arrived there some twenty thousand years ago to the most recently settled colonist. By contrast, Richard Leakey insists there are no indigenous people in Kenya. Are the Karen, Hmong, Akha, and other hill tribes of Southeast Asia indigenous to Burma, Thailand, and Laos or to Yunnan, China from where they migrated a few hundred years ago? To where are the Maasai, Qashqui, Bakhtiari, or the Tuareg pastorals indigenous?

The International Labor Organization's Convention 169 defines indigenous peoples as "tribal peoples in independent countries whose social, cultural and economic conditions distinguish them from other sections of the national community, and whose status is regulated wholly or partially by their own customs or traditions or by special laws or regulations." One problem with that definition is that many ethnic groups in Africa reject the term *tribal* when used to define them.

The International Work Group for Indigenous Affairs rejects all definitions. "We assert our inherent right to define who we are. We do not approve of any other definition," reads their official statement on the matter.

Since there is so much confusion about who is and who is not indigenous, for the purpose of this text I am using the following definition: A people are indigenous to an area if they occupied the land where they reside, or in the case of pastoral nomadics, if they grazed their livestock through a region before the particular area in question was absorbed by the nation-state or states within which it now exists.[2]

Introduction: "Enemies of Conservation"

First we were dispossessed in the name of kings and emperors, later in the name of state development, and now in the name of conservation.

—Indigenous delegates to the Fifth World Parks Congress, Durban, South Africa, 2003

Against the wall of a large meeting room in Bangkok, Thailand, packed with committed environmentalists, stands Martin Saning'o. The Maasai leader from Tanzania listens intently to a panel discussion of the human factor in conservation, and patiently awaits an invitation to comment. He stands out as the only black man in the room. When his turn comes Saning'o speaks softly in slightly accented but perfect English, describing how nomadic pastoralists once protected the vast range in eastern Africa that they have lost over the past century to conservation projects.

"Our ways of farming pollinated diverse seed species and maintained corridors between ecosystems," he explains to an audience he knows to be schooled in Western ecological sciences. Yet, in the interest of a relatively new vogue in conservation called "biodiversity,"[1] he tells them, more than one hundred thousand Maasai pastoralists have been displaced from their traditional homeland, which once ranged from what is now northern Kenya to the savannah grasslands of the Serengeti plains in northern Tanzania. They called it Maasailand. "We were the original conservationists," Saning'o tells the room full of shocked white faces. "Now you have made us enemies of conservation."

This was not what six thousand wildlife biologists and conservation activists from over one hundred countries had traveled to Bangkok to hear. They were there at the Third Congress of the World Conservation Union (also known as the International Union for the Conservation of Nature [IUCN]) to explore new ways to stem the troubling loss of biological diversity on an ecologically challenged planet.

Based in Gland, Switzerland, IUCN is an assembly of 77 states, 114 government agencies, innumerable conservation NGOs, and over 10,000 scientists, lawyers, educators, and corporate executives from 181 countries. The ICUN's mission is "to influence, encourage and assist societies throughout the world to conserve the integrity and diversity of nature and to assure that any use of natural resources is equitable and ecologically sustainable." To those who believe that ecological health trumps all other measurements of human security, IUCN stands among the most important international organizations in the world.

What drew Martin Saning'o and about four hundred other indigenous people to the November 2004 gathering was the congress's theme— "People and Nature—Only One World." It was not a title that all members of IUCN would have chosen, as there remains in that community a fair number of traditional conservationists who define wilderness as the U.S. Wilderness Act of 1964 does: "an area where the earth and its community of life are untrammeled by man, where man himself is a visitor who does not remain." It is a definition that expresses itself through a practice known in the field as "fortress conservation," wherein areas designated for conservation protection are bordered and guarded to keep wildlife in and unwanted humans out.

However, the word *People* in the conference theme was a long-awaited indication to Indians, pastoralists, bushmen, aboriginals, and forest dwellers on every continent that international conservation groups were reconsidering fortress conservation and trying a little harder to understand the historical role that most native peoples have played in stewarding the very ecosystems being selected for protection.

This was not the first foray of indigenous peoples into the elite and well-endowed world of global conservation. For a quarter of a century their leaders have been traveling thousands of miles to conservation, national park, and wilderness conventions around the world. The message they bring is clear and simple: "We have proven ourselves good stewards, otherwise you wouldn't have selected our land for conservation. Let us stay where our ancestors are buried and we will help you preserve the biological diversity we all treasure."

Here in Bangkok, in one thematic word, was a sign that their message was getting through—although not to everyone. There remain skeptics, and holdouts for that model of exclusionary conservation invented in the United States more than a century ago that spread gradually to every continent on the planet, and they were in Bangkok in force. This factor only heightened the congress as an opportunity not to be missed. In Bangkok native people from every continent found the largest gathering ever of scientists, activists, bureaucrats, donors, and bankers, many representing organizations that for more than a century had pretty much excluded tribal people from the conservation planning process. It was Martin Saning'o's moment. But it wasn't the first time he had traveled thousands of miles from his homeland in the Serengeti to watch indigenous peoples confront organized conservation, nor would it be the last.

The Beat Goes On

Every form of refuge has its price.
—Don Henley and Glenn Frey, The Eagles

In early 2004, a United Nations meeting was convened for the ninth year in a row to push for passage of a resolution protecting the territorial and human rights of indigenous peoples. The UN Draft Declaration on the Rights of Indigenous Peoples read in part, "Indigenous peoples shall not be forcibly removed from their lands or territories. No relocation shall take place without the free and informed consent of the indigenous peoples concerned and after agreement on just and fair compensation, and where possible, with the option to return."

During the meeting, one indigenous delegate rose to state that extractive industries, while still a serious threat to their welfare and cultural integrity, were no longer the main antagonist of indigenous cultures. Their new and biggest enemy, she said, was "conservation." Later that spring, at a meeting in Vancouver, British Columbia, of the International Forum on Indigenous Mapping, all two hundred delegates signed a declaration stating that "conservation has become the number one threat to indigenous territories."

A year later, the International Land Coalition (ILC) added "conservation" to its list of factors that were "negatively affecting" landless people, alongside "extractive industries" and "tourism." ILC later identified conservation as one of five threats to common-property regimes and condemned the "appropriation of common property for conservation."

Then in February 2008, representatives of the International Indigenous Forum on Biodiversity (IIFB) walked out of a Convention on Biological Diversity (CBD) annual meeting, unanimously condemning CBD (of which IIFB had been a formally recognized member since 1996) for ignoring their recommendations and interests. "We found ourselves marginalized and without opportunity to take the floor and express our views," read their statement. "None of our recommendations were included in [the meeting's report]. So we have decided to leave this process which clearly does not respect our rights and participation."[2]

These are all rhetorical jabs, of course, and perhaps not entirely accurate or fair. But they have shaken the international conservation community, as have a subsequent spate of critical studies and articles calling international conservationists to task for their historical mistreatment of indigenous peoples.

Transnational conservation's threat to indigenous land and lifeways has been an increasingly prominent theme at international conventions like the Earth Summit in Rio de Janiero, Brazil; the Convention on Biological Diversity; previous IUCN meetings in Caracas, Montreal, and Amman; and more recently at the World Parks Conference held in Durban, South Africa, in September 2003 where Nelson Mandela pled with conservationists not to "turn their backs" on rural economies, and to treat indigenous peoples more fairly in the course of creating new parks and game reserves.

Mandela was followed on the podium by his political protégé and successor, South African President Thabo Mbeki, who warned that "mere exhortations to poor people to value and respect the ecosystems contained within national parks will not succeed. It is critically important that alternative means of livelihood be found for the poor of the world, so that they are not forced to act in a manner that undermines the global effort to protect these ecosystems, driven by hunger and underdevelopment." To that Mandela added: "I see no future for parks, unless they address the needs of communities as equal partners in their development."

Mandela and Mbeki were bearing witness to an African conflict that had over the previous century poisoned relations between international conservationists and natives of the continent. It was in large measure symptomatic of a larger global conflict between science-based and rights-based conservation. Here is how Roderick Neumann, associate professor of international relations at Florida International University, describes the African conflict: "From the perspective of park officials and wildlife conservationist, the conflict is defined by livestock trespass, illegal hunting, wood theft, and consequent ecological costs such as species extirpation. For local communities the conflict revolves around reduced access to ancestral lands, restrictions on customary resource uses, and the predation of wildlife on cultivated lands."[3]

The discord between indigenous communities and "big conservation," which subsided for a while as the indigenous movement gained strength and volume through the 1980s, is heating up again as the once-dominant force of science-based conservation reemerges in the world. However, there remain some promising signs of peace and reconciliation, as conservation intellectuals like Kent Redford and Steven Sanderson, who for years sought to distance themselves from the social consequences of "fortress conservation," have come to see the folly of evicting people from protected areas,[4] and the worldwide indigenous rights movement has become more sophisticated about the use of international law.

In the chapters that follow I describe the direct experience of the following peoples with transnational conservation:

- The Miwok, Paiute, and Ahwahneechee of Yosemite Valley
- The Maasai of Eastern Africa
- The Pygmies of Uganda and Central Africa
- The Karen of Thailand
- The Adevasi of India
- The Basarwa of Botswana
- The Ogiek of Kenya

- The Kayapo of Brazil
- The Mursi of Ethiopia
- The Babongo, Bakoya, Baka, Barimba, Bagama, Kouyi, and Akoa of Gabon

Their stories differ in many ways, particularly in how they responded to the tendency of conservationists to ignore their basic rights, at times their very existence, in the course of protecting biological diversity. Some have failed and others succeeded in retaining land tenure, negotiating as equal players, and convincing modern, science-based conservationists of the strength and reliability of traditional ecological knowledge.

The Protected Area Strategy

This is the perfect place for us, which is why the Creator put us here, these few of us, and made us tough enough to stay.
—Upik elder

The central strategy of transnational conservation relies largely on the creation of so-called protected areas (PAs). There are several categories of PAs ranging from rigid exclusionary "wilderness" zones, off limits to all but a few park guards and an occasional scientist, to community-conserved areas (CCAs) initiated and managed by a local population. While the categories vary widely in style and purpose, the essential goal of all of them is the same: protect and preserve biological diversity.

From 1900 to 1950, about six hundred official protected areas were created worldwide. By 1960 there were almost a thousand. Today there are at least one-hundred-and-ten thousand, with more being added every month. The size and number of PAs are a common benchmark for measuring the success of global conservation.

The total area of land now under conservation protection worldwide has doubled since 1990, when the World Parks Commission set a goal of protecting 10 percent of the planet's surface. That goal has been exceeded, as over 12 percent of all land, a total area of 11.75 million square miles (18.8 million square kilometers) is now under conservation protection. That's an area greater than the entire landmass of Africa and equal to half the planet's endowment of cultivated land. At first glance, such a degree of land conservation seems undeniably good, an enormous achievement of very good people doing the right thing for our planet. But the record is less impressive when the social, economic, and cultural impact on local people is considered.

About half the land selected for protection by the global conservation establishment over the past century was either occupied or regularly used by indigenous peoples. In the Americas that number is over 80 percent. In Guyana, for example, of the ten new areas gazetted for protection, native people currently occupy eight. However the most recent and rapid expansion of protected area initiatives has occurred in Africa and Asia.

During the 1990s, the African nation of Chad increased its protected area from 1 to 9.1 percent of its national land. All of that land had been occupied by what are now an estimated six hundred thousand displaced people. No country I could find beside Chad and India, which officially admits to about one hundred thousand people displaced for conservation (a number that is almost certainly deflated) is even counting this growing new class of refugee. And existing quantitative studies of conservation evictions covered but a few hundred of the tens of thousands of enclosed parks and refuges, like Yosemite National Park, where human settlements once existed.[5] Thus world estimates range widely from five million to tens of millions of refugees created since Yosemite Valley was gazetted for protection in 1864.

Charles Geisler, a rural sociologist at Cornell University who has been studying the problem for decades believes that since the beginning of the colonial era in Africa there could have been as many as fourteen million evictions on that continent alone. The true figure, if it were ever known, would depend on the semantics of words like *eviction*, *displacement*, and *refugee*, over which parties on all sides of the issue argue endlessly. However, the point at issue is not the exact number of people who have lost their homeland to conservation, it is that conservation refugees, however defined, exist in large numbers on every continent but Antarctica, and by most accounts live far more difficult lives than they once did, banished from lands they thrived on, often for thousands of years, in ways that even some of the conservationists who looked aside while evictions took place have since admitted were sustainable.

Not to be confused with ecological refugees—people forced to abandon once-sustainable settlements because of unbearable heat, drought, desertification, flooding, disease, or other consequences of climate chaos—conservation refugees are removed from their homelands involuntarily, either by force or through a variety of less coercive measures. They have come to call the gentler, more benign methods of displacement "soft evictions," which they claim are as bad as the "hard" ones. "If you allow people to stay on land without the right to use it," said Cherokee leader Rebecca Adamson, "you might as well have taken their land from them. It's as bad as outright eviction."

Soft or hard, the common complaint heard at one international meeting after another is that relocation so often occurs with the tacit approval of one or more of five largest conservation organizations—Conservation International (CI), The Nature Conservancy (TNC), the Worldwide Fund for Nature (WWF), the African Wildlife Foundation (AWF), and the Wildlife Conservation Society (WCS)—which collectively have been affectionately nicknamed the "BINGOs" (Big International NGOs) by indigenous leaders.

The rationale for "internal displacements," as these evictions are officially called, usually involves a perceived threat to the biological diversity of a larger geographical area, variously designated by one or more BINGO as an "ecological hot spot,"[6] an "ecoregion," a "vulnerable ecosystem," a "biological corridor," or a "living landscape"—alternatives for categorizing what each organization hopes will be designated a protected area by the government of its host country.

The huge parks and reserves created in this fashion occasionally involve a debt-for-nature swap (some national debt paid off or retired in exchange for a parcel of sensitive land) or similar financial incentive provided by the Global Environment Facility (GEF) and one or more of its eight "Executing Agencies" (bilateral and multilateral banks), combined with an offer made by the funding organization to pay for the management of the park or reserve. Broad rules for human use and habitation of the protected area are set and enforced by the host nation, often following the advice and counsel of a BINGO, which might even be given management powers over the area through a World Bank- or GEF-funded contract.

In countries where evictions from ancestral homelands are illegal or otherwise unfeasible, the process is often sanitized by terms such as *voluntary relocation*, or veiled behind a so-called *co-management* project where a government imposes strict livelihood restrictions (e.g., no hunting, fishing, gathering of certain plants, agricalatural practices) to be enforced by a BINGO. Inducements are offered to refugees, often involving promises of compensation that are all too frequently unfulfilled or inadequate.

Until quite recently, most conservation leaders responded to the injustices of exclusion by denying they were party to it while generating unapologetic and defensive promotional material about their affection for and close relationships with indigenous peoples. That message was carefully projected toward a confused and nervous funding community, which has expanded in recent years beyond the individuals and family foundations that seeded early global conservation organizations, to include very large foundations like Ford, Packard, McArthur and Gordon and Betty Moore, as well as international financial institutions like the World Bank, the Global Environmental Fund, foreign governments, United States Agency for International Development (USAID), a host of bilateral and multilateral banks, and, most recently, transnational corporations. All but the latter have expressed concerns about the uneasy relationship between native people and transnational conservation, and have begun to insist on fairer treatment of native people who happen to be living in high biodiversity areas.

International funding agencies dedicate the equivalent of billions of dollars every year to land and wildlife conservation. The five largest conservation organizations absorb about 70 percent of that expenditure. The rest is scattered among thousands of local conservation NGOs, many of them created by the larger organizations when funders insist some money be regranted to local groups. Indigenous communities receive virtually none of it.

With that kind of financial leverage, five Euro-American nongovernmental organizations—the BINGOs, with chapters in almost every country of the world, strong connections to business and political leaders, millions of loyal members, and nine-figure budgets—have assumed enormous influence over the world's conservation agenda.

Commitment to People

Conservation will either contribute to solving the problems of the rural people who live day to day with wild animals, or those animals will disappear.
—Jonathan Adams and Thomas McShane, Worldwide Fund for Nature

All of the BINGOs and most of the international agencies they work with have issued formal and heartfelt declarations in support of indigenous peoples and their territorial rights.

The Nature Conservancy's "Commitment to People" statement states that "we respect the needs of local communities by developing ways to conserve biological diversity while at the same time enabling humans to live productively and sustainably on the landscape."

After endorsing the UN Draft Declaration on the Rights of Indigenous Peoples, the World Wildlife Fund International (WWF-I) adopted its own Statement of Principles upholding the rights of indigenous peoples to own, manage, and control their lands and territories (see appendix A for the full text). Shortly thereafter, the World Wildlife Fund United States (WWF-US) approved and adopted the principles.

In 1999 the IUCN's World Commission on Protected Areas formally recognized indigenous peoples' rights to "sustainable traditional use" of their lands and territories. The following year the IUCN adopted a bold set of principles for establishing protected areas, which state unequivocally, "The establishment of new protected areas on indigenous and other traditional peoples' terrestrial, coastal/marine and freshwater domains should be based on the legal recognition of collective rights of communities living within them to the lands, territories, waters, coastal seas and other resources they traditionally own or otherwise occupy or use."

Of course the UN draft declaration on indigenous rights became the prize, because it had to be ratified by so many nations, and because unlike the International Labor Organization, the Convention on Biological Diversity, and other international bodies that have weighed into this issue on behalf of indigenous peoples, the draft declaration has behind it the potential enforcement and sanction powers of the United Nations. Almost two decades after it was first proposed, the strongly worded

declaration was approved in 2007 by the UN Human Rights Commission in Geneva and two months later by the UN General Assembly.

Tribal people, who tend to think and plan in generations rather than weeks, months, and years, patiently await the consideration promised in these thoughtful declarations and pronouncements. Meanwhile, the human rights and global conservation communities remain at serious odds over the question of displacement, each side blaming the other for the particular crisis they perceive. Conservation biologists, many of whom still maintain that humans and wilderness are inherently incompatible, argue that by allowing native populations to grow, hunt, and gather in protected areas, their supporters become agents in the decline of biological diversity. Some, like legendary paleontologist Richard Leakey, maintain "the entire issue" of protected areas "has been politicized by a vociferous minority that refuses to join the mainstream."[7] Others, like the Wildlife Conservation Society's outspoken president Steven Sanderson, believed for some time that the entire global conservation agenda had been "hijacked" by advocates for indigenous peoples, placing wildlife and biodiversity at peril.

In contrast, human rights groups such as Cultural Survival, First Peoples Worldwide, Earthrights International, Survival International, and the Forest Peoples Programme accuse the BINGOs of complicity in destroying indigenous cultures, the diversity of which they argue is essential to the preservation of biological diversity.

Meanwhile, the public-relations spin placed on "market solutions" to this unfortunate divide has been relentless and misleading. BINGOs promote cooperative management plans, ecotourism, bioprospecting, extractive reserves, and industrial partnerships that involve such activities as harvesting nuts for Ben and Jerry's Ice Cream or plant oils for The Body Shop products as the best way to protect land and community with a single program. Websites and annual reports feature stunning photographs of native people harvesting fair-trade coffee, Brazil nuts, and medicinal plants. But few native names or faces can be found on the boards of the BINGOs, which have become increasingly corporate in recent years.

Market-based solutions, which may have been implemented with the best of social and conservational intentions, share a lamentable outcome,

barely discernible behind a smokescreen of slick promotion. In almost every case, indigenous people are moved into the lowest end of the money economy, where they tend to be permanently indentured as park rangers (never wardens), porters, waiters, harvesters, or, if they manage to learn a European language, ecotour guides. Under this model, "conservation" becomes "development," and native communities are assimilated into national cultures.

Assimilation invariably means taking a permanent place in society at the bottom of the ladder. Whole societies like the Batwa of Uganda, the Basarwa of Botswana, the Maasai and Ogiek of Kenya, the Mursi of Ethiopia, the Karen and Hmong of Southeast Asia, and the Ashinika of Peru are transformed from independent and self-sustaining to deeply dependent and poor communities. People who gradually become dependent on commercial markets, labor contractors, and governments operating under the ill-defined rubric of "development" are going to be easy prey for any new colonizer, even one as seemingly benign and worthwhile as a conservation organization.

It should be no surprise, then, that tribal peoples like the Maasai, who have seen their lands plundered for two hundred years by foreign colonizers, do regard conservationists as just another colonizer, an extension of the deadening forces of economic and cultural hegemony. Nor should conservationists be surprised to find central African communities associating plans to protect biodiversity with forced expulsion, or to hear Martin Saning'o once again declare himself an "enemy of conservation."

Close observers of evacuated areas on almost every continent have noticed other unfortunate consequences of the colonial model. Evictees, deprived of their usufruct rights are driven to desperate survival actions denounced as "criminal" by conservationists. Once accustomed to harvesting game with traditional weapons for their own community's use, expelled natives often buy rifles, reenter their former hunting grounds, and begin poaching larger numbers of the same game for the growing "bush meat," or the meat from wild animals, trade, which like almost everything else has gone global. Bush meat, even roast eland and sautéed howler monkey, can now be found on the menus of chic restaurants in Europe. Whose fault is that?

And who is to blame for what happened in Cameroon in 2003 after two "flagship" nature reserves that had expelled their inhabitants and consumed more than $20 million in international support both lost their donor funding? Overnight, impoverished and embittered refugees invaded both reserves and plundered their natural resources.

Banished Pygmies will sometimes sneak back into the forest to harvest medicinal plants and firewood at the risk of being legally killed by eco-guards hired and paid by conservation agencies. And much less desirable groups—colonists, renegade loggers, exotic animal hunters, cash-crop farmers, and cattle ranchers—are moving into unpatrolled protected areas the world over. As they often share ethnicity with the ruling class of the nation involved, the new settlers are generally favored in territorial conflicts with Indians and other aboriginals who are arrested or expelled for doing the same things.

Absent knowledgeable and responsible stewardship, these occupied lands have declined into anarchic decay. In such areas biodiversity ebbs closer to zero as species either leave or crash. International conservationists then issue reports lamenting the impending extinction and blaming the very poachers and timber thieves that their policies and actions created. Indigenous peoples' presence, it turns out, may offer the best protection that protected areas can ever receive. That's a possibility that international conservationists have begun to consider.

But large organizations are generally slow to learn, about other people or themselves. Thus many well-meaning conservationists are still willing to introduce native peoples to the money economy, then scorn them for craving consumer goods; deprive them of protein, then rebuke them for eating bush meat; or ply them with alcohol and call them drunks. On every continent indigenous peoples are still being driven into the deepest imaginable poverty, then tried as criminals for selling ivory, tiger pelts, bush meat, or turtle eggs to stay alive.

So it is true that some tribal peoples are abusing their habitat. But before condemning them, conservationists need to ask: Why is this happening? Why, for example, did that Quichua farmer I met on a bank of the Napo River in Ecuador sell his only shade tree, a three-hundred-year-old mahogany, to a renegade logger for $15—unaware that the milled lumber of his tree would fetch a thousand times that price in the retail market? Why do Cameroonian natives plunder what had been their homeland for centuries? And why have some Huarani, a people who lived productively in the Ecuadorian rainforest for thousands of years, suddenly turned against the very ecosystem that sustained them for centuries? What was their motive? What was the catalyst? Have they been corrupted by *petrolero* (oil worker) jobs and money? What is disrupting their kinship systems and social networks? What forces undermine their traditional livelihoods, their cultural identity?

Issues and Lessons

To say that Yosemite is Eden is to say that everywhere else is not.
—Rebecca Solnit, University of California

In structuring this book I have interspersed the aforementioned chapters documenting the experience of tribes and native communities with chapters discussing the issues that face both conservationists and indigenous peoples worldwide:

· Chapter 2, for example, confronts the tortured semantics of *nature* and *wilderness* and shows how widely varying definitions of both words, and conflicting views of wild nature itself, create a communications impasse between land-based people of the south and science-based conservationists from the north.

· Chapter 4 describes the rise of a global conservation "aristocracy," which eventually concentrates itself into five very large organizations headquartered in Europe and the United States.

· Chapter 6 traces the origins, philosophies, and eventual justifications for exclusionary "fortress" conservation.

· Chapter 8 traces the fascinating trajectory of traditional ecological knowledge from a discipline rejected by northern wildlife biologists as baseless superstition and "nonsense" to a major contributor to their own "sound science."

· Chapter 10 attempts to differentiate and document the impacts of positive and negative human disturbances on the world's ecosystems.

• Chapter 12 recalls the rise of the most remarkable social movement in history—the concerted global uprising of four thousand five hundred indigenous "nations."

• Chapter 14 describes the indispensable value of mapping to people struggling to establish and protect land rights and tenure.

• Finally, chapter 18 recounts the creation and success of several community initiated, -owned, and -managed conservation projects.

The obvious theme of these chapters and perhaps the central thesis of this book is that Northern, science-based conservationists still have more than they ever imagined to learn from the ancient ecological practices and accumulated wisdom of people who were residing in high-biodiversity areas of the planet long before they were "discovered" by conservation circuit riders, schooled, and credentialed as "naturalists" and "wildlife biologists."

History is burdened with stolen stories, particularly when human conflict has occurred. And as the rest of this book demonstrates, the history of conservation is fraught with human conflict. In fact, as chapter 1 attests, the early conservation movement was partly spawned in war. The record of that war, and Yosemite National Park's subsequent relationship with its original occupants, is replete with inconsistency and self-generated mythology. It is a classic stolen story, and as usually happens, the winners, in this case of both the war and the park, stole the story from the losers. I have tried to return part of the story to its rightful owners, with the thought that stolen stories are also truths that we hide from ourselves. So few of us know what "had to be done" to create the national parks and wildlife refuges we truly believe are ours to enjoy.

1
Miwok

Civilization must advance, though it tread on the neck of the savage, or even trample him out of existence.
—CommanderWilliam Lewis Herndon, United States Navy

The rude, fierce settler who drives the savage from the land lays all civilized mankind under a debt to him. It is of incalculable importance that America, Australia, and Siberia should pass out of the hands of the red, black, and yellow aboriginal owners and become the heritage of the dominant world races.
—Theodore Roosevelt

Yosemite National Park was spawned in war, a "war of extermination" declared by California's first governor, Peter Burnett, to rid the nation's newest state of Indians.[1] Burnett didn't accept the conventional prophesy of his day that the Native American, unable to survive the shock of European culture and technology, would either assimilate with the white population or simply die off as a race, leaving only mannequins dressed in buckskin to adorn recreated Indian villages and dioramas in America's museums of natural history. No, Burnett was an early advocate of ethnic cleansing.

There are scattered eyewitness accounts of battles and battalions from the Yosemite chapter of California's vicious Indian War. They are found in dozens of books, hundreds of articles, and countless journals and diaries kept by militiamen, pioneers, gold miners, conservationists, politicians, nature romantics, and historians. And there are the oral recollections of a few surviving Indians. Thus there are many, often conflicting versions of every event in the war—the soldier's version, the National

Park Service version, the conservationist version, and a few tiny fragments of the Indian version.

One episode no one seems to contest took place on March 27, 1851, when Major James Savage led a dozen or so men from the Mariposa Battalion into the headwaters of the Merced River to rout Chief Tenaya and about two hundred mostly Ahwahneechee Indians from their ancestral homeland in what is now called Yosemite Valley. Savage's battalion was a paramilitary force created by Mariposa County sheriff James Burney at the behest of the governor. Its particular mission in the statewide war against Indians was to make the Sierra foothills safe for gold miners.

The Ahwahneechee were a band of the Miwok tribe that had one generation earlier fled the valley to Mono Lake after an outbreak of disease. There they intermarried with the Mono Paiutes. Chief Tenaya's mother was a Paiute. His father was Miwok. Sometime around 1830, Tenaya led his three sons, a few wives, and some camp followers back into the valley where his father had been born. When he arrived he named the new band *Yosemite*, a Miwok word that appears to mean both "grizzly bear" and "those who kill" (which, of course, is true of grizzly bears). The valley itself had long ago been named Ahwahnee, which means "large mouth." Some historians believe that other Indians in the area gave Tenaya's people the name Yosemite, in recognition of their ferocity. Either way, the name fits, so Major Savage was braced for serious resistance.

Riding with Savage that day was his enigmatic and deeply conflicted friend Dr. Lafayette Bunnell—battalion physician, miner, and wilderness romantic. When they reached Inspiration Point and Bunnell saw El Capitan, a dramatic sheer wall of silver granite shrouded in mist, as it so often is today, he wept. "Haze hung over the valley that day—light as gossamer," he wrote in his journal, "and clouds partially dimmed the higher cliffs and mountains. . . . As I looked, a peculiar exalted sensation seemed to fill my whole being, and I found my eyes in tears with emotion. . . . I had seen the power and glory of a supreme being and the majesty of his handiwork."

As far as we know, neither Savage nor his soldiers shared Bunnell's emotions for the valley's beauty. Their interests lay in a fierce band of warriors they expected to find hidden among the trees and rocks on the valley floor. Some of them, Savage believed, had recently sacked his store near Mariposa and killed two of his men. He had warned Tenaya that if he found him in Ahwahnee his battallion would come in and kill every member of the tribe. Never mind that Savage was at the time married to at least four of their women.

Bunnell remarked at one point that to Tenaya this was no doubt "a veritable paradise." Savage responded: "I haven't carried a Bible since I became a mountain man, Lafayette, but I do remember well enough that Satan entered paradise and did all the mischief he could. I intend to be a bigger devil in this Indian paradise than old Satan ever was." When they descended onto the valley floor they found one old woman. Tenaya had slipped out with the wives and warriors the night before. Too feeble to flee with her people, the old woman had stayed behind to live out her days.

After Savage and Bunnell left, Tenaya circled back into the valley and settled in until May, when a second company of the battalion returned under the command of John Boling. This time five young braves were captured, three of them Tenaya's sons. When one of the boys was killed, Tenaya returned to the valley, surrendered to Boling and begged him to kill him, but warned that if Boling did so the chief's spirit would return to torment the white man forever. Boling passed on the opportunity to fulfill Governor Burnett's dream of an Indian-free state and let the chief go.[2]

Lafayette Bunnell had mixed feelings about Ahwahnee's inhabitants. At times he exalted the lifeways of Indians, calling them "nature's landscape gardeners." But he also described them as "peculiar living ethnological curiosities," and eventually came to believe, like his governor, that there was no room for Indians in the west, calling them "yelling demons" and "overgrown vicious children." The territory, he said, one day should be "swept of any scattered bands that might infest it." Bunnell and his musings presaged a century of ambivalence toward Native Americans by the people of California, the managers of Yosemite National Park, and the now legendary founders of America's soon-to-be vibrant conservation movement. Major Savage was more than willing to accommodate their atavistic side.

That day Bunnell stood aside and watched while his battalion mates burned acorn caches to starve the Yosemites out of the valley. That night, as they sat around a campfire at the foot of Bridal Veil Falls, according to his journal Bunnell proposed naming the valley "Yosemite," after "the tribe of Indians which we met leaving their homes in this valley, perhaps never to return." The name, he said, was "suggestive, euphonious and certainly American." At the time he had no awareness of what archeologists would later discover—that the Yosemites had thrived in that resplendent valley, on and off, for almost four thousand years.

Four years later, in 1855, San Francisco entrepreneur James Mason Hutchings traveled with artist Thomas Ayres and two friends into Yosemite. In a sense, they were the valley's first tourists. Hutchings began writing about the place almost immediately. He returned four years later with photographer Charles Leander Weed. Weed's photographs and Ayres's still-classic sketch of Yosemite Falls, published nationwide alongside Hutchings's lyrical descriptions of the valley's splendor, turned Yosemite Valley into a tourist magnet and a lure for new settlers. White settlers flocked from around the country, hotels were opened, homes built, and livestock grazed in surrounding meadows.

In 1860, Unitarian minister Thomas Starr King paid Yosemite a visit. Horrified by the commerce and homesteading he found in the valley, he wrote a blistering six-part series for the *Boston Evening Transcript*. When nothing came of it he proposed the creation of a public park. Legislators listened, but the Civil War occupied their attention.

However, landscape architect Frederick Law Olmsted, designer of Central Park in New York City, did take notice. Olmsted, who had always wanted to create a park in the wilderness, took a break from his work in New York and traveled west to manage a mining claim in Mariposa, a town about twenty miles southwest of Yosemite. But when he first wandered into the valley, he found a new purpose for his journey, and his life—to create "a wild park" representing "the greatest glory of nature." Furthermore, when Olmsted saw the destructive consequences of development in the valley, he immediately contacted Senator John Conness of California and pressed him to introduce a federal bill to protect the area, which Conness had never seen.

However, it was not the first Conness had heard about the splendors of Yosemite Valley. The railroad and steamship lobbies had already been to visit his office, asking the senator to consider the enormous tourist value of a scenic attraction in his state. The "Conness bill" passed both houses with ease, and on June 30, 1864, President Abraham Lincoln signed into law an act creating "The Yosemite Grant," a public trust ceded to California as a park "for resort and recreation . . . to be left inalienable for all time." Inalienable from what or whom was never stipulated, but the land was certainly alienated from its original human inhabitants.

Galen Clark, known throughout the state as the "discoverer" of the Mariposa Grove, a splendid stand of redwoods, who had also lobbied hard for the creation of Yosemite National Park, became its first guardian, reporting to Frederick Law Olmsted, first chair of the California Yosemite Park Commission. Clark's interpretation of "guardian" seemed to mean letting almost everyone into the park but Indians. And to him the most important words in the new law were *resort* and *recreation*. Commerce continued, tourists flocked, and more sheep managed to find their way into the park's meadows. Clark himself opened and ran a badly managed hotel near the Wawona area.

The only nonnative who could imagine allowing Indians to remain in a national park was artist and explorer George Catlin, who traveled west in 1830 to "immerse myself in Indian country" and record with paint and canvas "the manners, customs and character of an interesting race of people."[3]

"What a splendid contemplation," Catlin later wrote, "a magnificent nation's park containing man and beast in the wild and freshness of nature's beauty, where the world could see for ages to come, the native Indian in his classic attire, galloping his wild horse, with sinewy bow, and shield and lance, amid the fleeting herds of elks and buffaloes."[4] Although long regarded as a forefather of the national park idea, Catlin's vision of an "Indian Park" remained pretty much his own.

Dominating the drive toward Indian-free national parks was Samuel Bowles, an East Coast writer and proponent of "manifest destiny." In 1865, Bowles visited Yosemite Valley and praised the federal government for placing it under the protection of the California legislature. He also

approved strongly of the government's decision to create Indian reservations and place their residents under federal protection, advocating that
all Indians be removed from any area of scenic beauty.

"We know they are not our equals," Bowles wrote in his classic *Parks
and Mountains of Colorado*, "and we know that our right to the soils,
as a race capable of its superior improvement, is above theirs. . . . So let
us say to the Indian 'you are our ward, our child, the victim of our
destiny, ours to displace, ours to protect.'" Although he shared Burnett's
distaste for Indians, Bowles did not believe that proactive extermination
was necessary. They were, he said, "doomed to vanish." It was the government's noble responsibility to place the natives on reservations, to
feed and educate the Indian "to such elevation as he will be awakened
to, and then let him die—as die he is doing and die he must."[5]

The Godfather of Conservation

To protect the nature that is all around us, we must think long and hard about
the nature that is in our heads.
—William Cronon, environmental historian

In 1868 John Muir arrived in California. For two years he worked as a
shepherd in the high Sierra, at times side by side with the Northern
Paiutes. He called them "diggers" and regretted that they did not meet
his standards of dignity. They were, he said, a "fallen" people. The
Ahwahneechees he found to be particularly "ugly, some of them altogether hideous." They had "no place in the landscape," he said, and he
felt none of the "solemn calm" he expected of wilderness while in their
presence.

While allowing that Indian lifeways had minimal impact on the land—
"they walk softly and hurt the landscape hardly more than the birds and
squirrels"—Muir was revolted by the presence of ant and fly larva in
their diet (which also included venison, trout, bear, grouse, quail, acorns,
pine nuts, berries, and other edible plants that Muir himself lived on in
the mountains). "The worst thing about them is their uncleanliness,"
Muir wrote of the Ahwahneechees he met in Yosemite, for "nothing truly
wild is unclean. . . . A mountain mansion where nature has gathered her

choicest treasures to draw her lovers into close communion with her" was simply not the place for "such debased fellow beings." The Indians, Muir believed, had to leave Yosemite.

Thomas Starr King concurred. Yosemite's inhabitants he saw as "lazy, good-for-nothing Digger Indians," inconsistent with pristine nature. "Many a Californian, if the question were up between the Diggers and woodpeckers," King predicted, "would not hesitate in deciding the point of 'moral value' in favor of the plundered birds." He stood with Muir: even if the Indians had lived sustainably in that valley for a hundred or more generations, they should be evicted.

But they would not leave quietly. In 1890, Yosemite, Mono, and Paiute chieftains petitioned President Benjamin Harrison, complaining of hoteliers and ranchers who "have come into the valley to make money only. Yosemite is no longer a State or National Park," they wrote, "but merely a hay farm and cattle range. . . . The 'People's Park' is a thing of the past. It has now resolved itself into a private institution."

Asking for $1 million in compensation for their lost homeland, the chiefs closed their petition with this prediction: "It will only be a short time before they tell the Indians they must go away and not come back any more." Their petition was denied, and although it would take another eighty years to accomplish the task, their prediction came true in 1969 when the last Indian settlement in Yosemite National Park was evacuated and razed. Thus ended, once and for all, George Catlin's dream of an Indian park.

The Conservation Lobby

Fortresses do not enclose wilderness, they defend western life styles.
—Dan Brockington, New Hall, Cambridge

In 1892 Muir founded the Sierra Club, recruiting 181 members who began almost immediately pressuring the federal government to make Yosemite Valley and its environs into a national Park, devoid of all human settlement, with the exception of a few rangers and perhaps a naturalist or two. And they wanted the sheep, which Muir called "hooved locusts," driven from the area for good. However, the park trust was at the time administered by the 4th Cavalry Regiment of the United States Army, which was denied authority to arrest white sheepherders. Thus there were sheep in Yosemite's meadows well into the 1920s.

In his writings Muir insisted that Yosemite Valley and the Mariposa Grove had, before the arrival of Euro-American settlers, been unoccupied virgin wilderness. He claimed that any Indians on these lands were temporary nomads passing through. Nothing could be further from the truth. For thousands of years, before Savage and Bunnell "discovered" the valley, Indians cultivated it with seeds and bulbs to grow legumes, greens, flowers, and medicinal plants. They pruned the valley's trees and shrubs and weeded the meadows. And they periodically burned off the entire valley to recycle nutrients and clear the floor of unwanted brush.

It is true that no permanent shelter or fences were built, no fields plowed. So what Muir saw the first time he viewed that bucolic valley might have seemed like wilderness landscape, but it wasn't. It was a tended wilderness, a cultural landscape. In fact, for four thousand years the valley had been a productive, rotational garden cared for by hundreds of full-time gardeners that sustained generation upon generation of Miwok, Yokut, Paiute, and Ahwahneechees.

Muir must have known this or learned it at some point, if not from his friend, University of California geologist Joseph LeConte, who had spent years doing research side by side with Indians, then from Galen Clark. Clark also lived for many years among the Miwoks and became Muir's friend. Surely one of his associates mentioned to Muir that unremitting labor by Indians and their traditional land management practices had much to do with the valley's appearance. If so, Muir ignored him.

Yosemite Valley, the stubborn Scot opined, should remain as wild and open as it was and always had been, a place where overstressed urbanites and wilderness romantics like himself and Lafayette Bunnell could go to revere nature and, as Muir himself put it, "cleanse" their "souls of worldly evil."[6] Muir's denial of the Indians' heritage nurtured a historical fiction, which regarded Indians as "first visitors" who had decided not to reside in Yosemite for years before it and other national parks were formed. Photographer Ansel Adams fed the fiction by deliberately keeping nearby Indians out of his classic photos of pristine Yosemite wilderness.

In 1901 Muir began leading annual Sierra Club trips to Yosemite, with hopes of recruiting support for the creation of a unified national park. In 1903 he camped with Theodore Roosevelt for three days near Glacier Point. Muir spoke passionately about duplicating there what Ulysses S. Grant had already accomplished in Wyoming with the 1872 creation of Yellowstone National Park. Three years later, Roosevelt signed a bill taking control of the park away from the state and placing it in Washington, a vital step toward Muir's dream of creating Yosemite National Park, and toward Roosevelt's dream of passing American land "out of the hands of its . . . aboriginal owners [to] become the heritage of the dominant world races."

In 1914 Muir's inspired and persistent lobbying paid off, and the vast Yosemite area, which included the valley, Hetch Hetchy Canyon and the Mariposa Grove, became a national park under control of the recently created National Park Service, the stated mission of which was "to conserve the scenery and the natural and historic objects and the wildlife therein" and to "leave them unimpaired for the enjoyment of future generations." Muir died in December of that year.

In 1916 the National Park Service was moved into the Interior Department, which had recently inherited the Bureau of Indian Affairs from the War Department. For the next fifty years, federal policy toward Indians in Yosemite and other parks vacillated wildly from reluctant accommodation to outright expulsion, depending mostly on who was in charge of the park and the Park Service.

Holding On

The land is our culture.
—Kuna chief

Tiring of reservation life in Fresno, Chief Tenaya had more than once led his people back into the Yosemite park. In 1857 he led a large migration in to harvest a bumper crop of acorns. On such trips fish and deer were also harvested. White settlers, who often hunted and fished the area themselves, said the salmon and deer taken by Miwoks were "poached." In 1860 a deliberate fire was set in the valley, burning away the underbrush as Tenaya and his men watched from a distance. They knew the territory so much better than the park rangers and were so mobile that they could thrive in hidden valleys for months undetected. Permanent eviction seemed impossible, and the non-Indian public of California was beginning to disapprove of Peter Burnett's "final solution" for the state's Indians. After the Yosemite National Park was created, ways were sought to accommodate a few Miwoks within its borders, including the following.

An Indian village was built in the valley. Small (400-square-foot) shacks were occupied by six to eight people. Some of the Indians were employed in park maintenance, while others were expected to provide traditional Indian "color" for visiting tourists by openly performing routine tribal tasks like basket weaving and acorn grinding. The Indian village came perilously close to becoming a human zoo.

Every August 1 beginning in 1916, Indian Field Days were celebrated at the park. It was an opportunity for Indians to demonstrate their skills and crafts. Games, contests, races, rodeo events, and dances were conducted for monetary prizes. Indian Field Days was a popular tourist attraction. But when cowboys from outside the park got wind of the prize money, they insisted on competing in the rodeo and horse races. Things got testy. Fights broke out between cowboys and Indians. In 1924 the park administration ended Indian Field Days.

In 1929 Park Superintendent Charles Thompson, who regarded Indians as "less than desirable citizens [who] should have long since been banished from the park," met with Miwok leaders and told them that residence in the park was "a privilege, not a vested right." Employment was required of all residents. From then on, the Miwok became cheap labor for the Park Service, which gradually lowered their population by evicting miscreants and the unemployed, prohibiting new Miwok settlers to replace those who died or left, and allowing the Indian village infrastructure to deteriorate.

By 1960 the government had complete control over the few remaining Indians. When a head of household died, the Park Service vacated his house and expelled its residents from the park. In 1969 the last of the settled Miwoks were ushered from the park and their village was set on fire as a firefighting drill.

By then the exclusionary model of wilderness preservation was a well-established strategy in American conservation, even written into the 1964 Wilderness Act, which described "wilderness" as "an area where the earth and its community of life are untrammeled by man, where man himself is a visitor who does not remain."

When that act was passed most of the major parks created in America—most notably Yellowstone, Grand Canyon, Mesa Verde, Mount Rainier, Zion, Glacier, Everglades, and Olympic national parks—had already followed the Yosemite example by expelling thousands of tribal people from their homes and hunting grounds so the new parks could remain in an undisturbed "state of nature."

Yellowstone was a brief exception. It was originally intended to be a nature *and* Indian reserve, as envisioned by George Catlin, and for a few years after its creation seven native tribes—the Shoshone, Lakota, Crow, Bannock, New Perce, Flathead, and Blackfoot—lived, hunted, and fished there. But "strict natural protection" combined with wilderness romanticism to change policy, and by 1877 all Indians were ordered to leave the park for good. Resistance to eviction led to the deaths of hundreds of Indians—three hundred Shoshones in one particularly lethal encounter. By the early twentieth century, many of the parks we now revere were not only cleared of Indians but were also posted "Whites Only," a policy Muir's Sierra Club voted to sustain until 1920.

A Model for the World

When the Indians vanish the rest will follow.
—Guarani elder

Like most American inventions, the national park idea spread beyond its border and was emulated, first in Australia (Royal National Park 1879), then in Canada (Banff 1887), and then in New Zealand (Tongarivo 1894). Then as Europe colonized the wild reaches of Africa and Asia, it applied the Yosemite model in the Transvaal and Serengeti where parks like Kruger, Singwisti, Ambolseli, Garamba, the Maasai Mara, and Parc Albert sprung up. All of them bore remarkable similarities to Yosemite and Yellowstone national parks—natives likewise were cleared out so colonials could enjoy the aesthetics of wild nature, and in the case of Africa, selectively hunt the game for trophies.

New maps were drawn of the western United States where parks were created, with Indian artifacts airbrushed away and place names changed to erase the memory of native existence. How else could the myth of a frontier carved from pristine wilderness be preserved? And how else to defend the persistent legal doctrine of terra nullius, (no man's land) applied around the world to claim that the land where parks were placed was empty, owned by no one, and unaltered by human activity, thus permitting states to set it aside as a "protected area" for perpetuity?

North America's national parks were immensely popular attractions for priveleged white tourists, who swarmed west by rail and automobile to stay in extravagant lodges like the Ahwahnee in Yosemite and Chateau Lake Louise at Banff and be served by waitresses at Glacier National Park dressed in traditional Swiss costumes intended to make Europeans feel at home. But parks free of permanent settlements were also seen by conservationists as opportunities to study and protect wildlife and to preserve biological diversity. And in that regard, most parks appeared to work. Animals seemed to sense the safe and welcome atmosphere of these quiet, firearm-free zones. They even became accustomed to these strange and peaceful creatures watching them through binoculars and camera lenses. Wildlife flourished, particularly large mammals and their predators, both signs of a healthy, diverse ecosystem.

Thus what eventually became known as "exclusionary conservation" was aggressively exported from the United States to well-financed and powerful conservation organizations such as the Society for the Preservation of the Wild Fauna of the Empire, formed in London in 1903, and later to more familiar groups like Bird Life International. In subsequent eras new groups like The Nature Conservancy, Conservation International, the World Wildlife Fund (WWF), and the New York Zoological Society (now the Wildlife Conservation Society) would join the fray.

The American model of land and wildlife conservation spread first to Europe. Bernhard Grzimek, a German national whose midcentury campaigns to protect wildlife in Africa became legendary (see chapter 3), spawned a continent-wide initiative that led directly to eviction of the Maasai people from the Serengeti. Parks, according to Grzimek, should be much as Muir had envisioned Yosemite—wild places where nature lovers go for rest and inspiration, and conservation biologists to study the mechanics of evolution. Colonel Mervyn Lowie, who helped Grzimek create Serengeti National Park, regarded a protected area as "a cultured person's playground."

The International Union for the Conservation of Nature (IUCN), the umbrella of world conservation based in Switzerland, has grappled since its very beginning with a definition of *national park*. Its first stated definition was: "A large area where . . . ecosystems are *not materially altered by human exploitation and occupation*, where plant and animal species, geomorphological sites and habitats are of special scientific value, education and recreative interest . . . and where the highest competent authority of the country has taken steps to *prevent or eliminate, as soon as possible, exploitation or occupation* in the whole area, and to enforce effectively the respect of ecological, geomorphological and aesthetic features that lead to its establishment" (emphasis added).

John Muir could have drafted that a half century before it was written—the Yosemite model writ large. In 1992, the IUCN would soften its definition to reflect attempts made around the world to put a human face on conservation. The harsh, exclusionary language would be changed to "exclude exploitation or occupation inimical to the designated purposes of the area."

Although that language would theoretically allow indigenous people who were living "sustainably" to remain in a national park—and that has happened in some locations around the world—the Yosemite model survives. And soft, less violent evictions from new parks continue to this day, as does the occupation and exploitation of existing parks by road builders, bioprospectors, tourist concessions, and luxury "ecolodges" like Yosemite's Ahwahnee Hotel, a four-story architectural tour de force constructed at the foot of Half Dome, the defining geomorphological icon of Yosemite Valley.

The globalization of American conservation has been so successful that there are today thousands of national parks, biological reserves, and wildlife sanctuaries on every continent. And there are millions of "conservation refugees"—ancient civilizations like the Yosemite Indians, evicted from ancestral homelands in the interest of that unique model of preservation inspired in the early twentieth century by the creators of Yosemite National Park, and promoted by men like William Hornaday, director of the New York Zoological Society, who in 1913 appealed to his members to "take up their share of the white man's burden," by preserving the nation's forests and mountains.

In December 1996, the last Yosemite Indian to reside in the Yosemite National Park, Joe Johnson, left his birthplace for a home in Mariposa. Johnson had stayed on as a ranger after the Indian village was razed. Years earlier his grandfather Bridgeport Tom had prophesized that after the last Yosemite left the valley "the walls will come tumbling down." On New Year's Day, 1997, the Merced River surged over its banks and the worst flood in recorded history tore through Yosemite's manmade structures. Massive rockslides closed the valley for days and changed its contours forever.

The design of national parks and other protected areas throughout the world has been inspired by a now familiar blend of wilderness romanticism and a self-generated mythology about humanity's relationship with nature created by wildland preservationists. But behind this strange admixture of ideas, which so strongly influences modern conservation, lies some deep confusion and a lot of disagreement about the meaning of the very word nature, and what we mean by wild.

2

"Nature"

Perhaps the most complex word in the English language.
—Raymond Williams, Cambridge University

One way to guarantee a conversation without a conclusion is to ask a group of people what nature is.
—Rebecca Solnit, University of California

In the course of "preserving the commons for all of the people," a frequently stated mission of national parks and protected areas, one class or culture of people, one philosophy of nature, one worldview, and one creation myth has almost always been preferred over all others. These favored ideas and impressions are at some point expressed in art. And it is through art that our earliest preconceptions and fantasies about nature are formed.

The mystique of Yosemite, for example, was largely created by photographers like Charles Leander Weed, Carleton Watkins, Ansel Adams, and Edward Weston, all of whose magnificent images of the place are completely bereft of humanity or any sign of it having been there. Here, they said (and they all knew better) is an untrammeled landscape, virgin and pristine, not a bootprint to be seen, not a hogan or teepee in sight. Here in this wild place one may seek and find complete peace.

They and their friends who sought to preserve an idealized version of nature called it "wilderness," a place that humans had explored but never altered, exalted but never touched. It was the beginning of a myth, a fiction that would gradually spread around the world, and for a century or more drive the conservation agenda of mankind.

They all knew better, the portrayers of wilderness; in fact, Adams assiduously avoided photographing any of the local Miwok who were rarely out of his sight as he worked Yosemite Valley. He filled thousands of human-free negatives with land he knew the Miwok had tended for at least four thousand years. And he knew that the Miwok had been forcibly evicted from Yosemite Valley, as other natives would later be from national parks yet to be created, all in the putative interest of protecting nature from human disturbance.

One can be fairly certain that Weed, Watkins, Adams, and Weston had all at one time in their lives read George Perkins Marsh's 1864 classic *Man and Nature* and recalled Marsh arguing passionately for the preservation of wild virgin nature, which he said was justified as much for artistic reasons as for any other. Marsh also believed that the destruction of the natural world threatened the very existence of humanity. We know that Muir read Marsh and so did Teddy Roosevelt. They both say so in their journals and memoirs. So when the topic of a park in Yosemite came up Muir and Roosevelt were, so to speak, on the same page.

Dueling Sciences

Natural science is just one way of understanding nature.
—Bill Adams, Cambridge University

The Yosemite model of conservation, which still expresses itself in a fairly consistent form, has sparked a worldwide conflict between two powerful scientific disciplines: anthropology and conservation biology. These two august sciences remain at odds with one another over how best to conserve and protect biological and cultural diversity, and perhaps more perplexing, how best to define two of most semantically tortured terms in both their fields—*nature* and *wilderness*.

Cultural anthropologists spend years living in what many of us would call "the wild," studying the languages, mores, and traditions of what many of us would call "primitive peoples." Eventually the anthropologists come to understand the complex native cultures that keep remote communities thriving without importing much from outside their immediate homeland.

"We do not ask if indigenous peoples are allies of conservation or what sort of nature they protect," write Paige West and Dan Brockington, two anthropologists who have spent most of their careers researching the impact of protected areas on indigenous cultures; "instead we draw attention to the ways in which protected areas become instrumental in shaping battles over identity, residence and resource use."[1] Their experience has convinced them that the best way to protect a thriving natural ecosystem is to leave those communities pretty much alone, where and as they are, doing what they've done so well for so many generations—culturing a healthy landscape, or what development experts would call "living sustainably."

Wildlife biologists also spend much of their careers in remote natural settings, but tend to prefer landscapes void of human hunters, gatherers, pastoral nomadics, or rotational farmers. They find anthropologists somewhat "romantic" about indigenous cultures, particularly tribes that have become partly assimilated and modernized; which generally means the tribes are in possession of environmentally destructive technologies such as shotguns, chainsaws, and motorized vehicles, conveniences that Western naturalists know from their own civilization's experience can wreak havoc on healthy ecosystems.

These two disciplines are also at odds over what they mean by nature and the degree to which humanity is part of it. And they have a different sense of wildness and wilderness. It is in this regard that one is more likely to hear anthropologists calling naturalists "romantic." Listening to this exchange of insults one might conclude one is witnessing a clash of romantic tendencies.

William Cronon, an environmental historian at the University of Wisconsin, has spent much of his intellectual career grappling with these conflicts. His thinking on the subject eventually came together in 1995 with publication of a widely read and controversial essay titled "The Trouble with Wilderness, Getting Back to the Wrong Nature."

"The time has come to rethink wilderness," Cronon begins his essay. He goes on to challenge the widely held and decidedly romantic notion of environmentalists that "wilderness stands as the last remaining place where civilization, that all too human disease, has not fully infected the earth." That concept, Cronon believes, gives credence to "the illusion that we can somehow wipe clean the slate of our past and return to the *tabula rasa* that supposedly existed before we began to leave our marks on the world." That fiction, which Cronon believes is based on a profound misunderstanding of nature, and our place in it, creates a force that is antagonistic to conservation. "The myth of wilderness," he writes, "is that we can somehow leave nature untouched by our passage." He goes on to challenge the shopworn and often misunderstood shibboleth of Henry David Thoreau that "in wildness is the preservation of the world."

Cronon concludes: "The more one knows of its peculiar history, the more one realizes that wilderness is not quite what it seems. Far from being one place on earth that stands apart from humanity, it is quite profoundly a human creation—indeed, the creation of very particular human cultures at very particular moments in human history. It is not a pristine sanctuary where the last remnant of an untouched, endangered, but still transcendent nature can for at least a little while longer be encountered without the contaminating taint of civilization. Instead, it is a product of that civilization."

These are fighting words to a "civilization" that has set millions of square miles of valuable land aside as "wilderness," passed a national law—the 1964 Wilderness Act—to both define and protect wilderness, and still supports a dozen or so well-heeled national organizations to lobby for more wilderness set-asides and convince the public that figuratively walling off large expanses of unoccupied land is the only way to preserve nature and biological diversity. But how natural is wilderness? To Cronon, not as natural as it seems.

"Wilderness hides its unnaturalness behind a mask that is all the more beguiling because it seems so natural," he says. By glorifying pristine landscapes, which exist only in the imagination of romantics, Western conservationists divert attention from the places where people live and the choices they make every day that do true damage to the natural world of which they are part.

So the removal of aboriginal human beings from their homeland to create a commodified wilderness is a deliberate charade, a culturally constructed neo-Edenic narrative played out for the enchantment of weary human urbanites yearning for the open frontier that their ancestors "discovered" then tamed, a place to absorb the sounds and images of virgin nature and forget for a moment the thoroughly unnatural lives they lead.

So What is Wild?

What counts as wilderness is not determined by the absence of people, but by the relationship between people and place.
—Jack Turner, philosopher

On several occasions during my research, an interview would be brought to a dead stop after I included the word *wild* or *wilderness* in a question. The word simply didn't exist in the dialect of the person I was interviewing. My interpreter would stare at me and wait for a better question.

When I tried to explain what I meant by wild to Bertha Petiquan, an Ojibway woman in northern Canada whose daughter was interpreting, she burst out laughing and said the only place she had ever seen what she thought I was describing as wild was a street corner outside the bus station in Winnipeg, Manitoba.

In Alaska, Patricia Cochran, a Yupik native scientist, told me "we have no word for 'wilderness.' What you call 'wilderness' we call our back yard. To us none of Alaska is wilderness as defined by the 1964 Wilderness Act—a place without people. We are deeply insulted by that concept, as we are by the whole idea of 'wilderness designation' that too often excludes native Alaskans from ancestral lands." Yupiks also have no word for *biodiversity*. Its closest approximation means *food*. And the O'odham (Pima) word for *wilderness* is etymologically related to their terms for *health*, *wholeness*, and *liveliness*.[2]

Jakob Malas, a Khomani hunter from a section of the Kalahari that is now Gemsbok National Park, shares Cochran's perspective on wilderness. "The Kalahari is like a big farmyard," he says, "It is not wilderness to us. We know every plant animal and insect, and know how to use them. No other people could ever know and love this farm like us."

"I never thought of the Stein Valley as a wilderness," remarks Ruby Dunstan, a Nl'aka'pamux from Alberta. "My Dad used to say 'That's our pantry.' Then some environmentalists declared it a wilderness and said no one was allowed inside because it was so fragile. So they put a fence around it, or maybe around themselves."[3]

The Tarahumara of Mexico also have no word or concept meaning *wilderness*. Land is granted the same love and affection as family. Ethnoecologist Enrique Salmon, himself a Tarahumara, calls it "kincentric ecology." "We are immersed in an environment where we are at equal standing with the rest of the world," he says. "They are all kindred relations—the trees and rocks and bugs and everything is in equal standing with the rest."[4]

When wildness is conflated with wilderness, and wilderness with nature, and nature is seen as something separate and uninfluenced by human activity, perhaps it's time to examine real situations and test them against the semantics of modern conservation. Are Maasai cattle part of nature? Perhaps not today, but when they wandered through the open range by the thousands, tended by a few human herdsman whose primary interest was to keep the biota healthy for their livestock and other wildlife, one might say they were "wild," certainly as wild as the springbok, eland, elephant, and buffalo that daily leave the open pasture to ravage Maasai farms for fodder.

And Who Is Nature?

We forget the reciprocity between the wild in nature and the wild in us.
—Jack Turner, philosopher

In one of the many conversations about nature I have been part of over the past three years, I said to a man—an educated, erudite, and generous supporter of international conservation, whose view of nature differed considerably from my own—"*You* are nature." He looked at me and laughed nervously. I had not insulted him, he assured me. He just didn't appreciate the notion that he was part or product of a system that also created "snails, kudzu, mules, earthquakes, grizzly bears, viruses, wildfires, and poison oak." It turned out also that his younger sister had, years before, been badly mauled by a mountain lion.

Well, how do you convince someone with that experience that he is kin with the lion? Perhaps you can't, I thought, but he seemed interested in continuing the conversation. Others joined in, and by the end of the evening he had accepted himself as an equal in the same creation with the lion that mauled his sister, a creation he was willing to call "nature," a creation of which he was not apart, but a part.

When one perceives humanity to be something separate from nature it becomes easier to regard landscapes in their "natural state" as landscapes without human inhabitants and aspire to preserve wilderness by encouraging the existence and survival in landscape of as many species as possible, minus one—humans.

The valuable contribution anthropology has made to conservation is perhaps best expressed by Paige West and Dan Brockington, who advise conservationists to be more aware of "local ways of seeing," and that the practice of conservation will be more successful "if practitioners learn local idioms for understanding people's surroundings before they begin to think about things in terms of nature and culture." There is a need, they say, for conservationists "to grasp the complicated ways that people interact with what they rely on for food, shelter, as well as spiritual, social and economic needs."[5]

Enrique Salmon believes that "language and thought works together. So when a people's language includes a word like 'wilderness,' that shapes their thoughts about their relationship to the natural world. The notion of wilderness then carries the notion that humans are bad for the environment."[6]

Certainly someone who regards the forest as his "pantry" is going to see the flora, fauna, soil, and water in a somewhat different light than the tourist, biologist, miner, or logger. But is there not something that can be seen by all of them, some common ground on which the forest's intrinsic value can be considered and agreed upon?

One example of a very different local idiom that Western naturalists have difficulty understanding is that of the Gimi, one of the hundreds of remote, Stone Age cultures in central Papua New Guinea. The Gimi "have no notion of nature or culture," say West and Brockington. "They see themselves in an ongoing set of exchanges with their ancestors [who they believe are] animating and residing in their forests, infusing animals, plants, rivers, and the land itself with life. When people die their spirits go back to the forest and infuse themselves into plants, animals and rivers. When the living use these natural resources they do not see it as a depletion but rather as an ongoing exchange" of energy and spirit.

When the Gimi kill and eat an animal "they understand it to be generated by their ancestors' life forces and it will work to make their life force during this lifetime. When they die that force will go back to the forest and replenish it."[7] This is an admittedly difficult cosmology for the Western mind to contemplate or accept. But the fact that every atom in every living thing has existed since the beginning of time gives some scientific grounding to the Gimis' belief that spirit is simply reorganized force and matter. That said, their understanding "of the relationship between humans and their surroundings [remains] extremely difficult to reconcile with arguments about the decline and loss of biological diversity."[8]

However, if Western conservationists in central Papua New Guinea know that the Gimi believe all matter is here for eternity, that it simply changes form over time, they will be better equipped to work with local communities in the preservation of biodiversity. But if they dismiss that cosmology as primitive animism and seek to impose Western science and religion on the Gimi people, their conservation initiative will almost certainly fail.

Of course, the final arbiters in this scientific conflict should be indigenous peoples themselves, the very people that early advocates for Yellowstone Park said had no interest in raw nature or the park area. They were alleged to be afraid of the geysers and fumaroles (Not true. They cooked over them). The truth is that much of what the rest of us know about nature and have incorporated into the various sciences we use to protect it—ecology, zoology, botany, ethnobotany—we learned from the very people we have expelled from the areas we have sought to protect.

American land conservation strategy has hardly inured to the benefit of the American native. Why would anyone expect it to work for native people in other parts of the world?

While the rank, outspoken discrimination of the nineteenth century has disappeared from the writing and oratory of contemporary conservation leaders, the notion that people living too close to nature are somehow inferior, savage, even dangerous, has survived, particularly in Africa.

3

Maasai

We conserve nature because we live in it, because it is our life.
—Maasai elder

A National Park must remain a primordial wilderness to be effective.
No men, not even native ones, should live inside its borders.
—Bernhard Grzimek, Frankfurt Zoo veterinarian

In 1908, a well-educated young Englishman named Winston Churchill traveled to Africa. It was a fairly common voyage for privileged children of the Commonwealth to make before settling into university or a career—a rite of passage, a pilgrimage to the outer reaches of the British Empire. In one letter home to his mother Winston describes a train trip from Mombassa to Nairobi, throughout which he was seated on a bench in front of the engine, a rifle across his lap. "As soon as we saw anything to shoot at, a wave of the hand brought the engine to a standstill," he wrote. "On the first day I killed one zebra, one wildebeest, two harte-beest, one gazelle and one bustard." Churchill doesn't say in that letter what became of all that protein, but there can be little doubt that trophies were taken, and one can only hope that local natives managed to harvest the meat.

Even the most enthusiastic big game hunter today would shudder at such senseless carnage, which was common throughout the African continent at the height of British colonization. Colonial settlers and even their children were permitted to kill wildlife at their pleasure, while Africans were forbidden to own or carry firearms and allowed to hunt only with spears and arrows in areas of minimal interest to safari guides and their customers. One might call the early twentieth century the pre-conservation era of African settlement.

But gradually, over the half-century that followed Churchill's visit, colonials realized that the bounty of wildlife they had found on the continent was beginning to thin out. Some species were even threatened with localized extinction. A new urgency to protect wildlife and preserve its habitats evolved in concert with a nature aesthetic that had been blooming in both Europe and North America over the fifty years since the "discovery" of the Yosemite Valley. Wildlife was to be more than a target for sharpshooters, and the habitat of Africa's charismatic mega-fauna (large, rare, and attractive animals, mammals mostly) was regarded as something worth preserving. Conservation had gone global. But while the sensibilities of the "great white hunter" were softening, the politics of conservationists were not.

Bernhard Grzimek, veterinary surgeon, Adolph Hitler's director of the Frankfurt Zoo, and if not the "father of African conservation," certainly one of its forefathers, said that he would be willing to sit down with Joseph Stalin if he thought it would help protect the majestic animals of the Serengeti. He could even find good reasons, he said later, to work with Idi Amin. "It can be easier to work with a dictator on these matters of conservation than with a democracy," he believed. "You don't have to deal with parliaments."[1] Nor did Grzimek believe he would have to deal with the Maasai, a proud and fierce tribe of pastoral nomadics who had been herding their cattle up and down the Rift Valley for a millennium or more. British colonial rulers in the countries where he worked would handle that challenge. But he would have to convince them to do so.

Although the Serengeti[2] is regarded by most anthropologists as the longest-inhabited place on earth, and although when he first saw it in 1954 there was no scientific evidence that the few Maasai who lived there threatened the wildlife, Grzimek declared the Serengeti a "primordial wilderness" and said that no one, "not even natives," should live within its borders. It was as if John Muir was writing his script. Grzimek and his son Michael, a pilot, flew the Serengeti together following migratory birds and ungulate herds. They wrote books and made movies about

African wildlife that generated interest and money from the elites of Europe and America to protect the flora and fauna of an area that both Grzimeks sincerely believed was doomed. Michael was killed in 1959 when his plane collided with a vulture. In grief his father wrote *Serengeti Shall not Die,* a bestseller, in which he said: "Large cities continue to proliferate. In the coming decades and centuries, men will not travel to view the marvels of engineering, but they will leave the dusty towns in order to behold the last places on earth where God's creatures are peacefully living. Countries which have preserved such places will be envied by other nations and visited by streams of tourists. There is a difference between wild animals living a natural life and famous buildings. Palaces can be rebuilt if they are destroyed in wartime, but once the wild animals of the Serengeti are exterminated no power on earth can bring them back."[3]

Grzimek was convinced that all pastoral societies, even those comprising people who had lived and thrived on the same nomadic pathways for countless generations, would eventually destroy their habitats. "We Europeans must teach our black brothers to value their own possessions," he wrote, adding that this should not happen "because we are older or cleverer, but because we do not want them to repeat our mistakes and our sins."[4]

Grzimek had a strange way of convincing his black brothers to value their possessions. "Perhaps one day in the future the new park could be fenced in," he wrote in 1960. "Then the animals would have to remain inside it. They would be protected from the settlers near the park and prevented from dying from hunger and thirst when all the timber around their water holes had been felled and their pastures all overgrazed by native cattle." Again, the colonial conservationist knows what is best for Africa and the Africans.

Legendary paleontologist Lewis Leakey had similar things to say about the Maasai. Responding to fellow colonial Alan Moorhead, who in his classic tribute to African wildlife, *No Room in the Ark,* wrote of the Maasai: "They never wash . . . [and they] disdain all forms of trade and ordinary labor," Leakey wrote "I am not one of those who consider that the Maasai should be treated with contempt and disdain or that they are unfit to survive." That said, Leakey argued that the Maasai had no right to remain in the Serengeti, which he described as "a major potential source of wealth to the territory and for its inhabitants of all races for many centuries to come, provided that it is not destroyed now."[5]

British colonists of Tanyanika (now Tanzania) and Kenya whose friends and relatives had, since the turn of the twentieth century, taken home and adorned the walls of their elegant Victorian mansions with thousands of wildlife trophies from the Serengeti plains, eventually supported the conclusions of Leakey and Grzimek, as did members of the London-based Society for the Preservation of the Fauna of the Empire.[6] At their behest thousands of square miles of savannah on both sides of the border were mapped and enclosed.

A protracted debate continued about exactly what to do with this land, who to keep out, who to let in, and for what use and purposes. On the Tanyanikan side, the 5,700-square-mile (14,700-sq.-km) reserve eventually became Serengeti National Park, first of its kind in the British Empire, and the largest wildlife refuge in Africa. On the Kenyan side, the reserve was to be called Maasai Mara. While the 1948 ordinance creating the Serengeti Reserve permitted the passage of "people whose place of birth or ordinary residence is within the Park," all inhabitants were eventually evicted from both parks. Entrance fees for hunters and tourists were stiff, so the reserves became de facto "whites only" parks.

Upon opening the Serengeti National Park, British colonials in Tanyanika promised fifty thousand Maasai herders living and grazing there that if they left the new park they would be allowed to continue grazing and cultivating in the Ngorongoro Game Reserve. It was a promise that would be severely challenged in the years to follow, as a new myth appeared about the Serengeti, expressed in phrasing like "original Africa," "Africa, undamaged and unspoiled," and a "wild Africa" that must be maintained in its "original wildness." By using such rhetoric, repeatedly, Bernhard Grzimek led an aggressive campaign to have the Maasai evicted from the Ngorongoro, to create, he said, "another area free of human impact."

Box 3.1

Who are the Maasai?

Who is and who isn't a Maasai is still debated by historians, archaeologists, anthropologists, and the Maasai. Oral history and the archaeological record place the original Maasai near Lake Turkana in what is now northern Kenya. They have always been pastoral nomadics and have resisted the urging of all governments in their homeland to adopt a more sedentary lifestyle. They claim land and grazing rights to many of the national parks in what are now Kenya and Tanzania, relatively new additions to their geography that they once called Maasailand. They still routinely ignore international boundaries as they move their great cattle herds across the open savannah with the changing of the seasons.

While there are university graduates, professors, and ministers of state among the Maasai, most have avoided modernity and in many ways live pretty much as they did for the centuries when Maasai warriors dominated eastern Africa, distaining permanent settlement and peace.

Traditional Maasai culture revolves around cows. In fact, contemporary Maasai herders regard themselves as the original cattlemen, the world's first cowboys. Some still believe that they are the legitimate owners of all beef and dairy cattle in the world. They were, after all, the first people to domesticate wild ruminants, with an assist from their rain god Enkai who gave them their first small herd. All breeds developed since descended from stock stolen from Maasai herds over centuries of raids carried out by the Taita, Shamba, and other cattle rustlers. Then there are the *Kwavi*, a term of derision used to describe a stock-poor community of people who regard themselves as Maasai.

Cattle are also central to Maasai economy. They are rarely slaughtered, but instead are accumulated as a sign of wealth and either traded for vegetables, sold to settle debts, or given as marriage dowry to a daughter's husband. The rare exception would be for a rite of passage, such as a young boy's arrival in adulthood.

Young men tend their fathers' herds, frequently moving their mobile camps in a constant search of water and good grass. When they find a suitable graze they settle temporarily in small huts built of cattle dung inside thorn barriers that protect them from predators. Maasai are efficient cattlemen, rarely owning more animals than their range will carry. That said, they can also be ruthless capitalists, and to recover the stock they believe is theirs they remain notorious cattle rustlers.

While they spend most of their lives on the savannah, Maasai do travel into towns and cities to purchase goods and supplies and to sell their cattle at regional markets. Maasai also sell their beautiful beadwork to the tourists with whom they now share their grazing land.

Maasai social structure is based on an age and gender system that separates young men and prepubescent girls from older men and their families. When a young woman reaches puberty she is usually married quickly to an older man. Until this time, however, she may live with and have sex with youthful warriors. After they are married, women often maintain close ties, both social and sexual, with their former boyfriends.

In order for men to marry, they must first acquire wealth—cattle. Women, on the other hand, are married at the onset of puberty to prevent children being born out of wedlock. All children, whether legitimate are not, are recognized as the property of the woman's husband and his family.

Maasai spiritual leaders, known as *laibon*, have earned a reputation as the best healers in Tanzania. Even as Western biomedicine gains ground, people search out the traditional remedies of the laibon. Laibons are easily found peddling their knowledge and herbs in the urban centers of Tanzania and Kenya.

The Maasai have no chiefs. Laibon hold the power. Maasai have always worshipped one god who dwells in all things, and who like the Judeo-Christian God may manifest Himself as either kindly or destructive. Their theology has made the Maasai relatively easy targets for Christian evangelism. I saw many Maasai men in the traditional long red robes also sporting a small wooden or silver cross.

What is perhaps most relevant to conservation efforts with regard to the Maasai and their religion is their strict prohibition against the killing and eating of wild animals, except in times of famine. This a most unusual tradition in Africa.

The African governments that took over from colonial rule have as their avowed aim the abolition of tribal distinctions and the blending of all Africans into one united people. Tribal pride, customs, and separateness must go. Assimilation is the price of survival. The Maasai will have none of it.*

---

* For more on the Maasai read: Thomas Spear and Richard Waller, *Being Maasai: Ethnicity and Identity in East Africa* (Ohio University Press, 1993); Dorothy L Hodgson, *Once Intrepid Warriors*, (Indiana University Press, 2001); James Igoe, "Becoming Indigenous People," *African Affairs*, Oxford Journals (July 2006): pp. 399–420.

Ngorongoro

How is it that supposed experts and "guardians of nature" come here after having failed to conserve trees and wildlife in their places of origin?
—Maasai community leader

The Ngorongoro compromise would evolve into an early experiment in what would eventually be called "Integrated Conservation and Development Projects" (ICDPs), a World Bank-funded joint venture of environmentalists and social scientists attempting to put a human face on conservation. A few ICDPs would achieve some measurable success, particularly in Australia and Zimbabwe, but the Ngorongoro experiment would not. (For more on ICDPs see chapter 8.)

The 3,200-square-mile (8,300-sq.-km) Ngorongoro Conservation Area (NCA) is a unique geomorphological mix of volcanic craters and wide plateaus existing at elevations reaching 13,000 feet (4,000 m). Rain is plentiful and the grass is rich in vital nutrients. Artifacts found in the region indicate that pastoralists, including the Maasai, have grazed the area for 2500 years or more. The mandate of the NCA was to create a multiple-use area that would foster conservation and preserve the pastoral culture of the Maasai. The latter became a particularly difficult challenge for Tanzania's Conservation Authority, as the Maasai insisted that although they were essentially pastoral nomadic cattle herders, cultivation was an important and traditional aspect of their culture. Conservationists wanted no cultivation in the NCA.

However, an even greater challenge to the Maasai arose when the Ngorongoro population of wildebeest grew in just over a decade from 240,000 to 1.6 million. Wildebeest calves carry a virus in their nasal mucous that is harmless to their own kind, but fatal to domestic cattle. To avoid contact with the virus, which the wildebeest calves leave on grass blades, the Maasai are forced to constantly move their herds to ranges where they know the wildebeest has not been grazing that season, including at times into the protected Northern Highland Forest, which is strictly off limits to cattle and their tenders.

In the early 1970s pressure mounted from conservation organizations, particularly the Frankfurt Zoological Society that had sponsored the

Grzimeks' forays to the Serengeti, to renege on the compromise and kick the Maasai out of the NCA. Henry Fosbrooke, a former conservator of the NCA, remembers an early morning "in March of 1974, when three Land Rovers entered the Crater, one going to each boma [Maasai settlement]. They carried the personnel of the paramilitary Field Force Unit. Without explanation and without notice they ordered the immediate eviction of the inhabitants and their cattle. Their possessions were carried out by transport of the Conservation Area Authority and dumped on the roadside at Lairobi. No explanation was given and no arrangements made for the resettlement of the evacuees."[7]

The demise of the NCA compromise coincided with the creation of new parks in Tanzania. Tarangire National Park was created in 1971. In the mid-1980s, a group of European and African conservationists attempted to expand park boundaries to the east, a move that has galvanized community opinion against the park.

Tanzania now has about 25 percent of its land under some form of conservation protection. By itself that fact is impressive, and the international conservation organizations active in Tanzania deserve some credit for the biological diversity that has been preserved. However, they also deserve part of the blame for the impoverishment of once-prosperous nomadics made refugees by their policies and actions.

Mkomazi

Conservation based on myth is bound to fail.
—J. S. Adams and T. O. McShane, Worldwide Fund for Nature

Financial contributors in Europe and the U.S. have found the myths of Africa more attractive than the realities.
—Robert Nelson, historian

When the Mkomazi Reserve was first gazetted in 1951 on the northeastern border of Tanzania, there were a few pastorals grazing a few small herds of cattle in the reserve. They were allowed to stay on. However, as in most of the rest of the world, their numbers, both people and cattle, grew. By 1985, there were over one hundred thousand head of cattle and wildlife numbers were falling. In a clear revision of both history and anthropological records, conservationists declared that the pastoralists were not indigenous to the area and that their cattle were destroying both the scenic beauty and the biological diversity of the area. They lobbied the government to remove all residents and their livestock from the Mkomazi.

First to go were nonpastoral cultivators, the Pare, Kamba, and Sambaa, who were moved out of the reserve and settled on or near its borders. After rebuilding complex irrigation systems and enriching soil to grow their food, a new crisis arose for the early evictees—elephants and other animals ranged out of the unfenced reserve in search of food and destroyed the settlers' crops. But evictions affected the pastoralist Maasai even more. Cattlemen who for centuries had relied heavily for their survival on the excellent water sources in the Mkomazi were driven into arid pastures with relatively bad grass and water. Many were forced to give up the herding life and drifted into urban centers and menial labor.

By 1988, all cultivators and pastoralists and their cattle were evicted from the Mkomazi Reserve. Although the Tanzanian Supreme Court later proclaimed these evictions illegal, they were never overturned and local people were never meaningfully compensated. In 1994 some herders petitioned the government to be allowed back into the reserve, claiming that they were natives of the area whose ancestors had grazed cattle there for generations. The government denied their petition. The herders appealed to the High Court, which ruled that they were wrong to claim long-term tenure in the Mkomazi area and thus did not qualify for "ancestral customary rights."

Unfortunately for the conservationists who had lobbied for evictions, the Mkomazi Reserve did not recover its biotic health in the absence of pastoralists. Two international NGOs, the United Kingdom-based George Adamson Wildlife Preservation Trust and the American Tony Fitzjohn/ George Adamson African Wildlife Preservation Trust[8] then stepped in with staff and money to rejuvenate the ecosystem, build new roads and airstrips, and import Black Rhinos from South Africa and wild dogs from the Pangani River valley in Arusha province.

The message put forth by both organizations, at toney London and Hollywood fundraising soirees, is that the environmental health of the Mkomazi Reserve was severely threatened by the activities and practices of people who were "not indigenous too the area" and "in order to the save the remaining wildlife and reverse the years of deterioration they were relocated outside the reserve."[9] Sorrow was always expressed for the evicted people, who were promised compensation, new housing, clinics, schools, and medicine.

British anthropologist Dan Brockington, who lived and worked in the Mkomazi after the evictions, observes that

These three elements [put forward by the Trusts] are typical of a broader vision of Africa's environment, history and society that drives conservation throughout the continent. Its premise is a belief that people have harmed the environment, buttressed by scientists' interpretation of environmental change. It is powered by the emotive and mystical appeal of wilderness, stunning landscapes and the aura of extraordinary biodiversity. It is grounded in the interpretations of the history of protected areas that play down the presence of people before gazettement. It is characterized by concern to provide for people's needs around protected areas in order to win local support. It is a powerful, persistent and popular vision. Fortunes are invested in its promotion, multitudes absorb the books, films, television documentaries and glossy magazines that endorse and reproduce it. Millions of tourists spend billions of dollars visiting the parks set up to preserve it. It is a vision that can be harmful, unjust and unnecessary."[10]

The Mkomazi episode raises once again that troublesome question about the consequences of conservation evictions. Is it preferable to have people scattered about a protected area, foraging and cultivating under reasonable conservation restrictions, than to have them clustered and embittered in ramshackle makeshift camps and villages on the boundary of the reserve or park? The last Tanzanian census counted forty-eight thousand people living close enough to the Mkomazi Reserve to enter and make some use of it every day. Many of them are conservation refugees, evicted from the reserve. Most of their villages suffer water shortages. There is much bitterness among them, and the evicted people have lost much of the respect and reverence they had for the land when they lived in the reserve. Like so many other protected areas around the world, the opportunity costs are borne by the poorest people, as the benefits from creating a park or reserve don't come close to covering the cost of the evacuees' lost revenues.

There is no question that the biotic health of the Mkomazi Reserve was in serious decline between 1950 and 1980, largely due to overgrazing. But the wholesale eviction of thousands of people and their cattle was an extreme, violent, and unnecessary solution. With enough encouragement and incentive, people can change their lifeways and agricultural practices to enhance the biological diversity of wildlife and to conserve endangered species; in fact, they are more likely to do so if allowed to remain in their traditional homelands rather than forcibly removed to strange landscapes with less productive soil and scarce water.

Twenty-seven percent of Tanzania's land eventually became national parks, game reserves, or national forests, most of it off limits to human habitation. A booming tourist industry does employ some former residents of the reserves as guides, watchmen, porters, and staff at ecolodges, but the overall wealth of the livestock economy plummeted as thousands of traditional pastorals were forced to reduce or completely sell off their herds and learn to cultivate grains and legumes on small plots of arid land. Some turned to poaching for a living, others to prostitution. The painful lesson from Mkomazi, as in so many places like it in the world, is that the rural poor will only support conservation when it improves their lot in life. Attempts to educate indigenous people about conservation, or convince the educated among them, like Martin Saning'o, that it's a worthy pursuit they should be part of, will only succeed if the people perceive that their standard of living is being improved.

The response to the obvious social catastrophe of what Dan Brockington calls "fortress conservation" was to experiment with community conservation, or at least to claim to do so. The aforementioned trusts have led the way, under the dedicated direction of Tony Fitzjohn, a man of high ideals and integrity who truly believes his organizations' persistent mythology about Mkomazi being a former wilderness area, only recently spoiled by human activity, and thus something to be "saved" by the intervention of well-meaning Euro-American conservationists.

Mkomazi provides a useful test case in the evaluation of community conservation. It is frequently held up as a success by conservationists eager to prove that the protected-area strategy can include local communities in the process to everyone's benefit. A closer examination of the effects of eviction and sedentarization on an ancient pastoral culture raises some doubts about real success. Maasai, Parakuyo, Pare, and other traditional Mkomazi cultures have in fact deteriorated in every measurable way. Young men who sold their herds turned to profligate lives, and when their money ran out they became low-wage farm workers and small-time hustlers. Young women facing a shrinking pool of potential husbands sell community essentials such as charcoal, traditional medicines, milk from borrowed goats, or, saddest of all, themselves. Older men who sold their herds have turned to drink. A successful few evacuees bought some land and learned to cultivate it. Now they indenture the less successful. The bottom-line impact of the pastoralists' eviction and economic strangulation is a gradual community and cultural meltdown, though not total demise, for these cultures are strong and so are their people. But many more people are living in hardships that were unimaginable before the evictions.

Sincere attempts have certainly been made in and around Mkomazi to improve the lives of local people and involve them directly in the conservation effort, but in large measure these attempts have failed, at least in the estimation of former pastoralists and the social scientists who study and work with them. "If community conservation only appears to address material needs, and gives only the semblance of power sharing," says Brockington, one of the few scientists to carefully study the impact of evictions from the Mkomazi, "then community conservation will just perpetuate the injustices under new guises."[11]

The Ujamaa Community Resource Trust, a local NGO based in Arusha, Tanzania, tries to mediate conflicts between indigenous peoples and conservation organizations. "Conservation organizations have huge resources," Maanda Ngoitiko, a manager of the trust points out, "but they are dependent on staying in the good graces of central government and will readily run over people's rights for narrow conservation agendas. White-washed gains and hidden or twisted failures are 'marketing norms.'" Despite the massive influx of donor money from Europe and America, conservation NGOs and the Tanzanian government do not have the capacity to manage the 27 percent of the country under protection. "Isn't it time to incorporate people into the equation?" asks Ngoitiko.[12] Meanwhile, the once proud pastoralists of the Serengeti can be found selling handmade trinkets from makeshift homes along the desert road between Ngorongoro and Mkomazi. Most of the proceeds are used to buy water.

Box 3.2

Uncle Sayyaad Speaks

Sayyaad Soltani is the elected chair of the council of Elders of the Kuhi subtribe of the Qashqai Confederation, one of the largest pastoralist communities in Iran. He feels a strong affinity for the Maasai, as this September 2003 speech to the Plenary of the World Parks Congress Durban, Republic of South Africa, attests.

Ladies, gentlemen, and honorable excellencies, my people are nomadic herders. The memory of our tribe goes as far back as five thousand years and the livelihood of our mobile communities has always been sustained by raising goats and sheep. We never stay in one pasture long enough to do it damage. We may now be a pale remembrance of what we were, but we see signs of resurrection, signs that are very important for conservation.

The tale of my tribe is a long one. We used to graze large herds of sheep and goat on vast pastures and grasslands, which sustained the livelihoods of thousands of mobile households. The plant diversity of our pastures and the health of our wetlands endured over generations. We grazed on higher-elevation pastures in the summer and returned to lower elevations in winter. Twice a year, we moved through magnificent migration routes carved, known, and improved through centuries of care. We shared our landscape with wildlife—deer and gazelles, wild goats and sheep, lions, leopards, cheetahs, caracals, foxes, jackals and wolves, and resident and migratory birds. We told the stories of these animals in our tales and our songs and our migration time has been, for centuries, a time of celebration, learning, and spiritual renewal. It has also been a time to connect people and nature in the landscape.

Unfortunately, throughout the twentieth century forced sedentarization was inflicted upon us. Pastures and natural resources were seized from us by various governments. Our migratory paths were interrupted by all sorts of "development" initiatives including dams, oil refineries, and military bases. Our summering and wintering pastures were consistently degraded and fragmented by outsiders. Not even our social identity was left alone. Our tribal foundations were forcibly "restructured" and our image has been cast as that of backward, stubborn peoples who do not wish to adapt to modernity. Our story is similar to the story of nomadic pastoralist peoples all over the world, under all sorts of regimes that do not bear to let us manage our lands and lives. In fact, in recent times some of our people have nearly forgotten the magnificence of our pastoralist lifestyle, but not yet entirely!

Honorable Friends: We pastoral peoples have always considered our land what you would call a "protected area." We have always embraced "conservation" not as a professional activity but as intimate duty and pride of every member of our tribes, as the heart of our livelihood, because our very subsistence depends on it. I hear you talk of ecosystems, landscapes, and connectivity. We have always known about this without using your terms. Our migration patterns transfer seeds. Our grazing patterns shape the landscape. We subsist on our land; we know and care for its diversity of plants and animals. We pray on this land, and we guard its many sacred spaces. For the land provides us also with spiritual well-being. But we can no longer do it alone. In the world of today, we need the concurrence of our governments and all the support that others can give.

Let me give you an example. In the summering grounds of my tribe is a marvelous, life-giving wetland called Chahar Tang-e Kushk-e Zar. It is surrounded by tall reeds, and fields of lush grass, and for hundreds of years it has been used and protected by our ancestors. Today, the water is being diverted for unsustainable agricultural purposes. The wetland's migratory birds, coming from lands far away, are hunted down as soon as we leave for the wintering season. We have been witnessing the shrinking of this wetland, and the destruction of its flora and fauna. I am proud to announce—however—that the Kuhi pastoralist community has discussed this with our government. We have agreed that our wetland will soon be legally recognized as a "Community Conserved Area." When its management will be entrusted to us we will know how to protect it, and we will do our best to restore it to its past splendor.

[For more on Community Conserved Areas see Chapter 17]

Honorable Friends: Before the beginning of this congress, the representatives of mobile peoples from many countries convened and reflected on how to solve our common problems. We have drawn several action points, which we will further refine during this congress, but basically we are here to extend our hand to you. Together, we can be very powerful allies for conservation. Alone, we are likely to act at cross-purposes and waste the best of our energies.

Please help us maintain our nomadic lifestyles. This is not only the heart of our livelihoods. It also creates the biocultural corridors that you conservationists need as much as we do. Stand on our side in opposing the forcible settlements of our people and herds. Allow us to preserve the splendid genetic diversity of our herds, as well as the wildlife diversity that depend on it. Help us preserve our cultural integrity and build our capacities. Talk to us, involve us in decisions, refuse to understand us by stereotypes, and tell us how we can help you. We, the mobile peoples and pastoralist communities of the world, are prepared to be your strongest allies in conservation. Are you?

Translated by Aghaghia Rahimzadeh

Amboseli

The European appropriation of the African landscape for aesthetic consumption is inseparable from the appropriation of African land for material production.
—Roderick Neuman, Florida International University

The Amboseli ecosystem is primarily open savannah grassland. River systems north of the basin, the watershed of Kilimanjaro, form a seasonal floodplain that hosts millions of migratory birds after the rainy season, and natural springs throughout the basin provide a permanent source of water during the dry season. The basin is ideal open range for a livestock culture and uncountable generations of Maasai pastoralists have grazed their cattle, sheep, and goats in Amboseli following the migratory patterns of the area's wild ungulates, which the herdsmen regard as "second cattle" to be harvested during droughts and times of protein scarcity.

The Amboseli also supports an impressive array of charismatic species that are used as tourist attractors and as funding mechanisms by global conservationists—elephants, lions, rhinoceros, giraffes, cheetahs, zebras, buffaloes, wildebeests, impalas, gazelles, hyenas, baboons, bats, and over four hundred different birds. The prominent geological formation is Mount Kilimanjaro. Thus the region has always had enormous tourism potential.

As with the Yosemite and Yellowstone national parks, the creation of Amboseli National Park was gradual. Early in the twentieth century Amboseli was a game reserve, formed to protect wildlife from excessive hunting. During this period the Maasai retained full land rights and were permitted to graze their livestock throughout the reserve, making it one of the few multiple-use systems in Africa. It was in fact stated Kenyan government policy not to "interfere with indigenous people or stand in the way of legitimate human development" in protected areas. With sound range management and traditional ecological knowledge a harmonious balance was maintained between nomadic humans and wildlife.

However, in 1945 the colonial governments of Kenya, seeking to protect "our" natural heritage and preserve some of the earth's most magnificent creatures, passed a National Parks Ordinance that called for a drastic change in conservation policy from "protection through legal hunting to preservation through land protection." African wildlife was placed under foreign control, and grazing rights were severely restricted.

The Maasai were furious. But despite their protests, the Amboseli National Reserve was created in 1947 with the hope that it would one day become a national park. Although the Maasai were allowed to remain in the reserve, they viewed grazing restrictions as a seizure of their land—a taking. Their hostility led to open confrontations with conservationists and park authorities.

In 1971, by decree of President Jomo Kenyatta, the reserve was declared Amboseli National Park, new restrictions and management policy to be effective by 1974. Hunting was banned outright. The Maasai were promised compensation for loss of their pastures. It was very slow to come, however. Poverty spread through their communities, and tourism degraded their culture, bringing with it disease and illicit drugs. The ecosystems and lifeways of the Maasai began to collapse, and very few tourist dollars remained in their communities. Maasai leaders began pressuring the government to restore some of their pastures. A second, 600-square-kilometer "Maasai Park" was proposed, to be owned and managed by the Maasai. The plan was rejected.

Retaliation was swift and brutal. Maasai warriors began spearing lions, leopards, and rhinos, leaving their carcasses near favored tourist campsites. The government had to negotiate. In a tentative compromise the Maasai agreed to stop killing animals and grazing their livestock in Amboseli National Park if the boundaries were shifted to free up some good grass and water and fairer compensation was paid for lost range. When government leaders failed to deliver on their promises, the Maasai simply returned with their herds to the park.

Eventually, the New York Zoological Society (now the Wildlife Conservation Society) and the World Bank stepped in, providing some community compensation and funding a pipeline from Ol Tukai, a favored Maasai watering hole, to a new site outside the park. A school and a clinic were also built. At the same time, a national plan was developed to promote wildlife education, park management training, and tourism. Although the water system broke down almost immediately, tempers subsided and some Maasai actually began to accept the park, although with some hesitation.

"We have to be hopeful" said tribal leader Paul Ntiati, "but to the Maasai there is a positive and a negative value to wildlife conservation. Before, when we were masters of most of southern Kenya, we used to look upon wildlife as our own. Many of our songs are about animals and the beauty of them. Now, we are told that they belong to the government. And we have to put up with someone else's property on our grazing lands; and when they kill our livestock and we are not allowed to kill theirs, it makes us angry and resentful."[13] Wildlife in the ecosystem gradually increased, Kenya eventually boasting more rhinos than any other country in Africa.[14] Elephant numbers rose significantly due to reduced poaching, while zebras and wildebeests thrived with less competition from domestic stock. And tourism boomed. Amboseli became a continent-wide model for new national parks—for a while.

Two problems arose that still exacerbate each other today. First, the elephant population grew far beyond the carrying capacity of Amboseli National Park. In search of food, elephants vandalized the woodlands, plucking seedlings and stripping the bark off mature tree that soon died for lack of water. While the loss of woodland provided more space for grazing animals like zebras and wildebeests, elephants remained a serious problem. Even legendary elephant protector Cynthia Moss, who at one point had named all eight hundred elephants in Amboseli, eventually admitted there were too many, and supported a cull. And the Maasai who lost their pastures gradually shifted their lifeways from cattle grazing to agriculture, which they carried out on seven communally owned "group ranches" of fifty- to two-hundred-fifty-thousand acres surrounding the park. While their livestock once roamed the savannah side by side with elephants, sharing watering holes with eland and gazelle, today Maasai farms are routinely raided by buffalo and trampled by elephants. In a bad season a family can lose three-quarters of its crop in a single night.

In 2005, the Kenyan government floated the idea of converting Amboseli back to a county-run wildlife reserve. That would place management responsibilities and powers back into the hands of local, mostly Maasai, Kenyans. The move was strongly opposed by park officials and conservationists who said that county leaders lack the ability to manage a reserve. They also feared that the Maasai would be allowed back in to graze and water their cattle, and that security, both for tourists and wildlife, would be compromised. Nevertheless, Amboseli was degazetted.

Box 3.3

Human-Wildlife Conflict

Traditional wildlife conservation has been slow to assess and build on cultural values of coexistence with and tolerance of wildlife. The historical treatment of the Maasai and their vast herds of cattle provide one of the best examples.

For centuries the Maasai herded their livestock along the established migratory routes of wildlife, with whom they coexisted in relative peace. They called the wild ungulates their "second cattle," as they would rely upon them for sustenance during times of severe drought when their own herds would be seriously depleted. Thus the Maasai developed a friendly symbiosis with wildlife. However, the forced transformation of the Maasai from pastoral herders to settled farmers has radically changed their relationship with the wildebeest, zebra, gazelle, impala, and elephants which frequently raid and trample their crops, and which they are no longer permitted to hunt for food. They now refer somewhat bitterly to wildlife as "the government's cattle."

By fracturing a positive long-term relationship with wildlife, conservationists and East African governments have contributed to a serious decline in the economic wellbeing of the Maasai, who remain quite resentful.

Documented examples of human-wildlife conflicts that are being created or exacerbated by modern conservation policies and practices are forcing conservationists to carefully consider the cultures of indigenous peoples living in or near the margins of new protected areas, particularly those cultural features that support peaceful coexistence between humans and wildlife.

The Maasai today are regarded as symbols of revolt against a conservation paradigm that either distorts or ignores the traditional use of protected areas. Whenever the opportunity arises at small or large gatherings of international conservationists, Maasai leaders like Martin Saning'o are present to remind the audience that they have gradually and unnecessarily been turned into "enemies of conservation." And the Maasai are not alone in that regard. In fact the entire African continent is dotted with embittered communities of people who describe themselves as such.

Colonial conservationists like Bernard Grzimek, Dian Fossey, John Waithaka, George Schaller, David Western, George and Joy Adamson, and Louis and Mary Leakey regarded the protection of Africa's natural heritage to be a moral duty. But for most of them the morality seemed to stop at the border between wildlife and humanity. Thus Africans have been suspicious of conservationists whom they perceive as insensitive to their right to make a living from the land. How else to interpret native hunting bans in vast reaches of Tanzania, Zambia, and Zimbabwe where safari hunting is still allowed?

And what are Africans to make of parks and game reserves imposed on their most productive lands in Kenya, a country that boasts over fifty national parks and reserves, or Botswana where 34 percent of the country's surface is under "Wildlife Management"? And how should they respond to conservationists who argued that 50 percent of the entire continent needs to be placed under "protection" if global biodiversity is to be preserved?

Box 3.4

The [Other*] Arusha Declaration

We the Indigenous peoples of Eastern and Southern Africa assembled in Arusha 10–22 August 2003, reaffirm the Kimberly Declaration, Kari-Oca Declaration of Rio 1992 and the World Summit on Sustainable Development Plan of Action.

• Indigenous Peoples of Africa demand the recognition, acceptance and protection of our cultural identity and diversity, languages, ways of life and all other fundamental human rights.
• As Indigenous Peoples we demand our inherent rights to self-determination. We further relentlessly assert for unconditional collective and holistic land use, ownership, control, and management of our ancestral lands, forests, wildlife, and other resources utilizing our unique traditional resource management systems.

• Indigenous Peoples' lands are endowed with diverse natural resources. We have a [sic] long-time experience [in] managing and using them for different purposes. The continued process of reckless mining and logging [and] over-fishing and hunting causes a lot of danger for human and wildlife as well as disturbances of whole ecosystem. We therefore condemn and urge governments, private sectors, particularly multinational companies, to desist from unsustainable practices, which cause environmental degradation.

• Indigenous knowledge, being an integral part of our heritage, defines our distinct identities as Indigenous Peoples. This is endowed to us by nature and bestowed by our ancestors. We denounce the loss of Indigenous Knowledge noting the extensive exploitation of our cultures and traditional knowledge systems and we urge governments, tourism sectors and other key players to device a participatory mechanism, which safeguards, develops and protects our heritage from misuse and [m]isappropriation.

• [With regard to] protected areas and to realize the principle of free, prior and informed consent, we demand the effective involvement of Indigenous Peoples in decision making, policy formulation, planning, implementation, monitoring and fair sharing of accrued proceeds.

• We condemn the human rights violation of Indigenous Peoples as a result of the creation of protected areas, which has led to the disintegration of Indigenous Peoples and their communities, integration and assimilation into the mainstream society.

• The denial of social amenities, harassment and subsequent displacement of the Bushmen from the Central Kalahari Game Reserve by the Botswana Government. We therefore call upon the government of Botswana to provide basic social amenities to communities still residing in the reserve and to restart negotiations with the concerned San/ Bushmen. [For more on the San see chapter 10.]

• The displacement of the Batwa people from the Bwindi and Mgahinga National Parks without compensation has led to landlessness and near cultural and physical extinction. We demand the government of Uganda to recognize the Batwa Indigenous Peoples as citizens of Uganda eligible to social services, their land and the right to the benefits accruing from the parks and forests. [See chapter 5 for more on the Batwa eviction from national parks in Uganda.]

• The deliberate forceful eviction of the Pastoral Maasai from Mkomazi Game Reserve and the intended eviction of the Maasai from Ngorongoro Conservation Area who were initially relocated from the Serengeti National Park. We strongly urge the Tanzanian government to stop the intended eviction and restore to the victims their original ancestral land, provide basic social amenities, and adequate compensation for the loss of life and property.

Noting the widespread violation of human rights as illustrated by the above cases, we strongly denounce the ongoing displacement of Indigenous Peoples, the loss of biodiversity and environmental degradation in respect of conventional conservation. We call for the effective participation and integration of our traditional practices and knowledge in modern conservation.

To understand and appreciate the international processes pertaining to Indigenous peoples, we urge the African Governments to fully participate in different discussions and fora on Indigenous Peoples. Among them [are] the United Nations Draft Declaration on Indigenous Populations which requires advancement, the ongoing permanent Forum for Indigenous Peoples' issues and ILO convention 169 which calls for ratification;

We call upon the United Nations to convene a World Conference on Indigenous Peoples in order to evaluate the progress of Indigenous Peoples decade and extend it to enable more visibility and advancement of Indigenous Peoples worldwide.

---

* Not to be confused with the Arusha Declaration of 1967, a speech given by Tanzanian President Julius Nyerere on the future of socialism in Africa, this "lesser" declaration was drafted and signed by indigenous peoples from Tanzania, Uganda, Kenya, Sudan, Botswana, Namibia, and Ethiopia in Arusha, Tanzania, on August 21, 2003.

As evictions of pastoralists and other indigenous communities around the world continued, transnational conservation became increasingly concentrated in the offices of five enormous, largely U.S.-based organizations. While somewhat distinct in their cultures and approaches to conservation, these well-funded, science-driven organizations are in large measure designing the global strategy and setting the agenda for biodiversity protection worldwide.

4

BINGO

A great strength of the conservation movement in the twentieth century was its capacity for self-criticism.

—Bill Adams, Cambridge University

In November 2004, a seasoned anthropologist named Mac Chapin rocked the world of global conservation. In a detailed and trenchant article entitled "A Challenge to Conservationists," published in *World-Watch* magazine, Chapin took three large organizations "that dominate the world's conservation agenda" to task for their close ties to transnational corporations and international banks, and their distant, often hostile relationship with indigenous peoples "whose lands they are in business to protect."

What made Chapin's report so threatening to big conservation was that he was targeting the money that supports it. Here's how he opened his report:

In June 2003 representatives of major foundations concerned with the planet's threatened biodiversity gathered in South Dakota for a meeting of the Consultative Group on Biodiversity. On the second evening, after dinner, several of the attendees met to discuss a problem about which they had become increasingly disturbed. In recent years the foundations had given millions of dollars of support to nonprofit conservation organizations, and had even helped some of those groups get launched. Now, however, there were indications that three of the largest of these organizations [Conservation International (CI), The Nature Conservancy (TNC), and the Worldwide Fund for Nature (WWF)] were increasingly excluding from full involvement in their programs the indigenous and traditional peoples living in territories the conservationists were trying to protect. In some cases there were complaints that the conservationists were being abusive.

That paragraph hints at a story that millions of indigenous people around the world had been waiting for nearly a century to see in print, as they had been trying through all those years to deliver the same message to the kinds of representatives who were at that meeting in 2003. "We knew that the foundation community would listen to things said in a highly respected journal that we had been saying for years," remarked Rebecca Adamson, a Cherokee leader of America's native rights movement and founder of First Peoples Worldwide, an indigenous advocacy organization based in Virginia.

Native people on every continent, Chapin wrote, were becoming increasingly hostile toward international conservation organizations based in the United States and Europe—groups they had nicknamed the BINGOs (Big International Non-Governmental Organizations). These NGOs, with their singular, science-based interest in creating vast protected areas, seemed to have little interest in the land rights or respect for the traditional lifeways of peoples who had been living in the areas for centuries, in some cases millennia. What native people found particularly distasteful was the tendency of some BINGOs to express support and affection for indigenous peoples, then "partner" with extractive corporations that, according to Chapin, "are directly involved in pillaging and destroying forest areas owned by indigenous peoples." Indigenous ownership was, of course, challenged by those very corporations and the national governments that sought their business. And the BINGOs either concurred or looked the other way as evictions proceeded, often under the cover of "conservation."

The BINGO justification for partnering with oil, gas, pharmaceutical, logging, and mining interests is and always has been that those partnerships assure that the corporations involved behave more responsibly, more "sustainably," in their extraction of resources. Here's the way CI words its policy: "Since its inception, Conservation International has held the belief that engaging industry is an effective way to make progress toward addressing the rapid decline in the world's biodiversity. Conservation International takes a pragmatic view in this respect. The real world fact is that companies will continue to be granted concessions by governments to operate in high biodiversity areas." Another real-world fact is that the tacit approval of CI and other BINGOs, purchased with donations that are a fraction of extractive costs, adds environmental respectability to both the extractive project itself and the relevant company's public image. And it removed a potentially powerful adversary from the opposition to logging, drilling, and mining in wildlife sanctuaries and other protected areas.

So it's a win-win-lose situation, with local, land-reliant people losing. Even the most carefully constructed drilling rig, pipeline, logging road, or luxury ecolodge has no bearing on sustainability from an indigenous point of view. These infrastructure encroachments pass through or are situated on hunting grounds and food stocks decline. The combination of displacements and outside resource use inexorably leads to local poverty and prompts traditional conservationists like Maasai leader and spokesman Martin Saning'o to consider themselves victims of a new form of colonialism and "enemies of conservation."

The essential contradiction of the conservation-corporate partnership reaches a crisis point when the extractive corporation wishes to explore or harvest a truly sensitive ecosystem. What can the conservation "partner" say—"No, you can't explore it, or go ahead, but if you find what you're looking for you must extract it sustainably"? That's naive. Extractive industries can't make money extracting resources slowly, nor can they do so without compromising the ecological integrity of the area in question. Airstrips, drilling rigs, and bulldozers are rarely eco-friendly. If an ecological hot spot is too sensitive for an ancient tribe of hunter-gatherers or pastoralists, is it not too sensitive for Texaco?

Big conservation rose in unison against Chapin's allegations. Their worry was not that his views would reach indigenous peoples or their advocates. They had been saying the same things for years. In fact, Chapin, a working anthropologist, heard his arguments first from people he had studied. The BINGOs' fear was that new funding sources they had so carefully cultivated—like the Gordon and Betty Moore Foundation, the John D. and Catherine T. MacArthur Foundation, the French and Japanese governments, United Nations Development Program (UNDP), USAID, and the World Bank and its Global Environment Facility (GEF)—would believe Chapin and reconsider their generous support of a transnational establishment that had come to dominate the global conservation agenda.

"Imperial Conservation"?

Encounters between conservationists and indigenous people are never between equals.

—Jim Igoe, University of Colorado at Denver

Oldest of BINGOs, The Nature Conservancy was launched in 1946 when a small group of scientists from the U.S.-based Ecologists' Union resolved to take "direct action" to save threatened natural areas. In 1950 the union changed its name to The Nature Conservancy, which began buying conservation easements on private land. TNC, which eventually turned to buying land outright, grew to be the largest of all conservation NGOs, with assets exceeding $3 billion. Rapid growth began in 1965 when the Ford Foundation made a small grant to pay TNC's first full-time president, Dr. Richard H. Goodwin. During the 1970s the organization expanded into all fifty states. Its first international division opened in South America and the TNC has since spread to other continents.

But rising internal tensions at TNC's Washington, DC, headquarters came to a head in 1987, when all but one of the forty members of the international division left work one night intending never to return. The leadership—including Peter Seligmann, Rachel Gomez, Spencer Beebe, and Liliana Madrigal—met for drinks at the legendary Tabard Inn and started a new organization called Conservation International. Today Seligmann is chairman and CEO of CI; Gomez, Beebe, and Madrigal have moved on. The positions they left, and other slots, were filled by another exodus in 1989, this time from the Worldwide Fund for Nature.

TNC remains the largest BINGO, but no conservation organization in history has raised money faster and more creatively than CI, which grew from a budget of $27.8 million in 1998 to $144.2 million in 2005. Credit for that goes partly to brilliant spinning of CI's ecological "hot spot" strategy, but mostly to Seligmann, who is regarded in the nonprofit sector as one of the most aggressive and successful fundraisers in the business.

One young colleague remembers Seligmann handing him something to read the night before they were both to call on a major donor. It turned out to be an article about how German Field Marshall Erwin Rommel prevailed in World War II by destroying enemy tanks in such a way that their fuel was not burned. Rommel would then siphon the fuel into his own tanks, enabling them to drive deeper into the desert and destroy more enemy tanks.

"Peter, I think you gave me the wrong thing to read," the young associate said the next morning. "This is about Rommel stealing gas from enemy tanks in North Africa to fuel his own."

"Exactly," said Seligmann. "That is the art of fundraising."[1]

After one such call, delivered standing in a Rocky Mountain trout stream in 1998, Intel founder Gordon Moore, who had retired from his company and created a foundation with his wife Betty, promised CI the largest single private grant in conservation history—$261 million. It was the first installment of what may eventually total $500 million.

Second oldest of the BINGOs is WWF, originally called the World Wildlife Fund, but later, under the same initials, renamed the Worldwide Fund for Nature. Launched in London on September 11, 1961, with a small office in Switzerland, WWF's work was at first limited to raising funds for the IUCN, a process that began with a front-page story in the London *Daily Mirror* featuring a black rhinoceros and its calf under a banner headline reading "DOOMED to Disappear from the Face of the Earth due to Man's FOLLY, GREED and NEGLECT." A week later, WWF had sixty thousand pounds in the bank and big game hunter Prince Phillip, the Duke of Edinburgh, had agreed to head up WWF's British chapter, joined soon thereafter by his old friend Prince Barnard of the Netherlands, who became president of WWF International.

At the 1961 launch WWF issued a seven-step "World Wildlife Charter" that promised to:

1. prevent any extinction of wildlife,

2. make sure that room shall be left for wildlife,

3. protect all wildlife from unintentional or wanton cruelty,

4. encourage children to develop a love and understanding of wildlife,

5. make certain that all those whose work has an impact on nature recognize their responsibility to wildlife,

6. help those nations in need of it in order to preserve their wildlife, and

7. work together to save the world's wildlife.

The message was clear. The global goal of conservation would be to promote a worldwide moral agenda of responsibility to wildlife, particularly charismatic mammalian fauna like the panda, which eventually became WWF's totem and subject of the most ubiquitous logo in the conservation industry.

With two high-profile royals on the letterhead, global business celebrities like Robert MacNamara, Agha Hasan Abedi, Lew Wasserman, Robert Vesco, Augie Busch, Lord Kagan, Daniel Ludwig, Nelson Bunker Hunt, Thomas Watson, and Henry Ford II became generous donors in the 1960s. WWF fundraisers clearly did not consider a potential donor's environmental record, or criminal history, before approaching him or her. Nor did people like billionaire Daniel Ludwig, whose companies ravaged the Amazon, pass up an opportunity to "greenwash" his reputation with a generous gift to save Chi-Chi the panda, one of the WWF mascots then in residence at the London Zoo.

For the next twenty years or more, WWF remained largely a fundraising entity using desperate predictions of wildlife extinction, particularly of the panda, tiger, elephant, and rhinoceros, to raise millions for wildlife conservation. The organization grew rapidly, opening offices in the northern-hemisphere nations where fundraising potential seemed strongest. Although the original impetus for WWF's creation was Sir Julian Huxley's passionate 1960 series in *The Observer*, celebrating the undeniable beauty of large animals in Africa, it would not be until the early 1980s that WWF, with over a million supporters worldwide and a $10 million "Nature Trust" created by Prince Bernhard, would begin to part ways with IUCN and open its own offices in the developing world. Today WWF operates in 130 countries and employ over four thousand people working out of twenty-eight fairly autonomous chapters in as many different countries.

The first test of WWF's influence and loyalty began in the late 1980s over the question of whether or not to support a worldwide ban on ivory trading to stem the demise of elephants, which for a century had been ruthlessly slaughtered to feed a worldwide demand for fancy combs, figurines jewelry, and piano keys. The controversy unfolded first over whether or not to declare the elephant an endangered species, and later over whether or not to ban all trade in ivory. The ensuing debate bitterly divided WWF leadership and eventually ignited a firestorm both in Africa and throughout the global conservation movement. The eventual conflict turned out to be less about ivory and more about money—not only the money made from poached ivory but also the money that could be raised by conservationists by promoting the undeniable charisma of elephants.

Inside WWF that divide expressed itself in an intense battle between professional conservationists convinced that a limited cull of elephants ("sustainable utilization") was essential not only to the health of Africa's ecosystems but also to the elephants' future as well, and fundraisers who believed that opposing a ban would drive contributing members away. The two sides hammered it out internally, in an endless series of what were later described as "blood and guts" meetings. WWF-US was flooded with thousands of letters supporting the ban. The struggle persisted until June 1989, when money and PR prevailed over science and the WWF board voted to support an outright ban on the trade of ivory.

That did not mean that WWF would be opposed to culling elephants when "it was absolutely necessary for the conservation of the species," only that elephants should never have their faces mangled with chain saws after they were killed, and their bodies left to rot in a meadow. Ban all purchasing of ivory, worldwide, and that poaching would stop. Of course it hasn't.

There are two other, slightly smaller conservation groups that deserve mention, as they are frequently included in the BINGO category. First is the Wildlife Conservation Society, formerly the New York Zoological Society that founded and still owns the world-renowned Bronx Zoo. WCS, which now has operations on every continent, and gets very mixed reviews from indigenous peoples and their supporters, is currently focused on the Congo Basin where their high-profile adventurer Michael Fay has inspired a massive initiative to save the second-largest rainforest on the planet. The homelands and livelihoods of countless forest communities hang in the balance. (Chapter 18 details the WCS Congo Basin initiative.)

If the number of BINGOs were to be limited to five, the fifth in size and stature would be the African Wildlife Foundation. Although exclusively focused on African animals, as its name implies, AWF was conceived (by big game hunter Russell Train and his socialite friends), founded, headquartered, and managed in Washington, DC. Opened the same year as WWF (1961), the African Wildlife Leadership Foundation, its original name, was likewise founded on the principle that whites had to intervene in African wildlife management or the game would be destroyed. Realizing early in its existence that there was big money in elephants, and that culling would be a hard sell to a membership universe of species preservationists, AWF joined the counter-science bandwagon, ignored the wishes of every nation in Africa, the position of every member of IUCN, and aggressively promoted an ivory ban.

Money

Conservation refugees are invisible because visibility raises the price of conservation.
—Charles Geisler, Cornell University

While the global budget for conservation has been shrinking fairly steadily since 1990, the BINGOs have been growing exponentially. This indicates a level of preference and trust held toward them by the seven-, eight- and nine-figure funders of conservation—national governments, government agencies, bilateral and multilateral banks, large foundations, transnational corporations, and international foreign aid agencies like UNDP, UNEP, and the GEF, all of which are attracted to the "large-scale conservation" approaches formulated by the BINGOs. As in every level of philanthropy, banking, and public funding, big money seems to prefer big projects.

The GEF, which is now the financing mechanism for the Convention on Biological Diversity (CBD), in fact strictly limits its financing to large projects with a clear global (as opposed to local) impact. By global the GEF means initiatives that effect biodiversity, climate, international waters, the ozone layer, land arability, and persistent organic pollutants. But the main emphasis is biodiversity, and most grants addressing that objective go toward the management of protected areas, particularly national parks and biosphere reserves. Between 1991 and 2001, the GEF spent almost a billion dollars on protected-area management.

Like the World Bank and the aid agencies, the GEF does not make direct grants to international conservation NGOs contracted to "manage" conservation projects, but does allow them to draw appropriate operating expenses from grants that are frequently in the tens of millions of dollars. WWF, which between 1990 and 2001 received about 45 percent of USAID's $271.3 million appropriation to conservation,[2] is complimented by critics of this system whenever they allocate less than 50 percent of a bank-funded project's budget to internally operated projects. That rarely happens any longer. As other sources of funding have diminished, the portion of government and bilateral banking money going to internally generated WWF projects has often exceeded 80 percent, and WWF, which in 1990 received one percent of its total revenue from development banks and agencies, had by the end of the century increased that portion to 24 percent. What is clear is that the BINGOs have become increasingly reliant, financially and politically, on institutions like the World Bank, USAID, and a host of multilateral banks whose primary global interest is economic development. That unexpected engagement has changed both the nature and practice of global conservation, as conservation NGOs absorb the culture of their major donors, and withhold verbal criticism of industries and businesses that they know are affecting the ecological health of the planet.

It is the hope, sometimes the insistence, of large donors to the BINGOs that these organizations regrant a portion of their appropriation to

Table 4.1
Nonphilanthropic global funding for conservation—2004

Agency	Period	Amount
Global Environmental Facility (GEF)	Active projects 2004	$2,161,000,000
World Bank	Active projects 2004	$5,623,670,000
USAID	Active projects 2001	$129,762,138
European Commission	Fiscal year 2004	$88,000,000
Total		$8,002,432,138*

* Some of the projects represented in this total are not entirely concerned with conservation, but they all have strong conservation emphasis.

smaller, more local conservation NGOs. This saves the funding agencies from burdensome paperwork and oversight, which they assume will be handled by the prime grantee. There appears to be little concern about the power and influence this gives to WWF, CI, and other organizations, or the lack of accountability inherent in the regranting process. In many places, when CI or WWF are unable to find a compliant local NGO to receive regranted funds, they simply create a new one of their own, hire a reliable national to run it, and grant it the funds to operate.

While the BINGOs claim to be fostering local conservation efforts around the world, the truth is a declining portion of their grant money is finding its way through to local NGOs, even the self-generated ones. Take for example CI's Critical Ecosystem Partnership Fund (CEPF), a $150 million partnership with the GEF, the government of Japan, the John D. and Catherine T. MacArthur Foundation, and the World Bank. CEPF "provides funding to engage civil society in safeguarding biodiversity hot spots," according to CI's website. The avowed purpose of CEPF is to strengthen local conservation NGOs. According to its founders' guidelines a minimum of 50 percent of total grant money is to be passed through to local groups. However, in the first two years of its Latin American operation, $6.9 million of $8.9 million granted by CEPF went directly to CI. Local organizations, including several created by CI, received the remaining $2 million, or 22 percent of the total allocation.[3]

In 1998, WWF and the World Bank formed a smaller but similar partnership called the Global Forest Alliance, which now operates in over 30 countries. And like CEPF, the public description of the Alliance is noble and unimpeachable: "By working with partners in government, civil society, and the business sector, the Alliance partners leverage support and results to reverse the process of forest loss and degradation, increase forest cover and quality, and harness the potential of forest lands to secure livelihoods and bring about lasting reductions in rural poverty, sustainable economic development, and the protection of vital local and global environmental values and services."

Regranting also creates an accountability problem, particularly for the original grantor who is unable to follow the money down to its final recipient. When this created serious friction between the Gordon Moore

Foundation and CI, Peter Seligmann asked for and received from Moore an additional $17 million grant to expand their financial reporting functions in a way that would satisfy the donor. Seventeen million dollars granted directly to local conservation groups or indigenous communities could accomplish a lot of conservation, but granted to CI's accounting department in Washington, DC: not much.

Greenwashing

Among the most controversial of big conservation's supporters is a growing number of transnational corporations, among them some of the most aggressive resource extractors in the world. TNC claims almost two thousand corporate sponsors donating about $300 million a year. CI lists over two hundred and fifty partnered corporations in its Center for Environmental Leadership and Business (CELB), which "promotes business practices that reduce industry's ecological footprint, contribute to conservation, and creates value for the companies that adopt them. The result is a net benefit for the global environment and participating companies." CELB has brought millions into CI's coffers from donors such as McDonald's, Boise Cascade, Chiquita Brands, CEMEX, Chevron Texaco, Mitsubishi, Exxon-Mobil, Ford Motor Company, Newmont Mining, Rio Tinto, Shell Oil, Weyerhauser, and the coal-burning AES Energy Corp. WWF, which raises most of its money from individual donors, receives proportionately less from corporations, but the amount is significant and the influence is real.

As more corporate sponsors and partners are drawn into the global conservation strategy and business sponsors insist that their grants be managed in a businesslike way, employing corporate accounting and timeframe planning techniques, the culture of big conservation becomes inexorably more corporate. One recent sign of that trend was the appointment of Peter Seligmann as chairman *and* CEO of Conservation International, a title virtually unheard of in the nonprofit sector but all too common in the business world, where managers rather than owners rule the roost. CI also rewarded its largest donor, Gordon Moore, with a seat on its board and for a while the chair of its powerful executive committee.

Conservation annual reports, slick and glossy, are indistinguishable from those of their new corporate sponsors. Outcomes are predicted from strategy, strategies are increasingly "market driven," and financial reports are presented in a classic balance-sheet/income-statement format. Descriptions of long-term planning are rigidly economic and political in their orientation, and specific goals and targets are clearly stated.

What appeals to corporate donors and their favorite banks is not only the BINGOs' willingness to work side by side with extractive corporations, and to reshape their organizations, but also their ecoregional approach to global conservation. Rather than address the entire planet as a holistic ecosystem endangered by industrial practices, the BINGO approach maps for protection of vast areas of "wild" landscape, high in biological diversity and low in population. CI calls them "biodiversity hot spots"; WWF, "priority places", and TNC calls them "functional conservation areas" and refers to them collectively as their "portfolio." African Wildlife Foundation, which still relies more heavily on the generosity of wealthy individuals, prefers the homier term *heartlands*, which they define as "large landscapes of exceptional natural value." Definitions vary slightly and there is considerable geographical overlap, but the hot protected areas increase in number year by year as new parks and reserves are added.

If a protected area happens also to be rich in resources, all the better to have a business-friendly conservation group in the mix to contain local outrage and assure the world that minerals, fuels, and fibers are being extracted from nature in an environmentally responsible manner.

Indigenous leaders deride the business-conservation partnership as a mutually convenient mix of corporate "greenwashing" and BINGO PR. They pointedly cite a recently issued WWF memorandum instructing "ecoregion conservation programmes [to] develop a bold, engaging, and ambitious vision for an ecoregion in order to set direction and arouse support. This vision should contain an inspirational message to motivate and engage stakeholders and partners."[4] Meanwhile, the message to potential corporate donors claims "independent research shows that consumers have a high regard for a company that invests in its social and environmental responsibilities." Among WWF's "conservation partners" attracted by this message are Exxon Mobil, Dow Chemical, Chevron Texaco, Monsanto, and Weyerhauser.

Of course there is nothing inherently wrong with trying to encourage extractive corporations to behave better than most of them do, and it is laudable for any organization attempting to protect biodiversity to work in close cooperation with indigenous peoples. But can the same organization do both? Why not leave the corporate reform work to the groups that do it best, like Environmental Defense, which was created for that very purpose, and instead concentrate on helping local communities create and manage new protected areas? The answer, of course, is money.

Territory

Wapiganapo tembo nyasi huumia.
(When elephants fight the grass suffers.)
—Swahili proverb

Being fiercely competitive with one another—over money and global influence—each BINGO has carefully chosen territories that are respected by the others. CI, for example, claims Suriname and Guyana as its domain. TNC works almost exclusively in Nicaragua and Wildlife Conservation Society acts alone in the Gran Chaco region of Bolivia. Even within organizations there is territorial scuffling. WWF-US, for example, recently moved out of Tanzania, replaced by WWF-International, which is based in Switzerland. Most indigenous communities would prefer to work with the International arm of WWF, as its representatives are more sensitive to traditional cultures and less beholden to politically and economically influential donors.

The competition for funds has had a lamentable effect on big conservation. Here is the way Tom McShane of WWF-International describes it: "Biodiversity conservation's devil is the competition for donor funding. We all know that successful conservation requires money. Unfortunately in the pursuit of funds, conservation organizations find themselves making claims based on little more than theory. This marketing of conservation approaches has resulted in a dogmatic debate, outwardly over how best to conserve the world's biodiversity, which is a necessary question, but behind the scenes over how to get the funds before someone else does, which is not."[5]

As the preponderance of funding for conservation has shifted from individuals and family foundations to larger government and quasi-government entities, so too have the priorities and strategies of biodiversity conservation. One consequence is that the BINGOs have all been forced to work more closely and uncritically with national governments, many of them deeply corrupt and acting against any semblance of conservation. And it is generally those governments that, in the alleged interest of conservation, initiate evictions of indigenous peoples who are often living in logging, mining, and grazing concessions granted to extractive industries or well-capitalized ecotourism projects. These concessions can be an inconvenient place to also contain indigenous communities.

Hope in the Field

Those who wish to dance with wolves must first learn to live with wolves.
—Daniel Wildcat, Haskell Indian Nations University

As I discovered in South and Central America, Mac Chapin found a major disconnect between the field and headquarters of many conservation NGOs. "Unlike the braintrusts in the main offices, representatives in the field are not dealing with abstractions," said Chapin. "Some have realized that they can accomplish little of value if they don't work in partnership with local people. Some have commented that they see their community work as their focus of attention and pay little heed to the global pronouncements coming from on high. Unfortunately these field efforts are given little support in the home office and as the drift of high level support for indigenous peoples continues, future financial backing may be hard to find."

The June 2003 meeting Chapin described in his article prompted Ford Foundation executives to commission two studies on the matter. Ford officials had already been hearing bitter complaints from some of their indigenous grantees about the treatment they had been receiving from conservation NGOs, particularly Conservation International. There had been virtually no previous studies examining the impact of conservation on human communities. Here was an opportunity to "deal with the questions of livelihood, tenure and participation" alongside the challenge of large-scale conservation. The original assignment for the studies was to examine only the work of CI, but when Ford officials realized this might be perceived as unfairly piling on one organization, WWF and TNC were added to the studies' purview.

Both studies found that "the large landscape approach [has brought] conservation NGOs face to face with millions of impoverished people," that indigenous complaints were by and large accurate, and that "large conservation organizations, with notable regional exceptions, do not necessarily see it as their responsibility to make links between biodiversity conservation and local sustainable livelihoods."[6]

At the time the studies were submitted there were two prominent conservationists on the Ford Foundation Board of Trustees: Yolanda Kakabadse, former minister of the environment for Ecuador, a member of TNC's board, and then-president of IUCN; and Katherine Fuller, president of WWF-US, who also chaired the Ford Foundation board. When shown the terms of reference for the studies, Fuller at first had no objections to the research proceeding. But when Kakabadse read them she feared that TNC, which had recently weathered a blistering investigation by *The Washington Post*, was in for more bad publicity. She expressed her concerns to Fuller, who changed her opinion and agreed that the reports should not reach the public, or for that matter the eyes of the Ford Foundation board. The reports' authors, Arvind Khare and David Bray, were told not to give their reports to the board but were invited in to make a verbal presentation of their findings. A bland summary was presented to the board at the next meeting, some members of which asked for and did receive "confidential" copies of the full report.

Even well-paid researchers and their assistants hate to see their work buried to protect the powerful. Therefore copies were leaked and I was a fortunate recipient. The most startling finding of the studies was that during a time when financial contributions to conservation were rapidly declining, "the most positive and least recognized increase in conservation investment comes from communities themselves." Community investment in forest conservation alone, one study estimated, had increased over the most recent decade from $365 million to over $2 billion, a fact that "large conservations do not seem to take into account."[7]

Only the money the BINGOs raise and spend on conservation seems to count.

While the reports stated that conservation NGOs "are not directly involved in displacement activities," the authors did conclude that the NGOs are "intervening in very complex tenurial situations, taking positions in multistakeholder disputes and supporting displacement of 'illegal' communities." Particularly troubling to the authors are "very disquieting reports of large scale displacements for protected areas in the Congo Basin."[8] (See chapters 5 and 18 for more detail on the Congo Basin displacements.)

On April 20, 2004, realizing that word of the studies and some of their content was reaching the public, and worse, other foundations, Katherine Fuller convened an emergency meeting of three BINGO leaders—herself, Steve McCormick, president of TNC, and Peter Seligmann, chairman and CEO of CI—as well as most of the foundation executives who had met a year earlier at the South Dakota meeting of the Consultative Group on Biodiversity. No indigenous peoples or their representatives were invited (and within a short Metro subway ride from WWF-US headquarters are at least a dozen organizations advocating for the land rights and civil rights of native people throughout the world).

The meeting was closed and confidential, but again there were leaks. And Mac Chapin heard them. Conservationists were evidently somewhat testy, he reported. They were "unapologetic" and "pushed back" at accusations of insensitivity toward indigenous peoples, stressing once again the shopworn claim that their mission is conservation not "poverty alleviation," and arguing that community "capacity building" was integral to all their local work. When someone raised the point that big conservation was not standing up forcefully enough to extractive industries, particularly to some of their corporate supporters and partners, NGO leaders resorted to another tired demurrer—that they needed to remain "apolitical" on matters that were the purview of national governments. The meeting adjourned with an agreement that more studies would be performed and another meeting held sometime in the future.

Two months later the Consultative Group on Biodiversity met again, this time in Minnesota. Evidently not much was accomplished at that meeting, but shortly after it adjourned the Ford Foundation received two proposals to "move the debate forward." The first came from IUCN, whose president Yolanda Kakabadze promised to hold an "open dialogue session" on the issue at the upcoming World Conservation Congress in Bangkok, over which she would "personally preside." The other came from Katherine Fuller of WWF, which proposed an organization-wide evaluation of all of WWF's community-based conservation projects and production of training manuals for fieldworkers. Both proposals were submitted and approved in August 2004, a speed of decision making unusual in foundation management. Of course, both applicants were members of the Ford Foundation Board of Trustees.

In Bangkok in November 2004, I and other uninvited participants were barred from entering the "open dialogue session" by armed guards at the door, and at a later meeting at the same convention one indigenous representative remarked that the WWF grant was like "funding the Jangiweed to do relief work in Darfur."

Mac Chapin, who has spent much of his professional life in the field, often working side by side with international conservationists, acknowledges that "forming partnerships and collaborations with indigenous peoples and conservationists is no easy task, but it would seem to be one of the most effective ways to save the increasingly threadbare ecosystems that still exist."

It should also be recognized that transnational corporate executives, foundation trustees, and northern hemispheric conservationists are generally of the same race, class, and language group; and their children are often in the same schools. Thus there is a camaraderie and bond they share that will never be found between any of them and indigenous peoples.

Big conservation's response to Mac Chapin's WorldWatch report was immediate and subdued. "The article drives a wedge between conservationists and indigenous people," read a letter signed by CI Chairman Peter Seligmann, "thereby distracting attention from what really matters: protecting and maintaining biodiversity"[9] (emphasis added). Seligmann then proceeded to express support for native people. "Since its founding," he wrote, "CI has believed that conservation must benefit all people who live in the areas of high priority for biodiversity conservation, and there are no more meaningful places to demonstrate this than the homelands of indigenous and traditional peoples. Recognizing this, one of our five core organizational goals over the next five years is to continue increasing our partnerships with and support of indigenous peoples."[10] (See appendix B for the full text of the WWF Statement of Principles on Indigenous Peoples and Conservation.)

Carter Roberts, chief conservation officer of WWF-US, wrote to remind *World Watch* readers that WWF was "the first large conservation group to articulate and practice a policy affirming the central importance of working as partners with indigenous people." Acknowledging a strained relationship, Roberts resolved to "openly reevaluate the WWF policy on indigenous peoples ... and listen more closely" to their voices.

Stephen McCormick, president of The Nature Conservancy, politely reminded readers that one of TNC's "core values" is "a 'Commitment to People' which states that we 'respect the needs of local communities by developing ways to conserve biological diversity while at the same time enabling humans to live productively and sustainably on the landscape.'"[11] Read carefully, that and the preceding two statements say and do nothing to prevent conservation NGOs from stepping aside while national governments perform the unjust and often violent process of evicting people deemed unworthy of "partnership" in a conservation endeavor.

These messages are exactly what major conservation funders wanted to hear. Or as Sally Jeanrenaud, an IUCN researcher put it: "The search for market advantage in today's highly competitive environment tends to favor dialogue with donors and mass media in which nature and people are treated as resources. The rhetoric of people-oriented natural resource management is often reworked and absorbed into fundraising strategy." Focusing on WWF, Jeanrenaud observed that the organization began "using the language of participation and people-centered processes without significant organizational change or realignment of political, scientific and bureaucratic powers."[12]

That's no longer quite as true as it was when she wrote it. WWF now has an office in Washington, DC, staffed by an anthropologist with deep experience with and sensitivity to indigenous peoples. Some might say funding that office was a small investment in window-dressing. Others might call it a start. Either way, indigenous people and their supporters are still patiently waiting for the first BINGO to step forward and actively oppose an eviction executed anywhere in the world in the interest of conservation.

"We did not know they were coming. It was early in the morning. I heard people around my house. I looked through the door and saw men in uniforms with guns. One of them forced open the door of our house and started shouting that we had to leave immediately because the park is not our land. I first did not understand what he was talking about because all my ancestors have lived on these lands. They were so violent that I left with my children."
—Kwokwo Barume, A Batwa of Uganda

"We were chased out on the first day. I didn't know anything was happening until the police ran into my compound. They all had guns. They shouted at me, told me to run. I had no chance to say anything. They came at us and we ran, they came so violently. I was frightened for the children—I had eight children with me—but we just ran off in all directions. I took my way and the children took theirs. Other people were running, panicking, even picking up the wrong children in the confusion. I lost everything. I had thirty-one cows and some goats and hens. They were killed—twenty cows were killed and the rest taken. They burned everything, even the bed and furniture and the kitchen. We're poor now."
—Testimony of Joy Ngoboka, (Evicted from the Kibale Game Corridor in Uganda)

5

Forest People

We were born in the forest.
—A Batwa of Kisoro

Most of the traditional communities of Africa known as "Pygmy," and there are many, share a few words of language indicating a possible, though unconfirmed, common origin—"Ba" for example, an almost universal prefix that means *people*. Some also share a common creation myth. Pygmies were God's forgotten people. When they realized their fate, the myth says, they kneeled together before their creator and said: "You have given something to all other peoples—pastures to the pastoralists, savannahs for the bushmen, flocks and herds to the hunters and fruits to the gatherers. What have you for us?" And God gave them the forest.

Pygmy is the Greek word for cubit, an ancient linear unit of approximately twenty-four inches. The measurement was originally based on the length of a man's forearm. When bands of unusually small people calling themselves Batwa, Baka, Bagyeli, Basua, Bakola, Ba'Ak, and BaMbuti were first observed by European explorers of central Africa, they were lumped together as one subspecies, and called Pygmies, sometimes regarded as human, sometimes not.

Pygmy is not a term that the Batwa, Baka, or Bagyeli embrace with enthusiasm, particularly knowing that in Western culture it has become a term deriding low intelligence (*intellectual pygmy*), bad taste (*cultural pygmy*), and the ethically challenged (*moral pygmies*). And it has been applied as well to uncharacteristically small farm animals, such as pygmy goats and pigs. That said, many of the Batwa I met in Uganda referred to themselves as "Pygmies." It's a matter not of pride but convenience. They would prefer to call themselves "forest people," but unfortunately that's no longer true.

The Batwa of southwest Uganda, who in English call themselves "the Twa people," today comprise about four hundred families scattered through makeshift villages. They once thrived in nearby forests, which they regarded as the source of all abundance. They were mobile, only hunted for immediate needs, shared all kills, and did not accumulate property or store surpluses. Their culture was strong, their music haunting, and despite diminutive feet, their dancing shook the ground. Still does.

They lived in the forest for thousands of years, alone until the mid-sixteenth century when the Tutsis joined them. Together the Batwa and Tutsis lived in peace with another primate about eight times their size and weight, the Great Ape—the mountain "Gorillas in the Mist" beloved by legendary primatologist Dian Fossey, and identified by wildlife biologist and Conservation International president Russell Mittermeier as a "charismatic megavertibrate," one of a few "flagship species" to be utilized as poster-species in organized conservation's passionate quest for wildlife protection and biological diversity, and as a major draw for ecotourism, the fastest growing sector of the fastest growing industry in the world.

Back in the 1930s, when the Ugandan government became persuaded that the montane forest was a national asset threatened by loggers, miners, and other extractive interests, three national parks were created—the Mgahinga Gorilla National Park, the Echuya Forest Reserve, and the Bwindi Impenetrable Forest National Park. The 80,000-acre Bwindi park, largest of the three, is believed by most tropical biologists to hold the richest botanic community in east Africa with over one hundred different fern species and two hundred tree species including *Lovoa swynnertonii*, an internationally threatened species. This eventually led the IUCN to select Bwindi as one of the twenty-nine forests in Africa most important for conserving plant diversity. The forest is called "impenetrable" because the dense cover of herbs, vines, and shrubs on the valley bottoms make it virtually inaccessible to all but the smallest, most agile of people. It is considered the most important area in Uganda for biodiversity conservation with nine globally threatened species and one-third of the world population of mountain gorillas.

All three parks encompassed the ancestral territory of the Batwa, who lived in such close harmony with their environment that wildlife biologists who studied the flora and fauna of the area barely noticed their existence. These small and gentle people, for whom every sound in nature was part of a language they borrowed and sang back to the forest, were, as one turn-of-the-century naturalist noted, "part of the fauna."[1]

For sixty years the parks were neither mapped nor managed. They simply existed on paper. And the Batwa stayed on, living as they had for generations. When in 1964 the Bwindi park was declared an animal sanctuary, conservationists exerted some pressure to remove the Batwa from the park. It was ignored. However, when the parks were formally gazetted in 1991, and Bwindi was declared a Natural World Heritage Site in 1994, and a bureaucracy was created with funds provided by the GEF, a rumor arose, if not started then certainly circulated by Dian Fossey, that the Batwa were hunting and eating the mountain goilla, the "Great Ape," which by then was widely recognized as a threatened species and also, by then, as a profitable attraction for tourists from Europe and America. The hunting rumor was reminiscent of apocryphal stories of nineteenth-century Indian buffalo slaughters spread by early American advocates of national parks. And unsubstantiated and exaggerated claims of native abuse—poaching, fire setting, snaring, logging, and "slash and burn" agriculture—are still commonly used as justification for eviction.[2]

The Batwa adamantly denied killing gorillas, and still do, and for that matter they deny killing "any animal that has a human face," just as American Indians denied ever killing more buffalo than they needed to survive (and emphasized that all parts of the animal were used). Gorillas were being disturbed, and even poached, the Batwa admitted, but by Hutu, Tutsi, Bantu, and other non-Pygmy ethnic groups who invaded the vacated forest from outside villages. Nonetheless, under pressure from Fossey's devoted followers and traditional Western conservationists trained to believe that wilderness and human community were incompatible, about 1,700 Batwa Pygmies, officially describes as "encroachers," were expelled from the Bwindi forest, a homeland they still believe God gave them not long after the creation. Additional Batwa were evicted from the other two parks.

The GEF promptly created a $4.3 million trust fund to compensate and find land for the Batwa, but only 326 acres were provided for over three thousand people and the portion of the fund set aside for compensation was somehow "lost in the stock market."[3] Evictees from the parks whom I met in Kisoro are still complaining about the paltry compensation they received. Arable farmland in the areas now sells for about $2,000 U.S. per acre. Average payments have been around $30 per acre, with some farmers receiving as little as $6 per acre. The government's response: the payments were not for land; they were for hardships endured in the course of displacement.

A Shabby Life of Poverty

A desert strange and chill.
—John Clare, nineteenth-century English poet

The Bwindi Impenetrable Forest is so dense the Batwa lost perspective when they first came out. They would step in front of moving vehicles. They are now living in squalid refugee camps near the perimeter of the park, prohibited from gathering herbs or visiting the graves of their ancestors. A licensed few are allowed to harvest wild honey, but if they are mistaken for poachers they risk being shot on sight by "ecoguards" hired from neighboring communities, many of whom themselves poach fuel wood and other resources from the park.

The only people with legitimate claim to the park and its resources live in squalor at its edge. "Their villages are covered in human waste," says Kalimba Zephyrin, the author of the Rwanda case study for the Forest Peoples Programme. "They do not have plates, forks or beds. One dwelling of two square meters may be shelter for five to eight people—the majority of whom are children and orphans either poorly dressed or even without clothes. Some 70 percent of the people live by begging."

"It is better to die than to live like this," one Batwa leader told me.

In the camps is the first generation of Batwa who have never set foot in the forest. They're adapting slowly and reluctantly to modern agrarian life. Tomas Mtwandi, who was born in what is now the Mgahinga

Gorilla National Park and evicted with his family when he was fourteen, is employed as an indentured laborer for a local Bantu farmer. He is raising a family in a one-room shack near the Bwindi park border. Mtwandi is regarded as rich by his neighbors because his roof doesn't leak and he has a makeshift metal door on his mud-wall home, the only such door in the hovel he refuses to call "home." Home is the forest, but not the forest as park.

About the parks, he says, "all that I know is that soldiers came from far away to chase us out with guns. They said we could never return to the forest where we were forbidden to hunt or harvest honey, water, and wood."

As a "registered resource user" Mtwandi is now permitted to gather wild honey from the Bwindi once a week, and pay an occasional visit to the graves of his ancestors in the Mgahinga, but only when there are no tourists in the park viewing the gorillas. That's rarely the case in the Bwindi, which is defined by conservationists as "a climax ecosystem" containing most of Uganda's gorillas. Mountain gorillas have a fairly wide range. The same troop might be seen one day in adjacent parks of the Republic of Congo or Rwanda and the following week in Mgahinga. When they are sighted by trackers, tourists hike into mountain groves, six at a time, often accompanied by three or four times as many guides, bushwhackers, and bodyguards armed with assault weapons to protect them from Congolese rebels who frequently cross the border to attack both tourists and gorillas. Each tourist pays up to $500 for the visit. Friends who have done it tell me it's worth every penny. But few are aware of the sacrifices the Batwa have made for their adventure. I figured the gorillas had probably seen enough tourists, so I stayed in Kisoro and interviewed Batwa who had walked into town to barter at the weekly market.

As he is able to spend less and less time in the Mgahinga, Tomas Mtwandi told me that his forest knowledge is waning, and his family's nutrition is poor. In the forest they had meat, roots, fruit, and a balanced diet. Today they have a little money but no meat. "Life was healthy and good," Batwa elder Kwokwo Barume remembers, "but we have become beggars, thieves, and prowlers." In one more generation he fears that his forest-based culture—songs, rituals, traditions, dances, medicinal skills, and stories—will be gone.

Although the Batwa, like most Pygmies in Africa, are severely discriminated against, they have no word for *prejudice* in their language . . .and no word for *future*. Which perhaps explains why Kwokwo Barume laments: "Death is following us. . . . We are heading towards extinction."

I wanted to visit Barume's village. To do so I had to make arrangements with Penninah Zaninka, director of the United Organization for Batwa Development, one of many local support groups that have sprouted in southwest Uganda, competing vigorously for scarce resources. When I told her about my project, she launched into a long, scolding diatribe about "research fatigue," saying how fed up the Batwa were with people like me haunting their villages, asking the same questions over and over, and in effect "stealing" their story.[4] I was traveling at the time, with a representative of a U.S.-based donor NGO. With him Zaninka was warm and solicitous. Yes, she said, of course he could come to her village. They would dance and sing for him. I tried to explain to her that he was there because he had read reports written by "obnoxious researchers" like myself. "I know," she said, "but the Batwa have had enough." I stayed behind in deference to their research fatigue, but somewhat saddened that these once proud and independent people were reduced to dancing for donors.

Forest People of the Congo

Our cultural existence would be empty, it would become folklore if our harmonious relationship with nature was broken.
—Statement of indigenous peoples attending the 1996 Buenos Aires Biodiversity Convention

No one knows exactly when the Baka people arrived in the Congo Basin, but archaeologists and anthropologists seem certain that it was thousands of years before the dominant Bantu migrated there from Nigeria about two thousand five hundred years ago, pushing their rotational plantain and taro agriculture deeper and deeper into the forest. Today the Baka live as virtual slaves of the Bantu, who often describe them as property—"my Pygmies." They also refer to them on occasion as "speaking beef."

While Bantu men frequently take sexual liberties with Baka women, they rarely intermarry. And while both barter and trade food and fabric, a Bantu would never eat food from a Baka pot or touch a Baka eating utensil. Bantu children ruthlessly bully Baka children. So Bakas rarely attend school. As a consequence literacy and numeracy in Baka communities are generally very low.

Baka settlements of one hundred or so people comprising two to four extended family groups are generally found near Bantu villages and farms where Bakas labor in plantain and taro fields for a dollar or so a day, often being paid in used clothing or plum wine. Or they live in refugee camps on the border of Nouabalé-Ndoki National Park (NNNP), which, before they were evicted in 1993, was home and hunting ground to about four thousand nomadic Baka. Commercial logging around the park and the enforcement of wildlife protection measures inside it together have caused a depletion of, or reduced access to, forest resources that were the basis of the Baka economy.

A relatively new park, NNNP is located in the northwestern corner of the Republic of Congo (RoC), bordering the Central African Republic (CAR). At almost 2,000 square miles, it is one of the largest parks in Central Africa. It forms the eastern portion of a contiguous tri-national protected zone, the other parts of which are the Dzanga-Sangha Special Reserve in CAR, and the Lobeke National Park in Cameroon.

Studies carried out by the New York-based Wildlife Conservation Society (WCS) found large and healthy populations of elephants, gorillas, chimpanzees, and other primates, as well as the large forest antelope and the bongo. NNNP is widely regarded as a model for future protected areas in the Congo Basin, which is considered by most international conservationists to be an ecosystem equal in biotic value to the Amazon Basin. The park has received worldwide media attention, been visited by several American congressmen, and has brought conservation stardom to its legendary originator and chief lobbyist, Michael Fay of WCS (for more on Fay's work in the Congo Basin see chapter 18).

Fay's dynamic and persuasive personality has raised over a million dollars a year to manage NNNP. USAID has contributed over $3 million, as has the Global Environmental Facility, a project of the World Bank. The Swiss, Japanese, and French governments have contributed undisclosed amounts and the Liz Claiborne Foundation has made at least one generous grant to the project. And the Congo Gorilla Forest, a six-acre exhibit at the WCS-owned Bronx Zoo, boasting "over 300 animals, including the one of the largest breeding groups of lowland gorillas" in the world, has raised over $2.5 million partly to train and pay Bantu ecoguards who have reportedly shot and killed Bakas poaching bush meat in the NNNP.

The Bakas are legendary hunters, and except on the rare occasion that a Bantu loans them a shotgun in exchange for a slab of meat, they still hunt with nets, bows, and arrows. And until recently they traded bush meat in town for clothing and vegetables. This whole part of Baka culture has deeply bothered executives at WCS, more so it seems than the forestry practices of their corporate "partner" *Congolaise Industrielle des Bois* (CIB), whose logging concessions border the NNNP.

In 2005 a blanket ban on hunting was imposed in the Republic of Congo at the behest of WCS, enforced by the government, WCS, and CIB. While the ban is nationwide and applies to all peoples, it appears to be primarily threatening the health of a hunter-gatherer Baka community still eking out a living in the rainforests in the north of the country. The Baka say the ban threatens both their traditional way of life and their food security. They report increased malnutrition among children and vulnerable adults.

"This makes life very difficult for us since our livelihood depends essentially on the meat we hunt, as our ancestors used to do," said Edmond Mondzoumbe, a leader of Ibamba village, 150 km northwest of the industrial city of Pokola. "We have the feeling that the people who work for wildlife conservation have decided to kill us. They ransack our huts and even examine the meat in our cooking pots." The government and the Wildlife Conservation Society should be seeking a compromise, he says, one that supports sustainable wildlife management and conservation while preserving the livelihoods and customs of the Baka.

Suzanne Somboko, of the Congolese Observatory of Human Rights, toured Baka communities in the north, and reports that the ban is harming the Baka much more than the Bantu or prosperous urban communities. "While people face starvation in the middle of the forest," Somboko says, "game meat is served every day in restaurants in Pokola."

Box 5.1

Bush Meat

In an Ashaninka village in the Peruvian Vilcabamba, I noticed that the young children had dark reddish streaks in their coal-black hair. My first assumption was that they had been streaking it with peroxide or a dye. I bemoaned the encroachment of Western culture. When I ask him about it, my guide explained that the streaks were actually caused by protein deficiency. He said the only protein the children received now was some small fish caught in the heavily polluted river and an occasional howler monkey shot by the village hunter. The monkeys had moved far from the village at the sound of his first shot, so foraging protein for his people often required two to three days in the forest.

As fate would have it, the hunter returned to the village the day I was leaving, an adult howler monkey slung across his back. When he appeared the entire village broke into cheers. And I was invited to stay for the feast. I couldn't, however; I had to catch a riverboat that afternoon or wait another week. I could also see that there were not going to be very large portions of meat from that skinny monkey. The children needed every bite they could get.

Bush meat is a major issue with conservationists, and in some parts of the world it should be. When the tenderloins of endemically threatened species like eland and gorilla can be ordered up in European restaurants, Africa has a problem, and wildlife conservationists are rightly concerned about it. However, what is often overlooked in the bush meat discourse is the fact that wild animals are all too often an entire society's only source of protein. Should those people be prohibited from hunting?

Indignation is often expressed about the hunting of certain species. Primates seem to engender the strongest reactions, and usually from people quite comfortable obtaining a sizeable portion of their protein from animals that are considered sacred by about a billion people in India.

What is also often misunderstood by conservationists is that in many tribal communities hunting and fishing is culture, in some it's religion. Denying such people the right to hunt for food is worse than asking them to forsake their protein; it's like prohibiting an American from attending church.

Part of any contract that allows people to remain in an area where a species is in decline should be to limit hunting of that species to local consumption—no selling into the bush meat market. But an outright hunting ban, like the one imposed on the Baka in the Republic of Congo, is a short step toward genocide.

There are no laws or regulations in the Republic of Congo that protect the rights of indigenous peoples, nor has RoC ratified International Labor Organization Convention 169, article 14 of which provides that "the rights of ownership and possession of the people concerned over the lands which they traditionally occupy shall be recognized." However, RoC has ratified the International Covenant on Civil and Political Rights, article 27 of which stipulates that "In those States in which ethnic, religious or linguistic minorities exist, persons belonging to such minorities shall not be denied the right, in community with the other members of their group, to enjoy their own culture, to profess and practice their own religion, or to use their own language." Since hunting is a central part of Baka culture, in fact considered a religious practice, it could be argued that the forcible suppression of their hunting activities by the conservation authorities, even by foreigners paid by foreign governments, breaches RoC's responsibilities.

Moreover, U.S. legislation places specific requirements on USAID-funded projects to ensure that biodiversity conservation projects are conducted in close collaboration with local peoples. Section 119 of the Foreign Assistance Act, which governs USAID related to the "preservation of biological diversity" states: "To the fullest extent possible, projects supported under this section shall include close consultation with and involvement of local people at all stages of design and implementation."

WCS, the GEF, and USAID's way around these covenants is simply to claim there never were any permanent residents in what is now the NNNP: yes, the Baka and other ethnic groups would take extended hunting forays into the area, but they were nomadics so they never settled. It is therefore inaccurate, in the BINGO perspective, to claim they were evicted or displaced since they have been routinely and voluntarily displacing themselves for thousands of years. It was a page right out of the Yosemite playbook where similar claims were made about the semi-nomadic Miwok who would move out of the valley during its harsh winters and return every spring to replant their gardens.

The GEF also claims "several public consultations were held between the Government of Congo, the preparation team for this project and the local populations" (Pygmy and Bantu). The outcome of these meetings showed a strong desire on the part of the local populations to create a "reserve" on the condition that they were invited to participate in defining the limits for the core and buffer zones of the reserve and in determining the wages for local employment. The local populations welcomed "their participation in the management plan for the site," according to a 1993 GEF memo.

Notice that the memo says "reserve" not "park." Hunting and other conservation restrictions are much less strict in reserves. There are also no records or minutes of discussion regarding the expulsion of Baka from reserve territory.

Another 1993 GEF memo reads: "The concerns of local populations not yet weaned from poaching and other resource extraction in reserves will have to be mollified. Local populations, especially in the vicinity of most existing reserves, may be disadvantaged by a cut off of traditional sources of food and other products. Proposed GEF studies may be able to address this issue and examine alternatives. In general, there will have to be some allowance or mitigation for hunting and other resource extraction by Indigenous peoples in protected areas." Mitigation measures were, however, defined vaguely.

The memo continues: "The reserve's management plan would include designating core areas where no hunting or commercial extraction would be permitted and multiple use areas and buffer zones where some subsistence hunting and resource extraction would be permitted. The activities planned at the reserve level would include the development, with the local communities, of alternative activities to be funded through the project, and/or by other donors and in conjunction with other projects."

The alternative activities mentioned in the memo received $150,000 of a total $3.3 million granted by the GEF, hardly just compensation to a community of four thousand people who had lost their sole source of protein.

Various versions of the two episodes I describe in this chapter have occurred in at least eight other locations in five other countries in Central Africa—two in Cameroon, one each in CAR, Equatorial

Guinea, and Nigeria, another in RoC, and two in Gabon. All involve the creation of national parks and in Gabon, where the government has gazetted thirteen new parks, there is the threat of thousands more evictions, although indigenous rights advocates are present and active in the country. The driving conservation force in Cameroon, CAR, Gabon, and Nigeria has been WWF. WCS is also present and active in Gabon. ECOFACT, a European-based organization funded by the E.U. Development Fund has also been active in the Congo Basin.

The country to watch for the future of conservation refugees is Gabon. In its thirteen majestic new parks, which have been featured in *National Geographic* and other photo journals, live thousands of semi-nomadic hunter-gatherer forest peoples, Pygmies mostly. Their fates could be very much like the Batwa of Uganda and the Bakas in RoC—loss of livelihood, home, and protein combined with increased health risks and social discrimination from economically stronger, dominant groups. And the biological diversity of Gabon's forests could be threatened by the desperate responses of impoverished refugees returning to their former pantry to forage firewood, harvest honey, and poach bush meat. Or the government of Gabon and the international NGOs that have set up camp there could begin to change the way conservation is practiced in Africa. Conservation planners in Gabon are aware that indigenous peoples have been seriously abused elsewhere in the Congo Basin and that the World Bank (which funds the GEF) now offers clear guidelines on how indigenous peoples should be treated in the formation of GEF-funded parks and protected areas.

Anthropologists and other social scientists working in Gabon report that most of the people who were previously resettled from an older protected area, the Minkebe National Park, have been forced into sedentary lifestyles, marginalized, and impoverished. While there remains an opportunity in Gabon to reverse those unfortunate outcomes and allow people to return to their ancestral homeland, history suggests that that will not happen unless the well-funded and influential international conservation NGOs active in the country push for a more just and humane way to create national parks. (For more on Gabon see chapter 18.)

The impulse to remove humans from protected areas, while seriously questioned, first by anthropologists and now even by many conservationists, lives on. Its proponents argue hard, and in places effectively, that the only way to protect and preserve biological diversity is in wild and fecund places free of all human disturbances, even those, they argue, of the most primitive and caring people, who are often found living in voluntary isolation long after an area has been mapped and gazetted for protection.

6

Exclusion

The world of people is not attractive to me.
—Alan Rabinowitz, Wildlife Conservation Society

John Terborgh has a dream. The brilliant Harvard-educated biologist, professor of environmental science at Duke University, director of the university's Center for Tropical Conservation, and romantic dissident, spends about a third of his time in tropical rainforests, mostly in Manu National Park in remote the Madre de Dios district of southern Peru "The most beautiful place I have ever seen" Terborgh said of the nearby Apurimac Valley. There he is happy, in love, and complete. Between classes back at Duke, he dreams of vast wild places free of human disturbance, mass extinctions, or unnecessarily chaotic weather, a pristine world throbbing with fecundity, where nonhuman evolution can proceed at its own pace, where species grow not shrink in number, and the signs of a healthy biota are all vital.

It's a nice dream, as Edenic as any, an idyllic counterpoint to what Terborgh calls "biological Armageddon." And he will be the first to admit that that's all it is—a dream, and one that will probably never come true, at least not without some radical changes in the way global conservation is practiced.

After "a lifetime of roaming the tropics [of the world] in search of unspoiled nature," Terborgh had found only "inadequate parks, unstable societies, and faltering institutions." He has some solutions in mind for all three problems, but little hope that they will ever be implemented. In fact Terborgh predicts that his beloved tropical forests, which he sees as the last bastions of true nature, will not last through the twenty-first century. He says so forcefully in a powerful but very sad book called *Requiem for Nature*. "If the world does not soon experience a sea change in public policy regarding tropical forests," he writes, "the last tree of the primary forest will probably fall sometime before 2045."[1]

Terborgh still dreams that one day the world will come to its senses and realize that the total loss of what he calls "nature" would be the worst imaginable consequence of human existence, activity, and policy, and that we will view what is left of nature as a global commons. However, that's another dream, as unrealistic and unlikely as the first, but very consistent with Terborgh's view of nature.

Terborgh's nature is a "web of interactions involving plants and animals in different combinations and in different relationships." Plants and animals only? Humans do not appear to be part of the web, in Terborgh's view. In fact they are inimical, at times perversely hostile to nature. This, of course, contradicts almost all indigenous cosmologies, which Terborgh claims to respect.

So do Kent Redford and Steven Sanderson of the Wildlife Conservation Society, Katrina Brandon of Conservation International, and a host of loyal followers defending their notion that large, pristine, uninhabited parks are the best way to conserve tropical forests, and that removal of people from those forests is an essential first step in creating new parks.

"Traditional and indigenous people can claim incontrovertible rights to their land. As morally responsible humans we must support their struggle," Redford and Sanderson wrote in *Conservation Biology*. But "this responsibility does not mean that as conservationists we must count as conservation everything that these people have done and wish to do. As independent peoples with rights to self determination, their future should be in their own hands—whether that future meets our expectations or not."[2]

Always careful not to offend the oppressed, Sanderson and Redford politely assert that forest peoples and their representatives do not really speak for the forest. "They may speak for their version of the forest; but they do not speak for the forest we want to conserve."[3] Redford resurrects his old straw man "the ecologically noble savage," an essentially nonexistent hominid he says was invented by cultural romantics who have spent too much time in egalitarian village republics that cherish their land and forest (which do exist). Redford's former colleague and coauthor, Katrina Brandon, who now works for Conservation International in Argentina, casts the noble savage and their representatives as adversaries in a "struggle in which indigenous and traditional peoples [see] the potential to gain power and prestige at international fora by their claims of defending biodiversity."[4]

Terborgh is even tougher and less compromising. After the 2003 Parks Congress in Durban, South Africa, he complained openly that "countless workshops, lectures, and discussions delved into topics such as poverty alleviation, social justice, indigenous peoples' rights, community management of protected areas, and gender equality in conservation. All these issues have their place in the global agenda," he said, "but for me they dominated and drowned out the discussions of themes more directly related to conserving nonhuman life on this planet."[5]

Terborgh stands almost alone in his criticism of contemporary conservation, which does not spare the BINGOs from indictment. "What I have seen convinces me that the conventional wisdom now being applied to the conservation of tropical nature is misguided and doomed to failure," he says. "At issue is a moral dilemma that pits the rights of our own species against the survival of nature. It is a contest that nature almost always loses."[6] Uncontacted indigenous communities inside parks he calls "fugitive indigenous groups" and refers to them frequently as "the danger within." The BINGOs, he says, lack "a nonprofit mentality. They pay corporate salaries and live high, wide, and handsome."[7]

Terborgh is particularly troubled by the presence of humans, even the most ecologically gentle, low-impact natives in the Manu National Park, where he has a small personal research station. He challenges the notion that the tribes he knows of in the park are intent upon coexisting with nature and believes that as their populations increase and they acquire technology (outboard motors, shotguns, chainsaws, etc.) biodiversity will be reduced. Even without modern tools and engines Terborgh worries about the threat of ordinary hunter-gatherers to the balance of species in the Manu. This worry flies in the face of a recent study published in *Conservation Biology* that shows that the subsistence-hunting practices of the Matsigenkas in the park are sustainable at current levels despite a doubling of the human population since 1988.[8] So much for "the danger within."

A paradox in Terborgh's hypothesis on conservation has to do with his observation of top predators that he, like most in his field, believe are essential to the balance of nature and to optimizing biodiversity. However, while he does allow that when poachers kill off herbivorous animals some vital plants regenerate, he refuses to regard humans as top predators, potentially serving the same natural function as jaguars and wolves. Thus he will write persuasive essays about saving feline predators while human predators are being evicted from the same ecosystem.

"Having lost the luster that made it one of the world's premier rainforest parks, and swelling with an ever larger and more assertive indigenous population," he believes, "the Manu will imperceptibly pass from being a national park to being a reserve for its indigenous inhabitants."[9] His solution: voluntary relocation of the tribes, sustained by "the desire of contacted indigenous groups to acquire goods and an education for their children and to participate in a money economy."[10]

And with a suggestion that has had him more than once branded an "ecofascist," Terborgh proposes an international armed force to defend pristine wilderness from all human dangers. "If peacekeeping has been widely accepted as an international function," he says, "why not nature keeping? If local park guards are too weak or too subject to corruption and political influence to carry out their duties effectively, internationally sponsored guards could be called in to help." His solution is militant and authoritarian. "Active protection of parks requires a top-down approach because enforcement is invariably in the hands of police and other armed forces that respond only to orders from their commanders."[11]

Terborgh reserves most of his animus for conservation-as-development schemes supported by some conservation NGOs and funded by the World Bank, the Global Environment Facility, USAID, and a host of multilateral banks. He regards economic development and conservation as mutually exclusive goals. "The logic of economics is unassailable," he says, "but it is amoral."[12] Sustainable development is "little more than wishful thinking," he continues. And "the notion that [it] will lead inexorably to harmonious coexistence of humankind and nature is patent nonsense," primarily because "in developing countries appreciation of wild nature is minimal and public institutions are notoriously frail. Worse, wildlands are viewed as a national embarrassment, a mark of underdevelopment and immaturity as a nation."

Sustainable use, Terborgh believes, provides "no line in the sand" beyond which biodiversity loss has to stop, and that "starting down that slippery road to sustainable use is stepping back from that crucial line that defines one's beliefs and principles."[13] He also has no use whatsoever for Integrated Conservation and Development Projects (ICDPs), whether initiated by indigenous peoples themselves—"Restraint in the use of renewable resources will not spring up from the bottom"— or by well-meaning conservationists—"When conservation organizations begin to advocate sustainable use of tropical forests, it's a signal that conservation is on the run."[14] Of course, trashing ICDPs is facile. After hundreds of experimental attempts made on every continent, no one likes them.

While he laments that international conservationists have been drawn into development priorities, he also sympathizes with them, as they face the twin realities that humans will continue to use wild resources and that antipoverty development is a powerful global initiative. "To be fair, the officers of conservation organizations are obliged to walk a tightrope between the shifting whims of a fickle public on one side and the narrow agendas of major donors such as the billion dollar foundations, the US Agency for International Development and the World Bank, on the other. The freedom from financial concerns needed to enable them to stick to it simply does not exist. Conservation organizations thus become prisoners of the bottom line, much as corporations are."

Terborgh is not alone in his disdain for mixing conservation and sustainable development. In their widely read defense of national parks, *Parks in Peril*, Katrina Brandon joins Kent Redford and Steven Sanderson to say that "the trend to promote sustainable use of resources as a means to protect these resources, while politically expedient and intellectually appealing, is not well grounded in biological and ecological knowledge. Not all things can be preserved through use. Not all places should be open to use. Without an understanding of broader ecosystem dynamics at specific sites, strategies promoting sustainable use will lead to substantial losses of biodiversity."[15]

In a separate essay Sanderson and Redford assert "biodiversity, a concept originating in biology, has been wrested from its originators, first by conservation activists and then by economic actors." Both are committed to sustainable use, say the authors. "This appropriation of the biodiversity discourse by politically interested actors . . . means that the struggle has been converted into a discrete, if complicated, contest for ownership. Biodiversity has become a political term and its use now revolves around economic appropriation, not natural preservation."[16]

Terborgh is also not alone in his somewhat extremist positions on people in nature. Primate ecologist John Oates, professor of anthropology at Hunter College in New York, has spent over thirty years doing biological fieldwork in Africa and India. And he too has no use for the concept of sustainable development, bottom-up planning or "the corrupting influence of a utilitarian approach to conservation."

"The close relationship between economic development and conservation has led to a view of wildlife conservation as predominantly an exercise in materialism," Oates believes. He has even less faith than Terborgh in the ability or willingness of indigenous peoples to protect biodiversity. He considers the notion that conservation and development can be conducted together a seriously flawed myth perpetrated by people who want to feel good about conserving nature without enhancing poverty.

"The emphasis on 'communities' as functional units has led to a neglect of abundant evidence that human societies in rural Africa and elsewhere typically have a hierarchical structure dominated by a few powerful individuals who may wish to advance their own personal interests," says Oates. He adds, "most real communities do not conform to the harmonious ideal implicit in international conservation policy."[17]

Oates says that international conservation's recent tendency to empower local people and include them in the conservation process is a "form of paternalism [that has become] an entrenched feature of Third

World development and humanitarian aid projects planned and implemented by highly educated middle class Westerners." Although a relatively prosperous American, Oates carefully separates himself from this odious human subculture, which he accuses of simply wishing to "maintain (or improve) their own lifestyles while displaying attitudes that seem to be colored by both colonial-style paternalism toward people they regard as benighted peasants of the Third World, and by guilt for the perceived wrongdoings of their colonial antecedents."[18]

Oates, who as an anthropologist has observed, firsthand, the bitterness of displaced people, their attendant loss of respect for the land they once loved, and their tendency to "poach" the wildlife they once protected, does not stop at proposing that such people be removed from new parks. In fact, he strongly advocates siting refugee communities and economic development projects "at some distance from protected areas to draw people away from their boundaries and reduce pressure on their resources. The first priority for nature conservation should not be the fulfillment of human material needs but rather protection of threatened nature from the destructive effects of human materialism."[19] Again, Oates equates a basic quest for food security with the rank materialism of conservation and development mercenaries, many of which are headquartered in his hometown of New York City.

Oates and Terborgh share one quite unusual and admirable quality. Unlike so many of their fellow ecologists and conservation biologists, neither attempts to make the case that biological diversity is essential to human survival. "Let us recognize a fact of life," Terborgh writes, "wild nature and the biodiversity it perpetrates are not a necessity for humans; they are a luxury." And he harbors no illusions about the economic value of conservation.

Seeming to ignore the real economic value of so-called "environmental services"—water yields from forested catchment areas, protein from bush meat, revenue from ecotourism, and pollution control through marshlands—Terborgh considers attempts made by environmental economists to find monetary value in species and ecosystems to be a futile pastime. In fact, he argues persuasively that "if economics rules, most tropical forests are worth more dead than alive."[20] Thus, to Terborgh and his followers, the protection of nature is strictly a moral imperative.

Nature, Oates and Terborgh believe, should be preserved for its intrinsic and aesthetic values. "Ultimately nature and biodiversity must be conserved for their own sakes, not because they have present utilitarian value," Terborgh writes in *Requiem for Nature*. "Essentially all the utilitarian arguments for conserving biodiversity are built on fragile assumptions that crumble under close scrutiny. Instead the fundamental arguments for conserving nature must be spiritual and aesthetic, motivated by feelings that well up from our deepest beings. What is absolute, enduring and irreplaceable is the primordial nourishment of our psyches afforded by a quiet walk in an ancient forest or the spectacle of a thousand snow geese against a blue sky on a crisp winter day. There are no substitutes for these things, and if they cease to exist, all the money in the world will not bring them back."[21]

This view is shared by Colorado State University Distinguished Professor of Philosophy Holmes Rolston III, who expresses opinions on the matter that shock even some of the most dedicated exclusionary conservationists.

"Ought we to feed people first, and save nature last?" Rolston asks. "We never face so simple a question. The practical question is more complex." He then deconstructs the question:

• If persons widely demonstrate that they value many other worthwhile things over feeding the hungry (Christmas gifts, college educations, symphony concerts),
• and if developed countries, to protect what they value, post national boundaries across which the poor may not pass (immigration laws),
• and if there is unequal and unjust distribution of wealth and if just redistribution to alleviate poverty is refused,
• and if charitable redistribution of justified unequal distribution of wealth is refused,
• and if one fifth of the world continues to consume four fifths of the production of foods and four fifths consumes one fifth,
• and if escalating birthrates continue so that there are no real gains in alleviating poverty, only larger numbers of poor in the next generation,
• and if low productivity on domesticated lands continues, and if the natural lands to be sacrificed are likely to be low in productivity,
• and if significant natural values are at stake, including extinctions of species, then one ought not always to feed people first, but rather one ought sometimes to save nature.

Many of the "ands" in this conjunction can be replaced with "ors" and the statement will remain true, though we cannot say outside of particular contexts how many. The logic is not so much that of implication as of the weighing up of values and disvalues, natural and human, and of human rights and wrongs, past, present, and future.

Some will protest that this risks becoming misanthropic and morally callous. The Ten Commandments order us not to kill, and saving nature can never justify what amounts to killing people. Yes but there is another kind of killing here, one not envisioned at Sinai where humans are superkilling species. Extinction kills forms (species)—not just individuals; it kills collectively, not just distributively. Killing a natural kind is the death of birth, not just of an individual life. The historical lineage is stopped forever.

Preceding the Ten Commandments is the Noah myth, when nature was primordially put at peril as great as the actual threat today. There, God seems more concerned about species than about the humans who had then gone so far astray. In the covenant reestablished with humans on the promised Earth, the beasts are specifically included: "Keep them alive with you . . . according to their kinds" (Genesis 6.19–20).

There is something ungodly about an ethic by which the late-coming Homo sapiens arrogantly regards the welfare of one's own species as absolute, with the welfare of all the other five million other species sacrificed to that. The commandment not to kill is as old as Cain and Abel, but the most archaic commandment of all is the divine, "Let the earth bring forth" (Genesis 1).

Stopping that genesis is the most destructive event possible, and we humans have no right to do that. Saving nature is not always morally naive; it can deepen our understanding of the human place in the scheme of things entire, and of our duties on this majestic home planet.[22]

In a less religious vein, Rolston argues with peers challenging his misanthropy. He focuses on the Royal Chitwan National Park in Nepal, home to the endangered Bengal tiger, Asian rhinoceros, sloth bear, pygmy hog, swamp deer, black buck, Asian rock python, and gharial crocodile, the world's most endangered croc. Before 1950 the area was too malarious for human habitation and the animals flourished. But introduction of DDT pesticide changed all that, and from 1950 to 1991 the area's human population grew from thirty-six thousand to 8.6 million. No one was allowed to live in the Park, but pressure on its resources was nevertheless severe.

As the debate over human versus animal rights escalated, Rolston spoke his mind. "I put the tigers first," he wrote in 1998, "and morally approve the present policies, on grounds that tigers as a species ought not be sacrificed on the altar of human mistakes."[23]

"There are better ways to be humane," Rolston continues, "as humane as one can, but stopping short of extinguishing species, else we lose the species only to continue the human tragedy."[24] Acknowledging that such thoughts will engender more accusations of "astonishing misanthropy," he counters by saying that, "on this spectacular planet, with many millions of species, maybe it's astonishing anthropocentrism to hold that people always come first, no matter what their mistakes, no matter where their uncontrolled growth."[25]

Rolston persists that there are times when we humans must prioritize nature over culture. "Most of our decisions are made, I concede, with culture in the foreground; but some should be made bringing into focus the background that is, after all, our life support system, not only ours but that of many millions of other species."[26]

Often accused of being a "nature Puritan," Rolston confesses to finding "in my nature 'Puritanism,' not moral virtue, not 'purity,' but value worthy of respect in wild things, sufficient at times to take priority over human needs. I do run the risk of being misanthropic," he admits. But "that is better than to risk being an arrogant humanist. And I welcome continuing debate about how, in these dilemmas, to be most humane."[27]

Perhaps the last word from fortress conservation's old guard should come from Clive Spinage, an aging British elephant expert, now living in Farringdon, England. Spinage dismisses supporters of participatory conservation as "neopopulists" and those who advocate too loudly for community conservation as "Marxists" who are "sacrificing conservation to political correctness" by criticizing "inherited colonial game laws" in Africa, and misrepresenting "colonial attempts at conservation as ill-intentioned towards indigenous peoples."

"Cloaked in philosophical discourse, to give spurious weightiness to the author's views," Spinage writes, "the left-wing radicalism of the opposition to the practice of traditional conservation is exemplified by statements such as that of Krishna Ghimire and Michel Pimbert who state that local communities should be in a better position to assess what is good for them than American biologists, British conservationists, German and Scandinavian foresters, or members of European aristocracies," which Spinage says "can only be construed as a snide attack on former

Presidents of the Worldwide Fund for Nature, His Royal Highness The Duke of Edinburgh and Prince Bernhard of the Netherlands before him." Spinage wonders "how far the World Wide Fund for Nature would have got without such prestigious backing?"[28] (See chapter 4 for more detail on Princes Phillip and Bernhard's respective reigns at WWF.)

With their strange blend of utopianism and misanthropy, Terborgh, Spinage, Rolston, and Oates have become lighting rods for a growing coalition of reform conservationists, anthropologists, and cultural preservationists who believe that humans are as much a part and aspect of nature as any plant or other animals, and that humans aware of their place in nature can be far better protectors of biodiversity than national governments, park administrators, ecoguards, and idealistic biologists.

Antagonists

Listening is difficult. Hearing even more so.
—Hugh Brody, Scott Polar Research Institute

Chief among Terborgh and Spinage's antagonists is Marcus Colchester. Colchester's professional arc is emblematic of the changes that are taking place in global conservation. He began his professional life as a zoologist, with a master's degree from Oxford University, class of 1971. One of his first fieldtrips was to the Upper Orinoco in Venezuela where he worked for over a year with the several different peoples of the Ventuari, studying the flora and fauna in and around their homelands.

Over the months he spent with the Sanema (Northern Yanomami) people, Colchester became increasingly interested in their culture and began to suspect that they, not the contract conservationists who were managing protected areas around the world, might be the best human stewards of biodiversity. When he left Venezuela, Colchester enrolled again at Oxford University to carry out graduate studies in the Department of Ethnology. He then went back to the Amazon for two more years of field research into the social ecology of the Sanema and in 1982 received his doctorate in social anthropology from Oxford.

Under his new title Colchester has become one of the most prolific and articulate spokesmen for indigenous peoples confronted with fortress conservation. With a balanced mixture of sound social science and persuasive advocacy, he has created a body of literature that is fostering a new approach to conservation, a new paradigm that directly involves local people in the management of protected areas.

"Protected areas need human occupants to defend them," Colchester asserts. "In an increasingly globalized and liberalized world, conservationists cannot rely on beleaguered state bureaucracies to defend isolated protected areas of high biodiversity.... Protected areas need to be implanted within much larger managed landscapes occupied by human beings who also care about the environment and the wellbeing of future generations."[29]

Colchester agrees with Terborgh that "premodern indigenous people have not always been exemplary stewards of biotic resources,"[30] and with Spinage that "recognition of indigenous peoples' rights to own and manage their ancestral lands does not automatically mean that sustainable land use will result," and with critics of cultural romanticism that "it may be imprecise and unhelpful to characterize indigenous peoples as having a 'conservationist cosmovision.'" However, he does believe that native communities are likely to "be more respectful of their local environments than most societies, owing to their close ties with their ancestral lands, their common property management regimes, and their sense of holding land for future generations."[31]

And at a time when about 85 percent of the world's protected areas are already occupied by indigenous peoples, and most remaining areas of high biodiversity are also owned or claimed by them, Colchester believes "it makes more sense for conservationists to work with them, rather than cast them into the role of environmental villain and expel them from their homelands. The latter course," he says, "is a sure route to social conflict and political instability."[32] Indigenous peoples, of course, know this from bitter experience, and thus it is very much in their self-interest to practice conservation and seek sustainability on their ancestral lands.

The perplexing thing about fortress conservation for Colchester and his ilk is that to a degree it is working. If conservation values are measured in the absence of social and cultural consequences, then many unoccupied protected areas are biodiversity success stories. It is therefore essential to the cause of cultural diversity that Colchester and the indigenous people he represents keep a spotlight on the human consequences of exclusionary conservation, particularly when innocent people are being forcibly evicted from protected areas, and where nature-as-wilderness is seen as nature in its best and purest form.

The best argument for preserving cultural diversity in the interest of conservation is the rather clear correlation between cultural and biological diversity. While there is some disagreement between anthropologists and conservationists about cause and effect, no one contests the correlation. It seems clear now that traditional knowledge, evolved over millennia, embedding itself along the way in thousands of indigenous cultures as skill, value, and unwritten ecological science, was in every case developed to preserve biological diversity, and its most important product, biotic wealth. Every shaman, healer, chief, and elder knows that without biotic wealth there is no food security. Thus biological diversity becomes an expression of culture. They appear and disappear together.

Wildness and Wilderness

Nature rarely if ever stands still.
—Barton Worthington, Oxford University

It is almost impossible to find the true origin of "nature" or the Terborghian notion that nature as wilderness is best preserved in the absence of humans. Rummaging back though history, Marcus Colchester finds that most "urban civilizations from their inception have characterized nature as brutish and evil and yet contradictorily as a refuge from the ills of city life. Thus the Epic of Gilgamesh, the world's most ancient tale, recounts the primordial struggle between kingly civilization and the forest, the source of all evil. Yet even Gilgamesh admits that 'in the city man dies with despair in his heart.'"

In ancient Greece, Colchester observes,

Untamed nature was perceived as the domain of wild, irrational, female forces that contrasted with the rational culture ordered by males. In this world view, not only was nature a dangerous threat to the city state, but the wilderness beyond was peopled by barbarians, the epitome of whom were the Amazons—long haired, naked, female savages who represented the antithesis of Greek civilization.

In Judeo-Christian myths of origin God solves the problem of wild, unruly nature quickly by giving man dominion over beasts.

In Europe's middle ages the image was sustained of an ordered world of culture managed by civilized men, bounded by a chaotic wilderness peopled with savages, the abode of pagan warlocks and witches who drew their power from the dangerous, evil forces of nature, the realm of Beelzebub himself. Similar images continue to sustain the views of fundamentalist Christian missionaries who perceive the shamanism of indigenous peoples as "devil worship," and believe that as "Commandos for Christ" they have a God-given role to "reach the lost until they have reached the last." These views of nature were reinforced in every new settlement throughout the New World.

A century or so later Americans would seek salvation in bordered wildernesses, from which they had carefully and brutally extracted the savage places that the reclusive Henry David Thoreau would describe as "little oases in the desert of our civilization." However, unlike John Muir and other wilderness romantics, Thoreau believed passionately that it was "vain to dream of a wildness distant from ourselves. There is none such. It is the bog in our brains and bowels, the primitive vigor of nature in us that inspires that dream. I shall never find in the wilds of Labrador any greater wildness than in some recess of Concord."

Despite that fine advice, the idea that humanity is something apart from nature remains deeply rooted in the Western mind, which still expresses faith in an origin where man holds authority over all other living things. Taming the wild, both in nature and ourselves, became a fundamental aspect of the New World's manifest destiny. By contrast, indigenous cultures that have remained isolated from Judeo-Christian influence continue to see themselves and their cultures, as they always have, deeply embedded in nature, and nature even more deeply embedded in themselves and their cultures.

Westerners still revere nature as a place, rather than a cultural concept—a place to commune with the rest of the animal kingdom, discover themselves, and also, perhaps, the purpose of life. An antagonism between human society and nature continues to grow as humans urbanize their cultures and separate themselves from both the places and the concepts they regard as "nature."

The antagonism expresses itself in the growing popularity of new environmental philosophies like deep ecology, which embrace the romantic visions of John Terborgh and put wilderness (pristine nature) off limits to humanity. This exclusion is justified by the fact that "most of the Earth has been colonized by humans only in the last several thousand years."[33] Before humans evolved, the entire planet was pure and undefiled. We are the sole enemies of nature. Rid the planet of humans and it will flourish again. Wilderness romantics and deep ecologists seem either unwilling or unable to face the fact that if the entire planet Earth were to suddenly disappear from the universe, with all its occupants, nature would continue to exist.

Exclusion in Practice

Replacement of European staff by untrained, unqualified African men will spell disaster for game.
—Russell Train, former Agency Administrator of EPA

The creation and defense of exclusionary conservation was inspired, of course, by many of the forefathers of American environmentalism, most notably John Muir, who, as we have seen, frequently associated America's first settlers with "filth" and "depravity." But Muir didn't single out Indians. He in fact argued that "wilderness" should be cleared of all human inhabitants and set aside for recreation and fulfillment of the urbane human's need for spiritual renewal. It became a sentiment expressed as policy with passage of the 1964 United States Wilderness Act, which defined wilderness as an "untrammeled" place "where man himself is a visitor who does not remain."

One should not be surprised to find hardy residues of that sentiment in traditional conservation, where John Muir remains a demi-saint. That said, the situation is in flux, as younger conservationists, working close to the ground, are beginning to realize that many of the areas they seek to protect are biologically rich and diverse because the people who have been living there for hundreds or thousand of years have remained in close harmony with what both Muir and Terborgh would agree was "nature." The fortress model is thus coming under siege, at least at the field level of transnational conservation in South America, where I spent the spring of 2004.

Throughout the Andean-Amazon watershed I visited tribal villages facing the consequences of Western, science-based conservation. Along the way I met and interviewed staff members of CI, TNC, WCS, and WWF. I found them to be acutely aware that the spirit of exclusion survives in the headquarters of their organizations, alongside a subtle but real prejudice against "unscientific" native wisdom.

"We are arrogant," was the confession of a CI executive working in the southern cone who asked me not to identify her. I was heartened by her admission until she went on to suggest that arrogance was a minor institutional foible possessed by an otherwise worthy and constructive organization. Arrogance is in fact the essential problem of transnational conservation, cited by every other indigenous leader I interviewed as a major impediment to constructive cooperation. And arrogance is not only found in the spin-driven swagger of these organizations, it has also seeped down into policy and spills out daily in the practice of strict science-based conservation, which says to the native: "throw off your tired old traditions and beliefs, our way is better."

Luis Suarez, the recently hired director of Conservation International in Ecuador, seemed aware of that. It was Suarez's public challenge of CI's policy and arrogance in Ecuador and Guyana that landed him his job. From his office as president of a local NGO called Ecociencia, he recalls, "I started questioning CI's motives in public. Russ Mittermier, president of the organization, called one day and said he liked my questions. Why didn't I come to work for him? I did." And CI's reputation with most of the tribes in Ecuador has improved noticeably since Suarez assumed his CI post.

In neighboring Peru, Erick Meneses, director of CI's highly controversial Vilcambamba project, also admitted, on the record, that his organization had been insensitive to two tribes in the area, the Ashaninka and the Machuagenga, and that his bosses had "gotten too close" to the Camisea Gas Project, which is drilling wells and building pipelines throughout the Vilcambamba cordillera. At one point, CI got close enough to Camisea to prompt one indigenous leader to remark publicly: "protected area for what: business?" CI headquarters still promotes its close tie to Camisea as a triumph of enviro-industrial cooperation.

Suarez and Meneses also admitted to me that their organization had made some serious blunders with indigenous organizations in Ecuador and Peru, and that at that very moment CI was making new enemies in Guyana, where they had shown considerable disrespect toward a tribe living in an area slated to become a national park, in an episode that indicates exclusionary conservation has taken a new, more subtle form than the outright evictions of previous decades.

CI's Chairman and CEO Peter Seligmann publicly promotes his organization's mediating role in the creation of a vast protected area the size of New Jersey in southern Guyana, upholding the proposed park as an example of constructive collaboration between international conservation and indigenous peoples. That claim is based on a half-truth. CI did sign a three-way memorandum of understanding (MOU) with the federal government of Guyana and the Wai Wai peoples, who have lived within the proposed park boundaries for centuries. And CI's regional director, retired Guyanan Major General Joe Singh, did persuade two Wai Wai *Toshaos* (Chiefs) Efuka Muwesha and Paul Chekuma, both of whom had served under him in the Guyanan army, to sign the memorandum, in which the Wai Wai relinquish some hunting and fishing rights in return for CI's commitment of $1 million to cover costs CI will incur as "managing authority" of the protected area. "A key component of the process would be involvement of stakeholders, including the Wai Wais," reads a statement from Seligmann issued during discussions. The memorandum was not written as the verbal agreement was worded, and both Muwesha and Chekuna now admit that they really didn't understand what they were signing.

What Seligmann omits, in his relentless promotion of this accomplishment, is the fact that another tribe, the Wapishana, who have resided in the southernmost reaches of Guyana for centuries, and whose six communities would be partly encompassed in the proposed area, long ago wrote to the government proposing the creation of this very same protected area. For generations the Wapishana and the Wai Wai have lived in harmony, even intermarried. But the Wapishana were never asked to sign the MOU or consulted on creation of a protected area on land that CI insists rightfully belongs to a third party, the Tarumas, a tribe that most anthropologists familiar with the area believe died out over fifty years ago. The consequence of this oversight has been intertribal bitterness, even a threat of warfare between the Wai Wai and the Wapishana, who have threatened to behead Efuka Muwesha and float his headless body downriver in a canoe.[34]

The Guyana fiasco began in 1995 when the national government and the World Bank met to demark ten new protected areas in the southern reaches of the country, part of the Amazon watershed. There were several indigenous communities living in the designated areas, none of which were invited to the meeting. When word of the plan reached them, their *Toshaos* insisted on another meeting that they would all attend to demand full participation in development of the protected areas. That meeting was held in 1996 and the Amerindian Peoples Association (APA) was formally assured of equal partnership in the scheme.

That was the last any Guyanan Indians heard about protected areas until 1998, when they inadvertently learned that the plan was almost finalized and about to be submitted to the World Bank for approval. Twelve million dollars was pledged to the project by the Guyana government, the World Bank, the GEF, the German Bank for Reconstruction, and the European Union, none of it budgeted for indigenous communities.

What particularly alarmed the Indians was a map of a proposed Kaieteur National Park that contained the largest single-drop waterfall in the world, which happens to be a sacred site of the Patamona tribe, a member of the APA. After attempts to draw the attention of the government failed, APA wrote to the World Bank. The bank did respond, but its answer was disturbing. APA requested a meeting, which was held at World Bank headquarters in Washington, DC. A long dialogue ensued during which Guyana's Indians made clear their concerns about territorial rights and the new park. But no one in the government was listening, and in April 1999 the APA learned, again by accident, that a ministerial order had been issued to expand the Kaieteur Park from five square miles to 242 square miles, thereby enveloping the entire homeland and hunting grounds of the Patamona people.

When the World Bank shelved the project, the Guyana government turned to WWF and Conservation International, both of which had offices in the country and seats on the national park board of directors. Visits were paid to bank executives in Washington, and in 2001 the bank reversed its position and revived the protected area plan, but this time stipulated that indigenous peoples affected by a particular park or reserve could veto its creation.

Change in the Wind

Conservation efforts will never succeed if local people do not.
—Patrick Bergin, Africa Wildlife Foundation

Large international conservation groups are still inclined to think and act globally, valuing macro over regional ecosystems. In doing so they have come to emphasize globalized management systems over local ones, leaving indigenous peoples in virtually powerless roles, with tribal knowledge and environmental ethics less likely to be valued. But elsewhere in South America that model is changing, albeit slowly, one enlightened staffer at a time.

Dan Campbell, The Nature Conservancy's director in Belize, confessed, "We have an organization that sometimes tries to employ models that don't fit the culture of nations where we work." And Joy Grant of the same office declared, after a protracted disagreement with the indigenous peoples of Belize, that "people are now the key to everything we do." And the Wildlife Conservation Society, one of the slowest of all BINGOs to accept the potential value of indigenous stewardship, has recently mediated a dispute in Bolivia that gives ownership and management powers to the Izocenos, a tribe that prior to WCS's intervention was facing eviction from the new Kaa-Iya Gran Chaco National Park.

These are heartening signs that conservationists closest to the ground are beginning to understand the social consequences of exclusionary "fortress" conservation. They are attempting to pass their message to satellite cartographers and push-pin policymakers in Washington who are designating protected areas based on infrared maps of what appear from space to be unoccupied lands. Grady Harper, a brilliant satellite

cartographer for CI based in Venezuela, told me when I asked him about
the potentially explosive situation in an area of southern Guyana that
he had mapped, "I have no idea what's happening on the ground."
Although his head was figuratively in the clouds, he was intrigued
and concerned by what I told him I had learned from his associates
who did work on the ground in Guyana. "It's a whole 'nother picture,"
he said.

If field observations and fieldworkers' sentiments become embraced in
the headquarters of CI, TNC, and the other BINGOs, there could be a
happy ending to this story. And that appears to be happening, slowly.
In a chapter written for a WCS Working Paper on Protected Areas and
Human Displacement, Katrina Brandon of Conservation International
describes a cautiously worded, internal position adapted by CI's Policy
on Indigenous and Traditional Peoples (ITP): While "CI has no formal
organization-wide policy on either displacement or resettlement . . . the
ITP strongly recognizes ownership, governance and indigenous rights
and pledges that CI will 'support legal designation and management
authority over ancestral lands and their resources, while respecting issues
of national sovereignty. Where overlap exists with legally designated
parks and protected areas and lands customarily owned or used by
indigenous peoples, we support collaborative management initiatives
that recognize customary uses while ensuring that natural resources are
not depleted and that actively involve indigenous communities in planning, z eoning and monitoring.'"

In footnote 1, attached to the title of the paper, Brandon notes, "this
paper reflects the views of the author and does not reflect any formal or
informal positions of Conservation International, its staff, or its Board
of Directors," many of whom surely take comfort at inclusion of the
phrase "while respecting issues of national sovereignty," national sovereignty being the most commonly invoked excuse for looking the other
way while abuse of indigenous people and their rights take place.

---

*There are today positive working models of socially sensitive conserva-
tion on every continent, particularly in Australia, Bolivia, Nepal, and
Canada, where international conservationists have joined hands with*

indigenous communities and worked out creative ways to protect wildlife habitat, sustain biodiversity, and allow humans to thrive in traditional communities that they own. Even in Brazil, where scores of tribes have been brutally eliminated over the past century, there is now official recognition of indigenous boundaries, Indian-only parks, and extractive reserves that appear to be operating sustainably. I return to all these themes and examples in chapters to follow, but not before examining a country, Thailand, which continues to abuse its powerless minorities in the alleged interest of conservation.

7

Karen

The way strife makes people talkative is a gift to anyone who wants to write about it.
—Paul Theroux, author

November 2004: Khon Noi, matriarch of a remote highland village, huddles next to an open pit stove in the loose, brightly colored clothes that identify her as Karen, the most populous of the six hill tribes found in the lush mountain reaches of northern Thailand. Her village of sixty-five families has farmed and hunted in the same wide valley for over two hundred years. She chews betel, spitting its bright red juice into the fire, and speaks softly through black teeth. She tells me I can use her name, as long as I don't identify her village.

"The government has no idea who I am," she says. "The only person in the village they know by name is the 'Headman' they appointed to represent us in government negotiations. They were here last week, in military uniforms, to tell us we could no longer practice rotational agriculture in this valley. If they knew that someone here was saying bad things about them they would come back again and push us out."

The Karen occupy about seventy-five thousand small villages scattered about the lush green hills of Thailand. Most of them migrated gradually into Southeast Asia over the centuries from Yunnan province in China, escaping various dynastic assaults on their culture and livelihood. And recently Karen families have been fleeing Burma in large numbers for pretty much the same reason—cultural genocide.

In a recent outburst of environmental enthusiasm stimulated by generous financial offerings from the World Bank and its Global

Environmental Facility, the Thai government has been creating national parks as fast as the Royal Forest Department (RFD) can map them. Ten years ago there was barely a park to be found in Thailand, and because the few that existed were unmarked "paper parks," few Thais even knew they existed. When I traveled to Thailand in 2004 there were 114 land parks and 24 marine parks on the map. Almost 25,000 square kilometers, most of it occupied by hill and fishing tribes, was under RFD-protected area management. All those numbers have since increased.

Since the state cannot recognize two titles to the same land, the creation of a protected area under government control creates a problem for indigenous communities that have existed within a new park's boundaries before the park or the state existed, and whose members assume that although they may not have held title to the land, their traditional rights to farm, hunt, and gather will continue unchallenged as they always have been. This is what Khon Noi and her family believed. They were in for a rude awakening.

"They just appeared one day, out of nowhere, showing their guns and telling us that we were now living in a national park," Khon Noi recalls of the day the Thai military arrived. "That was the first we knew of it. Our own guns were confiscated . . . no more hunting, no more trapping, no more snaring and no more 'slash and burn.' That's what *they* call our farming—slash and burn. We call it 'crop rotation' and we've been doing it in this valley for two centuries. Soon we will be forced to sell rice to pay for greens and legumes we are no longer allowed to grow here. Hunting we can live without, as we raise chickens, pigs, and buffalo. But rotational farming is our way of life." She then described the experience of a nearby village she hoped I would visit.

At the behest of "some green group" advocating relocation of highlanders as a way of solving water shortages in lowland areas, armed national park and RFD officials entered the mountain village, tore down buildings, and evacuated the tribal inhabitants. In the months that followed, lowlanders demanding immediate removal of highland dwellers blocked roads leading to surrounding villages. Then in June another group of lowlanders accompanied by the director of Doi Inthanon National Park appeared at the same village and attempted to destroy agricultural pipes and canals. Later in the month, amid a well-orchestrated and astoundingly racist campaign of hill tribe bashing promoted by a nearby Buddhist monastery, the Thai cabinet resolved to relocate Karen, Hmong, Akha, Lau, and other tribal communities living in "ecologically sensitive" areas. That resolution reversed the previous government's stated support for the land rights of all communities established before protected areas were created, as well as its decision to explore environmental solutions that would allow mountain communities to remain in national parks and wildlife sanctuaries.

Box 7.1

Karen Mythology

The Karen are inveterate storytellers. They encircle the embers of their cook fires most evenings and regale their children with myths that have been passed from generation to generation for the 2800 or so years since the tribe first gathered somewhere in Tibet.

Resentment and distrust are prevalent themes of their folklore, reflecting the centuries of oppression and powerlessness that have besieged them as they gradually migrated south through China into Burma, where they have been subjected to endless genocidal oppression. Hundreds of families and small bands totaling about a hundred thousand Karen have crossed the Salween River into Thailand where they have been promised citizenship, but are treated more like farm animals.

A common character in Karen folk tales is a downtrodden orphan who is bullied and exploited by the rich and powerful. At the end of each story he cleverly escapes his oppressors and moves on to a supportive Karen settlement.

The Karen believe that one day, like the orphan, they will be liberated to live in peace and harmony forever. They have waited patiently for hundreds of years for this outcome. In the meantime, they call their stateless collective homeland *Kathoolei*, which means "land without evil."

I spent the rest of the day and well into the evening listening to similar accounts from other hill tribe leaders who had walked miles from their villages into Khon Noi's valley to put their fate on the record. One man who said he was about to be evicted from a nearby wildlife sanctuary wondered aloud how his fellow villagers would be treated had they cut down the forests, destroyed the land, and built a great city like Bangkok.

"Would we now be facing eviction?" Bangkok, he reminded me, was itself a tiny forest village two hundred years ago, when his ancestors moved into the mountain valley he and his kin were about to lose on an order from Bangkok. Another Karen leader complained that he and his family had recently been evicted from the Khao Yai National Park to make room for two golf courses built inside the park. "The poorest people in Thailand are being pushed off their land," he said, "so the richest can play. And what do golf courses have to do with conservation?"

The next afternoon I climbed a mountain on the periphery of Khon Noi's valley with my interpreter and his eldest son, a rite of passage for all Karen boys. As we stood and looked down at the distant village and its communal rice terraces, I thought I had never seen a greener, healthier place in my life. I couldn't imagine what the RFD and its park managers were so upset about. And I wondered why the international conservation leaders I had met the week before in Bangkok were so complacent in the face of such unnecessary violence and injustice.

They had been a short flight south of this village attending the week-long IUCN-sponsored World Conservation Congress, manning display booths adorned with larger-than-life photos of indigenous peoples in splendid tribal attire. At huge plenary sessions they shared in heaping praise on Thailand's beloved Queen Sirikit and her environment minister, who came accompanied by a sizable delegation from the Royal Forest Department. But if they had taken the time to attend some smaller panels and workshops, one held outside the convention center in a parking lot, the conservationists would have heard Khon Noi's story repeated a hundred times or more by Thai and other indigenous leaders, who came to Bangkok from every continent, at great expense, to lobby six thousand prominent conservation biologists, environmental activists, and government bureaucrats for better understanding and fairer treatment.

And they would have heard a young Karen father of two young children ask why his country, Thailand, whose cabinet had ordered its environmental bureaucracy to evict his people from their traditional homeland, was chosen by IUCN to host the largest conservation convention in history? It was a question that expressed the accumulated anger of almost five hundred native people who had found the time and resources to travel to Bangkok and share their stories with the few in attendance who would take notes and report them.

Science-based conservation is a good idea. However, the problem with too many of its adherents is the limits of their science. Ecology, wildlife biology, geography, oceanography, and biochemistry are all sound and sensible tools of effective conservation, but they are not alone in the diverse panoply of knowledge that has been brought to bear on the age-old challenge of assuring healthy ecosystems. Hard as it might be for Western scientists to believe or accept, there is a huge body of remarkably sound science that has never found its way into textbooks. Anthropologists and ethnobotanists call it "traditional ecological knowledge," or TEK for short, and those who pay close attention to its teachings are eventually amazed by its precision and sophistication.

8

Natural Capital and TEK

Anything should be studied not by what it is in itself, but by its relationship to other things.
—Gregory Bateson, anthropologist

Treat the land as a plate you eat from.
—Tingit wisdom

We are awed by the new economic concept of "natural capital"—the process by which the floral, faunal, and mineral components of Earth combine, without human assistance, to produce oxygen, forests, fresh water, arable soil, and other free and invaluable "environmental services"—a notion first put forth by eco-economists Robert Costanza and Herman Daly, and later popularized by Paul Hawken, Amory Lovins, and others. It's a new and refreshing way to regard classical capitalism. We ignore the existence and value of natural capital at our peril, our neo-Keynesians warn us, for without it our ecosystems will eventually collapse, and so will we.

Of course, people who have never been separated from land steward-ship have understood this for thousands of years. In some ways natural capital is their only sense of capital, as the other kind—finance capital—is barely part of their economy. They rely upon and respect natural capital in ways that modern industrial capitalists rarely if ever consider. In their world, fodder is more essential than cattle, the forest more important than its products, and the river more sacred than the water. For native peoples those principles are Economics 101, the curriculum for which is an ancient science developed and transmitted through count-less generations of ancestry.

"Traditional ecological knowledge," or TEK for short, is the collective botanical, zoological, hydrological, cultural, and geographical know-how, rooted in spirit, culture, and language essential to the survival of a particular tribe or community in a particular habitat. It is "knowing the country." The details and complexities of TEK are passed orally from generation to generation as a form of practical common sense. Possessing and understanding the particular TEK of a habitat it is the sine qua non of a community's survival, and of leadership among native peoples. Thus it is not only a science but also an authority system.

Ethnoecologists and ethnobiologists,[1] relatively new interdisciplinary scientists who study folk taxonomy and traditional ecological systems, tell us that while the four thousand five hundred or so surviving indigenous cultures of the world are remarkably different in many respects, there are some important similarities among them, particularly in their cosmologies, and most particularly in the parts of those cosmologies that deal with the meaning of land and nature.

For most indigenous cultures, land and nature are to some degree considered sacred. Land is revered and regarded as much more than an economic resource, and nature is seen as the primary source of life, the center of the universe and the core of culture. Nature not only supports, it teaches. And the lessons taught by nature combine to form TEK. The Tingit of southeastern Alaska teach their young to respect, balance, share, regulate, and pass on the values that form a code of conduct governing seal harvesting. "Food comes from the land and the sea," tribal elder Walter Soboloff tells his children. "To abuse either may diminish its generosity. In other words, don't break the plate."

It should be noted here that there is some concern among anthropologists and ethnobiologists over use of the word *traditional* in TEK, as it seems to imply something that is static and homogeneous. Neither is true. Tradition should be regarded here as a process through which discovery and innovation occur. The Four Directions Council of Canada explains: "What is traditional about traditional knowledge is not its antiquity, but the way it is acquired and used: in other words, the social process of learning and sharing knowledge that is unique to each indigenous culture. It's at the very heart of its traditionalism. Much of this knowledge is actually quite new, but it has a social meaning, and legal character entirely unlike the knowledge indigenous peoples acquire from settlers and industrialized societies."[2]

Although traditional knowledge differs widely from culture to culture, it all derives from lateral thinking, the central tenet of which is sustainability. Its practice is a constant search for new and better ways of preserving a sustainable landscape. Western knowledge is derived from vertical thinking.

TEK offers a complete taxonomy of plants, animals, insects, fungi, and microorganisms, and understands their dynamic relationship with every type of mineral, soil, liquid, and gas in a landscape. Thus all TEK systems are essentially holistic, and people who understand their entirety are considered the wisest and often the most powerful members of the community. There are many names for the possessors of TEK—shaman, medium, sage, medicine man—but they are all known in their societies as the "wisdom-keepers."

In most traditional knowledge systems all things, living and not living, are inextricably linked. Human beings are simply one form of life participating in a vast biological community regulated by a set of laws that we might call the laws of nature, which native people would say is the repertory of their particular knowledge. Since indigenous peoples generally have no written language, and certainly no printing facilities or textbooks, TEK is passed orally from one generation to the next. Thus, as Mexican ecologist Victor Toledo points out, "memory is the most important intellectual resource among indigenous cultures." And according to an old African proverb, "when a knowledgeable old person dies, a whole library disappears."

Open-minded conservationists who take the time to visit and listen to shamans and other tribal wisdom-keepers are coming to realize that much TEK is, in many respects, as scientifically sound as classical textbook ecology, and that without it the inhabitants of an area of interest would long ago have either perished or destroyed the health of their biota. Instead they thrive by staying in close harmony with natural resources, carefully preserving the diverse plants and animals they harvest for food, fiber, and forage.

There is much in common between TEK and Western science, more than either side often cares to admit. Both are the produce of dynamic and cumulative intellectual processes aimed at creating order out of chaos. Both begin with empirical observations in natural settings. Both employ inference and prediction. Both are reliant on inquisitiveness, perseverance, honesty, and open-mindedness. Both believe the universe is unified. Both seek verification through repetition. Both innovate from within, but do adapt some external knowledge, sometimes even from each other. Both seek to manage human activities. And both believe their body of knowledge is subject to ongoing modification as factors and variables change. In the context of conservation, both disciplines believe that an accelerating loss of animal or plant species is a sign of imminent ecological crisis. Once that observation is shared, there is an opportunity to integrate TEK with Western science. Easier said than done.

Where the two approaches to knowledge part ways is primarily with traditional emphasis on spirit, and with matters of cause, effect, and quantitative measurement, the three major obsessions of Western science. Native cultures tend to reject such concerns because they control and interfere with nature. Most, in fact, have no interest in controlling nature. They prefer to work within it, to thrive in a multidimensional landscape of complex interacting ecosystems where nothing is simply cause or effect, where every system is comprised of complex cycles of circulated energy, matter, and relationships. Therefore they are antireductionist, which is another serious problem for modern science, which tends to reduce ecosystems to discrete components valued primarily for their economic utility. Thus in the final analysis, it is in natural resource management where the two worldviews collide most forcefully.

Here is how Fikret Berkes, professor of natural resources at the University of Manitoba, describes the conflict: "Western resource management and reductionist science were developed to serve the exploitative, dominion-over-nature world view of colonists and industrial developers. Utilitarian sciences were best geared for the efficient use of resources as if they were limitless, consistent with the laissez-faire doctrine still alive in today's neoclassical economic theory. But utilitarianism is ill-suited for sustainability, which requires a new philosophy that recognizes ecological limits and strives to satisfy social as well as economic needs."[3]

Conflict

We in the world's dominant cultures simply cannot sustain the earth's ecological health without the help of the world's endangered cultures.
—Alan Durning, Sightline Institute

Not all TEK is sound science, and not all indigenous people are perfect land stewards. Only cultural romantics believe that. And even those who were good stewards in years past may cease being so due to population growth, erosion of culture, market pressures, and the misuse of destructive technologies. A favorite example cited by defenders of exclusionary conservation is that of Chupa Pou, a settlement of Ache foragers in eastern Paraguay. After acquiring legal title to their land, the Ache of Chupa Pou, who had previously seemed like exemplary land stewards, began selling off old-growth hardwood trees. In a few months the trees were gone, and so was the money, squandered on gambling and luxury goods. While cynics tend to indict the Ache as an irresponsible ethnicity, and even use the episode to generalize about Amazonian Indians, it turns out that Chupa Pou was an anomaly, even among the Ache. Not far from the village, another settlement of Ache people, Arroya Bandera, which had also gained title to their settlement, initiated a carefully planned and controlled sustainable forestry program, which remains in effect.

The fact that ancient human societies can still be found in biodiverse habitats where they have being living for millennia should be an indication that sound TEK works. And if a conservation biologist finds an area of land, large or small, with high biodiversity, and later discovers a community of people who have been living in that area for many generations, chances are there is a connection between the lifeways of those people and the health of the biota. And since most indigenous people would prefer to stay where they're living, close to food supplies, medicines, and ancestral burial grounds, the wisest thing, it seems, would be to allow them the stay on as proven protectors of the biota.

There are a growing number of well-documented incidents where TEK and Western science have come into conflict, and TEK has proven to be superior. Here are three involving the hunting practices of the Inuit in northern Canada:

• For thousands of years the Inuit have hunted the Peary caribou opportunistically, taking those of whatever gender or age seemed most convenient. Canadian wildlife managers sought to introduce a conventional mature-male-only hunting regime in the high Arctic. The Inuit, who had been watching the Peary caribou for millennia, pointed out to wildlife managers that the caribou depend for their survival through the winter on the social structure of small herds dominated by alpha males. Therefore the selective hunting of mature males would quickly result in a rapid decline of the caribou population. A government-monitoring project initiated in southern Ellesmere Island found the native view to be right—a victory for TEK.

• The "solitary and surplus"-male hunting policy had also been applied to musk oxen in the high Arctic. Again the Inuit had found from observation that these males actually play an important role in the survival of the species and that a male-only harvest policy would quickly decimate the herd. And again, independent observation proved them to be right.

• Scientific surveys conducted in 1977, at the behest of the Canadian government, concluded that the bowhead whale population was seriously depleted in the Beaufort Sea. There were, according to the official count, about eight hundred remaining in the area. A hunting moratorium was proposed. Since the survey was conducted from aircraft, the Inuit pointed out, only animals swimming near the surface, in open water, could be counted. The bowhead, they observed, were able to swim for long periods under the ice flows where they could not be counted from the air. There were, they contended, closer to seven thousand whales in the Beaufort. In 1991 a new census, using techniques that acknowledged Inuit observations, found that despite an annual harvest of between twenty and forty whales a year, the total population was stable at close to eight thousand.[4]

International conservation leaders, many of whom have been dismissive of TEK, are beginning to accept the fact that the long-term empirical observations of "uneducated" native people can lead to sound environmental science. In fact, principle 22 of the Rio Declaration on Environment and Development, drafted at an international gathering attended by thousands of prominent conservationists, states that: "Indigenous people and their communities and other local communities have a vital role in environmental management and development because of their knowledge and traditional practices. States should recognize and duly support their identity, culture and interests and enable their effective participation in the achievement of sustainable development."

One can only wonder what Yosemite would look like today were the descendants of Tenaya still thriving in the valley, sharing the native wisdom accumulated over 4,000 years in the ecosystem, and sharing, as equal partners in the stewardship and management of the park. What would be the state of its biotic wealth? Would the grizzly bear and bighorn sheep still roam its meadows and canyons? And would the scientific descendants of University of California biologist Joseph Grinnell have found more or fewer deer mice, voles, and montane shrews than they did in their surprising 2005 biologic inventory of the park, which found far fewer of those species than Grinnell recorded in his legendary 1915 biological assay of the park[5]?

The answer to that question might, of course, have nothing to do with the area's occupants. Humans have found so many ways to reduce biological diversity without going near the land in question. However, it seems evident that an ecologically better conservation strategy can be found than the tried-and-failed Yosemite model.

As the reprise of Grinnell's research seems to suggest, creating a public playground in a wild place is no guarantor of biodiversity. And there are "paper parks" all through the less-developed world that bear no resemblance whatsoever to a protected area. Take for example the Hukaumg National Park in Burma. Within its borders are seven government-supported gold mines and several ungazetted mines filling the park's streams with mercury.

Or consider Pedang Wildlife Reserve in Burma's Kachin Province. Established in 1918, it is now 40 percent deforested. Tigers, elephants, and rhinoceros that once roamed that park are gone. Army compounds and small college have been built in the park and a railroad runs right through it. "Reforestation" consists of planting lychee nut and fruit trees to feed soldiers stationed in Kachin to fight the only people who might have prevented this conservation atrocity—the Karen.

Given the fact that most of the biologically rich, ecological hot spots remaining on the planet currently are occupied by proven land stewards like the Karen, perhaps they should be part of any new conservation strategy. And so should traditional ecological knowledge play a major cooperative role in natural resource management.

However, "integrating traditional ecological knowledge into the environmental impact assessment process entails more than a transfer of information from one culture to another," warns John Sallenave, senior policy advisor at the Canadian Arctic Resource Committee. "[I]t will require a change in the mindset of policy makers and of many in the scientific community. If knowledge truly *is* power, then appropriate decision-making power must be transferred to those at the source of the knowledge being used."[6] The only national government that has come close to accepting that premise is Australia's.

Box 8.1

The Declaration of Belem

In 1988, the First International Congress of Ethnobiology was held in Belem, Brazil. More than six hundred delegates attended from thirty-five countries and sixteen indigenous communities and organizations. At the conference, the International Society of Ethnobiology was formed and a declaration was passed that states, "indigenous peoples have been stewards of 99 percent of the world's resources." And when their knowledge is lost due to displacement or other social pressures, biological diversity will decrease significantly. The declaration calls for an exchange of knowledge and cooperation between TEK and Western biological sciences.

The declaration reads:

Leading anthropologists, biologists, chemists, sociologists and representatives of several indigenous populations met in to discuss common concerns at the First International Congress of Ethnobiology and to found [the] International Society of Ethnobiology. Major concerns outlined by conference contributors were the study of the ways that indigenous and rural populations uniquely perceive, utilize, and manage their natural resources and the development of programs that will guarantee the preservation of vital biological and cultural diversity. This declaration was articulated.

As ethnobiologists, we are alarmed that:

SINCE
Tropical forests and other fragile ecosystems are disappearing; many species, both plant and animal, are threatened with extinction; Indigenous cultures around the world are being disrupted and destroyed.

AND GIVEN
• That economic, agricultural and health conditions of people are dependent on these resources;
• That native people have been stewards of 95 percent of the world's genetic resources; and
• That there is an inextricable link between cultural and biological diversity.

WE, MEMBERS OF THE INTERNATIONAL SOCIETY OF ETHNO-BIOLOGY STRONGLY URGE ACTIONS AS FOLLOWS:
• Henceforth, a substantial proportion of development aid must be devoted to efforts aimed at ethnobiological inventory, conservation, and management programs; mechanisms be established by which indigenous specialists are recognized as proper authorities and are consulted in all programs affecting them, their resources, and their environments;
• All other inalienable human rights be recognized and guaranteed, including cultural and linguistic identity;
• Procedures must be developed to compensate native peoples for the utilization of their knowledge and their biological resources;
• Educational programs must be implemented to alert the global community to the value of ethnobiological knowledge for human well-being;
• All medical programs include the recognition of and respect for traditional healers and the incorporation of traditional health practices that enhance the health status of these populations;
• Ethnobiologists make available the results of their research to the native peoples with whom they have worked, especially including dissemination in the native language;
• Exchange of information should be promoted among indigenous and rural peoples regarding conservation, management, and sustainable utilization of resources.

Belem, Brazil, July 1988

Country

Perhaps we have begun to see that the distance separating the scientist and the shaman is not so great as was once imagined.
—Colin Scott, author

Australian Aborigines call their environment "country." By that they mean pretty much everything around them, including people, animals, plants, earth, minerals, water, and dreams; dreams that coalesce to create a multidimensional and spiritual relationship with the land. But foremost in the relationship that forms country, the Aborigines say, are people. "The country needs its people," they say. And "healthy country means healthy people." Their entire existence is organized around a sophisticated awareness of the biological functions that keep "country" in good health.

Aboriginal cosmology is all about the kinship between people and the natural world. It's essentially their ecology. Their ecosystem is a web of relationships that inculcates nature into family. Vital trees are called brothers, less vital ones cousins. Large yams are mothers, small ones children. Owls are uncles.

Australians, native and nonnative alike, speak of the "two toolboxes" for natural resource management—the Aboriginal toolbox and the scientific toolbox. Unlike the scientific toolbox the native toolbox is loaded with philosophy, cosmology, and a body of ancient law that defines the tenure and responsibilities of people in country. While they find much value in Western science, Aborigines make great efforts to prevent it from subsuming or overwhelming their toolbox. It's a matter of integrating self-interest with the rest of the world. Here's the way Debbie Bird Rose, anthropologist at Australian National University, describes it: "The way Aboriginal cultures understand how the world works . . . the connections and kinship, mean that they do not have to draw a distinction between self-interest and other interest. The interests of self and of others are so mutually constituted that they look for what works well for everybody."

Australia's natives regard people and country as an interdependent whole, as two parts of a system that cannot survive the absence of either.

And they seem never to have thought about population and biodiversity in an abstract way. "They produced biodiversity," says Rose, "rather than work with an abstraction called biodiversity." And as in so much of the South Pacific, population has for generations been controlled proactively by women who prescribe and use medicinal contraceptives and abortifacients brewed from local plants.

While visiting northern Australia in late 2006 I met an old man named Allambie Bunderra, whose name, he said, means "remain awhile among the hills." He is a Djalakuru, born and raised in a village about three hundred miles inland from where we met in a small coastal town he had wandered into seeking medical attention. The land of his ancestry had changed ownership three times since his birth and was still in tenure limbo. He seemed remarkably resigned to the endless struggle that had taken place over ownership and control of his outback homeland during his lifetime.

"You white fellas will burn yourselves out eventually," he told me, smiling, "destroy your whole society and die off. Then we will have our land back forever. It may take another three or four hundred years," he said, "but we are patient because we can see so clearly what you are doing, and we know how to live forever in country. We've been here for over sixty thousand years. Another four hundred is the blink of an eyelash."

Allambie grew up in a community that practiced rotational cultivation, which he told me was stopped after "conservationists came from your country and told us it was bad for the land. Do they think we don't know what your farmers do, sterilizing their soil with one chemical then soaking it in another that poisons their watershed and creates death at the mouths of your rivers? We laugh watching your conservationists arrive with their scientists in private jets, travel around in air-conditioned Land Rovers, stay in expensive lodges, and look aside while their friends buy ten-thousand-dollar permits to kill animals they say they are here to protect." I promised Allambie I would repeat what he said. I read back my notes to be sure I'd heard him right. "That's what I said," he said.

In recent years there has been widespread international recognition of TEK. Chapter 17 of the United Nations Conference on Environment and Development (UNCED) agenda 21 instructs signatories to "develop systems for acquisition and recording of traditional knowledge concerning marine living resources and environment, and [to] promote the incorporation of such knowledge into management." Section 17.94 (b) of the same treaty requires signatories to "provide support to local fishing communities, in particular those that rely on fishing for subsistence, the technical and financial assistance to organize, maintain, exchange and improve traditional knowledge."

It is also heartening to note that the Convention of Biological Diversity, a binding treaty that has been signed and ratified by 171 nations, and is now managed by the United Nations Environmental Program, has formally acknowledged the conservation value of TEK. Article 8 of the convention states that each signatory nation "subject to its national legislation [will] respect, preserve and maintain knowledge, innovation and practices of indigenous and local communities embodying traditional lifestyles relevant to the conservation and sustainable use of biological diversity."

"The Convention recognizes the close and traditional dependence of indigenous and local communities on biological resources and the need to assure that these communities share in the benefits arising from the use of their traditional knowledge and practices relating to the conservation and sustainable use of biodiversity," reads a recent CBD communiqué. "Member governments have undertaken to 'respect, preserve and maintain' such knowledge and practices, to promote their wider application with the approval and involvement of the communities concerned, and to encourage the equitable sharing of the benefits derived from their utilization." It is sad, however, and perhaps ironic, that the nation hosting the five largest conservation organizations in the world has not ratified the convention.

The Eurocolonial concept of equality meant making the colonized society equal to Europe. This, of course, led to the gross mistreatment of lower castes in Africa and India. So when protected areas were formed, the colonial powers thought nothing of resettling natives outside their boundaries and cared less for the social consequences. Thus came the game reserve model, hundreds of which have been created in India, at the expense of the Adivasi.

9

Adivasi

We and the forests are one.
—Rallying cry of the Jan Sunwai

Conservationists who believe that wildlife can be protected in such circumstances are living in a fool's paradise.
—Ashish Kothari, Kalpavriksh

In the spring of 2003, about eight thousand tribal people and low-caste farmers living in the Kuno area of Madhya Pradesh, India, were summarily uprooted from the rich farmlands they had cultivated for generations and moved to twenty-four villages on scrubland outside the borders of a sanctuary created for a pride of six imported Asiatic lions. "I'll never forget when we left," recalled village headman Babu Lal. "Even the men cried that day. Is it fair to do this to 1,600 families for a few lions?"[1] By then almost 500 villages occupied by a total of 300,000 families around India had experienced similar forced relocation to protect the habitat of tigers, rhinos and Asiatic lions residing in the 580 national parks and sanctuaries that have been created in India since the colonial period.

Wildlife conservation in India has generally emulated the early American (Yosemite/Yellowstone) model, which regarded forests as pristine wilderness, excluded human beings from national parks and other protected areas, and saw its Aboriginal people as "marauders," "poachers," and "encroachers," all the while sanctioning the lifeways and hunting practices of elite sportsmen and urban tourists. Throughout rural India, tribal Adivasis, ancient forest dwellers who occupy thousands of villages, are routinely blamed for declines in local biodiversity. As a government training manual for foresters instructs its students: "Forest dwelling communities are invariably inveterate hunters and have in most areas practically annihilated game animals and birds by indiscriminate hunting and snaring. It is surely time to instill in the tribal mind a respect for the basic game laws of the country."

In the past three decades, twenty-eight major relocations of Adivasis have been documented, seven more are known to have occurred, but not officially recorded, and there are several more in early planning stages. There are no hard numbers available, but estimates of conservation refugees in India range from one hundred thousand to six hundred thousand, with millions more slated for future forced, voluntary, and induced displacements.

Fig Leaves

The Nagarhole National Park (now Rajiv Ghandi National Park) in the state of Karnatka is part of the larger Nilgiri Biosphere Reserve, one of 440 such reserves existing in ninety-seven countries. Several Adivasi communities have inhabited the Nilgiri reserve for centuries, including the reclusive Cholanaikans, the last surviving hunter-gatherers on the Indian subcontinent.

When the Nagarhole park was officially constituted in 1983, there were about nine thousand other tribal peoples living in fifty-eight small hamlets throughout the park. There were the Jenu Kurubas, a honey-gathering tribe, the Hakki Pikki bird trappers, the Betta Kuruba bamboo artisans, the Yeravas fishing tribe, and the Soligas goat herders,[2] There were also about twenty-five thousand other Adivasi living outside but near the park who relied heavily on the Nagarhole forests for their survival. In violation of UN policy for biosphere reserves, which calls for equal protection of forests, birds, agriculture, and human wellbeing, the Indian government began pushing the Adivasis out. During the 1970s six thousand were evicted.

Anger arose among the Adivasis who had begun to organize nationally and express their disapproval more boldly. In response, the Indian Forest Policy statement of 1988 recognized the role of Adivasis in the conservation and sustenance of India's forests. However, evictions continued from the Nagarhole, albeit in less violent and forceful ways.

Box 9.1

Adivasi Contributions to Indian Culture and Civilization*

Repulsed by how greed was instrumental in causing poverty, social exploitation, and unending warfare, Siddhartha Gautama saw hope for human society in the culture and lifeways of the Bhils, Gonds, Oraons, Mundas, Hos, Santals, Korkus, and Irulas, known collectively as the Adivasis (literally: "original inhabitants"). When the Buddha wandered through India, these "tribal republics" had not yet come under the sway of authoritarian rule and caste discrimination. Thus early Buddhist *Sanghas* were modeled on Adivasi patterns of social interaction that stressed gender equality and respect for all members. As Buddhism spread throughout Asia, members of early *Sanghas* resisted hierarchy and sought to emulate the egalitarian outlook and democratic functioning of Adivasi culture.

Adivasi society was built on a foundation of respect for all life forms including plants and trees. There was a deep recognition of mutual dependence in nature and human society. The possession of highly valued skills or knowledge did not lead to a permanent rise in status. This meant that no individual or small group could engage in overlordship of any kind, or enjoy hereditary rights.

Such a value system was sustainable as long as the Adivasi community was nonacquisitive and all the products of society were shared. Although division of labor did take place, the work of society was performed on a cooperative and coequal basis—without prejudice or disrespect for any form of work.

It was the simplicity, love of nature, absence of coveting the wealth of others, and the social harmony of tribal society that attracted the Buddha, and had a profound impact on the ethical core of his teachings. In matters of trade he observed that the Adivasis followed a highly evolved system of honor. Individual dishonesty or deceit was punished severely by the tribe. Anyone who acted in a manner that violated the honor of the tribe faced potential banishment and family members lost the right to participate in community events during the period of punishment.

As the money economy grew, tribal societies came under increasing stress. The extension of commerce, military incursions on tribal land, and the resettling of Brahmins amid tribal populations had an impact, as did ideological coercion or persuasion to attract key members of the tribe into "mainstream" Hindu society. This led to many tribal communities becoming integrated into Hindu society as new castes. Those who resisted assimilation were pushed into the hilly or forested areas where they were discriminated as outcastes and "untouchables." Those who accepted assimilation often became quite prominent. In Central India, ruling dynasties emerged from within the ranks of tribal society.

But assimilation was a two-way street. Adivasi traditions such as ancestor worship, fertility gods and goddesses, and totemic reverence all found their way into the practice of what is now considered Hinduism. The widespread Indian practice of fasting for wish fulfillment or moral cleansing also has Adivasi origins. The Hindu gods and goddesses Shiva, Kali, Krishna, and Ganesh were Adivasi deities. Many of India's regional languages—Oriya, Marathi, and Bengali —developed as a result of the fusion of tribal languages with Sanskrit or Pali and virtually all the Indian languages have incorporated words from the vocabulary of Adivasi languages.

Adivasis who developed an intimate knowledge of various plants and their medicinal uses played an invaluable role in the development of Ayurvedic medicines. In a recent study, the All India Coordinated Research Project credits Adivasi communities with the knowledge of nine thousand plant species—seven thousand five hundred used for human healing and veterinary health care. Dental care products like datum roots and condiments like turmeric used in cooking and ointments are also Adivasi discoveries, as are many fruit trees and vines. Ayurvedic cures for arthritis and night blindness owe their origin to Adivasi knowledge.

Adivasis also played an important role in such agricultural developments as crop rotation, fertility maintenance, and leaving land fallow for future pasture. The Adivasis of Orissa were instrumental in developing several of strains of rice.

Adivasi musical instruments such as the *bansuri,* a flute, and *dhol,* a drum, as well as folk tales, dances, and seasonal celebrations also found their way into Indian tradition as did their art and metallurgical skills.

---

* Drawn from Debiprasad Chattopadhyaya *What Is Living and What Is Dead in Indian Philosophy* (People's Publishing House Ltd., 2001) by; *Buddhist Logic* (New York, 1962); Papers of Stcherbasky (Calcutta, 1969, p. 71); Baidyanath Saraswati's review of P. K Maity, "Folk-Rituals of Eastern India," *The Indian Historical Review* 16: 1, 2; *Bulletins of the ICHR* (Indian Council of Historical Research); *Studies in the History of Science in India,* edited by Debiprasad Chattopadhyaya (Editorial Enterprises, 1982); and Mari and Stan Thekaekara, *Adivasi: A Symbiotic Bond* (Hindu Folio, July 16, 2000). .

While the alleged purpose of the evictions was wildlife conservation, teak and eucalyptus plantations eventually replaced more than forty of the evacuated hamlets. As it has in Botswana, Kenya, and elsewhere, conservation in India has become a convenient and respectable cover for less savory motives when the very same national government that removes native people from their land in the name of conservation has no compunctions about giving up ecologically sensitive areas to large-scale development projects.

The fig leaf of conservation was eventually spread to cover a World Bank-funded ecotourism lodge proposed by the Taj Hotel Group. In December of 1996, Adivasis filed for an injunction with the Indian High Court and called for a general strike in the Nagarhole to stop the Taj project. A month later the High Court found the Taj Hotel Group in violation of conservation laws, a ruling that was upheld on appeal. The half-finished, abandoned structures of the Taj in the Nagarhole represent one of the very few Adivasi victories anywhere in India.

However, people who were allowed to stay in the reserve after construction was halted were subjected to severe restrictions of their lifeways and food security. No cultivation of any kind was allowed, this despite the fact that local Adivasi farming practices never called for cutting down trees, plowing land, or using pesticides or fertilizers. In addition, all hunting was banned and no livestock or pets were allowed. The gathering of tubers, mushrooms, and wild vegetables was forbidden, and most sacred sites and burial grounds were placed off limits. However, all these limitations did not seem to satisfy all conservation NGOs.

In 1993 the World Wide Fund for Nature India (WWF-I) petitioned the Indian government to enforce its own Wildlife Protection Act. The act, which was passed in 1972, prescribes procedures for setting up and managing the country's protected areas, which at the time included about 80 national parks and 443 sanctuaries that made up about 4.8 percent of India's land mass, a little more than half the current area under protection.

India's protected areas harbor the hub of what remains of the nation's biological diversity, and perform critical ecological functions like regulating hydrological cycles, stabilizing river catchments, protecting soil, and maintaining land productivity. India's agriculture would be seriously threatened and its climatic patterns much more erratic if those areas did not exist. And industrial and commercial forces long ago would have occupied these habitats were it not for the protected status granted them by the Wildlife Protection Act.

WWF's petition focused on the fact that vital enforcement procedures were not being implemented in most protected areas, and that state governments were often allowing them to be opened for industrial development. Darlaghat Sanctuary in Himachal Pradesh, for example, was denotified (the term the Indian government uses where park status is removed) to host a cement factory. Very few protected areas had adequate management or equipment. The whole situation was becoming as bad for wildlife as it was for people. This was a lawsuit that had to be filed.

However, there remained the question of land and tenure rights in protected areas. Neither was mentioned in the WWF suit. In national parks all human activities had to cease; in sanctuaries, certain activities were allowed to continue, but only if they were shown to be of use to wildlife conservation. In August 1997, at the behest of WWF-I, the Indian Supreme Court ordered all state governments to complete settlement procedures within one year.

That order was a clear victory for WWF and regarded worldwide as a landmark event in the history of conservation. However, the ill-defined rights of Adivasis and local villagers remained a major problem in the management of India's protected areas. And as a result, unfortunately, the order caused nothing but trouble. When government officials issued unclear and confusing notices of new regulations inside protected areas, villagers interpreted them as attacks on their right to reside in traditional settlements.

Almost four million people were at that time living inside India's formally protected areas, and alongside several million others in surrounding towns and villages. Most of them resided there before the protected areas were created, and all were heavily dependent on local natural resources for fuel, fodder, medicines, fish, water, and nontimber forest products. "To pass an order that denies all 'rights and concessions' to such people, is virtually like telling them to pack up and go," proclaimed Indian environmentalist Ashish Kothari. "Both the WWF petition and the learned judges' order are, to put it bluntly, devoid of any sense of grounded reality. Even if the procedure for inquiry was to be done properly, it could be grossly unjust to villagers."

Strangely enough this all happened as the government of India was, at least rhetorically, endorsing and agreeing to abide by an agreement of the Convention on Biological Diversity that called for full participation of indigenous peoples in the management of wildlife conservation. The agreement commits all signatories to recognize the rights of local communities to participate in conservation planning, to respect their land and resource rights, and to seek prior consent to any resettlement of people in protected areas.

The Indian government was also ignoring its own 1990 report on Scheduled Castes and Tribes, which includes a clear framework to deal with the livelihood consequences of conservation for displaced Adivasis and other forest dwellers. And they were in violation of article 338 (9) of the Indian Constitution, which provides protection for tribal welfare and stipulates that the National Commission for Scheduled Castes and Scheduled Tribes should be consulted in conflicts over resettlement. Bijoy Panda, a tribal activist in Madhya Pradesh, called the Adivasis "azaad desh ke gulaam log" (slaves of a free nation).

Ashish Kothari predicted that there would be growing demands from Adivasis to do away with protected areas and unpopular wildlife laws. There would also, he said, be more acts of subversion and deliberate violation of conservation laws such as poaching and theft of timber. "Never mind the issue of human rights and social justice," he said. "Even from a purely conservation point of view, these moves are suicidal." He turned out to be right.

Increased resentment rose toward conservation, which often expressed itself in the setting of forest fires, colluding with poachers, and undermining conservation efforts in any way possible, similar in many ways to responses of the Maasai and other African pastorals to being pushed out of their grazing lands. A 2005 report commissioned by India's prime minister called the situation "truly a war within, imploding inside reserves and taking everything in its wake."[3]

In Semarsot, Kanha, and other sanctuaries of Madhya Pradesh, each village was sent a form that families were to use to claim compensation.

As most tribal villagers cannot read, they were dependent on interpretations of the notice offered by nongovernmental organizations, forest service staff, or the few semiliterate people in their village. Misunderstandings became rampant. In many places, villagers thought the notices were for eviction. History had given them ample reasons to believe that.

While the notices never mentioned the e-word, activists like Kothari believed that massive displacement could nonetheless become the unintended outcome of the process. "Once final notification is issued," he pointed out, "no one will be allowed to collect nontimber forest produce. For a tribal whose life and livelihood depend on things from the forest like fruits, gum, honey, leaves, thatch, etc., this is like the telling urbanites that they may continue to live in their houses, but without the use of water, electricity, or the kitchen. For forest dwellers, this is tantamount to forcible displacement."

Kothari was right again about the increasingly violent response to forced resettlement. In Madhya Pradesh, twenty thousand tribe members rallied to protest against what they considered an unfair abridgment of their rights, and a mass sit-in was organized in front of the Vidhan Sabha (legislative assembly) in the state capital of Bhopal. Conflicts between forest service staff and local people turned to open clashes and villagers began poisoning wildlife to eliminate the raison d'etre for protected areas. Eventually, the entire protected-area network of India came under attack as local people became increasingly hostile to all conservation efforts. Not all protests were violent, however. In Phoolwari ki Nal Sanctuary, Rajasthan, one village filed a petition to India's High Court asking for the sanctuary notification to be quashed. But violent or nonviolent, the Indian government had created a public relations nightmare.

The Wildlife Protection Act of 1972 and the Forest Conservation Act of 1980, later fortified by the WWF lawsuit, have set the stage for what still might eventually become the largest mass eviction of indigenous peoples in any one country. Millions of people are still threatened with displacement.

The Forest Conservation Act froze about 22 percent of India's land for conservation. Land claims of mapped and demarcated forests have been ignored. In fact, some of the areas set aside weren't forest at all. A May 2002 court order mandated the government to record all encroachments on forest lands, whereupon the Ministry of Environment and Forests issued an order to every state to evict "encroachers" in the nation's forests, with no consideration to be given to the age or tenure of a community.

Eventually the tense state of affairs in India's forests reached the attention of Delhi. In early 2005, The Scheduled Tribes and Other Traditional Forest Dwellers (also known as the Recognition of Forest Rights) Bill was drafted by the Tribal Affairs Ministry and introduced in the Indian parliament. The bill recognizes Adivasi tenure rights to ancestral forest lands and resources, and grants 2.5 hectares of forest land to each Adivasi, even if their current residence is in a designated wildlife reserve. Section 4(2) of the bill also lays out a set of six stringent conditions for removing anyone from any area for purposes of wildlife conservation. The bill would also entrust forest communities with some conservation responsibilities.

The bill, which affects about 68 million people (8 percent of the country's population), was severely criticized by the Ministry of Environment and Forests, which feared that it would hinder efforts to preserve India's dwindling forest cover. Some social groups were also concerned that the bill would harm the livelihood of forest dwellers not considered to be part of the Scheduled Tribes. Conservationists were apoplectic, saying the bill would cause irreparable damage to forest ecosystems and lead to class conflict throughout the country. In May 2005 the Indian cabinet removed the bill from its agenda. However, after extensive debate and discussion, and some refinements that aren't so popular with tribal people and their supporters, the bill now known as the Forest Rights Act (FRA) passed into law on December 18, 2006. Rules and amendments are being devised, after which the FRA will be enforceable.

Sariska

In early 2005 a national debate erupted in India over the future of its national animal, the Royal Bengal tiger. Media reports of a "tiger crisis" led to the creation of several "Project Tiger" sanctuaries around the

· Box 9.2

The Freedom Movement

Shortly after the British took control of Eastern India, tribal revolts broke out to challenge alien rule. In the early years of colonization, no other community in India offered more resistance to British rule or faced such tragic consequences as did the numerous Adivasi communities of Jharkhand, Chhattisgarh, Orissa, and Bengal. But their defeat in 1858 only intensified British exploitation of national wealth and resources. A forest regulation passed in 1865 empowered the British government to declare any land covered with trees or brushwood as government forest and to make rules to manage it under terms of its own choosing. The law made no provision regarding the rights of the Adivasi users. A more comprehensive Forest Act was passed in 1878, which imposed severe restrictions upon Adivasi rights over forest land and produce in the protected and reserved forests. The act ended the traditional common property regimes of the Adivasi communities and made them all state property.

Adivasi uprisings throughout the country—the Bhil Revolt of 1809, the Paik Rebellion of 1817, the Ghumsar uprisings of 1836 to 1866, and the Sambhalpur revolt of 1857 to 1864—were quelled by the British through massive deployment of troops. As punishment for resistance to British rule, "The Criminal Tribes Act" was passed by the colonial government in 1871, arbitrarily stigmatizing Adivasis as "congenital criminals" and their communities as "criminal tribes." Among the criminals were insurrectional heroes like Birsa Munda, Kanhu Santal, Khazya Naik, Thana Dora, and Thalkkal Chandu, all remembered in the songs and stories of the Adivasis but ignored in the official textbooks of the freedom movement.

A major revolt broke out in August 1922 in the hill tribal tracts of Andhra Pradesh. Led by Alluri Ramachandra Raju (better known as Sitarama Raju), the Adivasis of the Andhra hills succeeded in drawing the British into a full-scale guerrilla war. Unable to cope, the British brought in the Malabar Special Force to crush the revolt and only prevailed when Alluri Raju died.

As the freedom movement widened, it drew Adivasis into all aspects of the struggle. Many landless and deeply oppressed Adivasis joined in with upper-caste freedom fighters expecting that the defeat of the British would usher in a new democratic era. It did for some.

While independence has brought widespread gains for the vast majority of the Indian population, Dalits ("untouchables") have been left out, and new problems have arisen for the nation's 68 million forest-dwelling Adivasis, 85 percent of whom live well below the national poverty line. With the tripling of India's population since 1947, pressures on land resources, especially demands on forested tracks, mines, and water resources have played havoc on their lives. A disproportionate number of Adivasis have been displaced from their traditional lands while many have seen access to traditional resources undercut by forest mafias—renegade loggers and corrupt officials who have signed irregular commercial leases that conflict with rights granted to the Adivasis by the Indian constitution.

And now come the conservationists, who, like the rest of the country can learn much more than they have from Adivasi social practices, particularly their culture of sharing, their humility and love of nature, and most of all their deep devotion to social equality and civic harmony.

country. As one might expect, the sides taken on the status and protection of tigers included, on the one hand, wildlife conservationists intent on saving a truly magnificent species from extinction, and on the other, anthropologists and tribal activists intent on preserving the cultures of tribal people, 325,000 of whom still live inside the core and buffer zones of tiger reserves.

Indian wildlife conservation, which was still strongly influenced by WWF-International and other foreign conservation NGOs, has persistently embraced a model of Western practice that focuses on individual endangered species—"megacharismatic metavertibrates"—like elephants, rhinos, or tigers, rather than on whole habitats or ecosystems. Prominent Indian conservationist Valmik Thapar insists that tigers can only be saved "in large undisturbed, inviolate landscapes" unoccupied by human beings. "As far as I am concerned," he wrote, "tigers and forest dwellers cannot co-exist." Based on Thapar's advice, the entire Gujjar community of Sariska, a formerly posted tiger sanctuary, faced the prospect of total eviction and relocation, a process that had slowly begun over a decade before the creation of Project Tiger.

No one questions that Gujjar villagers, a traditional grazing community, have had an adverse impact on the wildlife conservation potential of the Sariska reserve and that at least some of this pressure on forests will have to be removed to save it. That is obvious to even the untrained eye. The question in Sariska is why relocation of the Gujjars was selected as the first option for solving the problem, without input from villagers, when so many other options were available for consideration. Moreover, the number-one cause of tiger depletion throughout India is poaching by organized networks of smugglers, none of whom live in the forests.

Gujjars and tigers have coexisted in Sariska for thousands of years. The decline in tiger population is a consequence of development—large dams, iron mines, and the shifting appetites of distant elites—not the lifeways of forest dwellers whose habitats have likewise been threatened by the same phenomena. "Why then punish one victim to save the other?" asks Indian commentator Ramachandra Guha.[4]

In almost every respect the relocation of Gujjars was badly planned and executed, and evictees were compensated at unbearably low rates. Those relocated inside the forest still had access to firewood, water, and livestock fodder. But for years they faced an uncertain future about the permanence of their new residence. Some evictees have returned to their original villages in search of better soil and water, forsaking schools, clinics, and other amenities built in relocation communities. The outcome, in a word, has been chaos. However, relocation has continued despite the real threat of pushing another traditional community into utter destitution, while accomplishing next to nothing for endemic wildlife.

"Conservationists who believe that wildlife can be protected in such circumstances are living in a fool's paradise," according to Ashish Kothari. "Even while the rest of the world moves toward environmental policies that reconcile wildlife conservation with human rights and justice, India is headed in completely the opposite direction."

Kothari, through his organization Kalpavriksh, has proposed a participatory approach to environmental planning that would have the central government, NGOs, scientists, and tribal communities working together in the design and management of conservation initiatives like Project Tiger. He is also lobbying the government to improve the terms and rules of the Scheduled Tribes Act. "In a decentralized natural resources governance structure," Kothari suggests, "the state should become a facilitator rather than a ruler" and people living in and around parks and sanctuaries should become "frontline defenders of the forests and protected areas, rather than being seen as antagonists."

Kothari is part of a global network of pioneers, many of them prophets-without-honor in their own countries, pushing for community based co-management of conservation and community conserved creas (CCAs) where local communities decide on their own to conserve local biodiversity for political, cultural, spiritual, or ethical reasons. There are thousands of de facto CCAs in India, but few have been officially recognized as conservation initiatives. CCAs have, however, been officially recognized by IUCN and other international organizations as a powerful tool to protect wildlife and the livelihood of indigenous communities. (For more on the work of CCAs see chapter 17.)

The Indian tribal experience with conservation has been mixed. While some of the most brutal forced evictions have occurred on that continent during and since the colonial era, there have also been signs that federal and provincial governments are beginning to realize that sound and sensitive governance of resettlement projects can pay off for all involved. Take for example the Melghat Sanctuary and Tiger Reserve in Maharashtra, which became a wildlife sanctuary in 1967 and a tiger reserve in 1973, part of which was spun off into a national park in 1987. Between 1999 and 2002, three Adivasi villages (ninety-two families) were voluntarily relocated outside the tiger reserve. By all accounts the entire project was well managed. Communication with the villagers was open and transparent. However, there remain nineteen villages that opted not to move from the sanctuary and fifty-eight more located in the tiger reserve that could be forcibly moved at some point in the future. And when this book went to press the villagers that did move voluntarily still had not been fully compensated.

Yet forest dwellers and their supporters do regard passage of the Forest Rights Act as a heartening though imperfect triumph, and look forward to some significant amendments in the future legislative sessions. As we went to press, there were at least six petitions (four in high courts, two in the Supreme Court) challenging the FRA. One particularly disturbing petition, filed by three conservation NGOs and one Assamese Adivasi group, argues that the FRA is constitutionally invalid, that it will impinge on the rights of every citizen of India to a clean environment, and that it will condemn Adivasis to a life of subsistence with no access to development facilities. According to Ashish Kothari, "the grounds used for this challenge to the FRA are not only flimsy, but also dangerous. It is argued, for instance, that the parliament does not have a right to pass laws on land matters, since these are exclusively the domain of state governments. If this argument were accepted, the very basis of most current environmental laws would be struck down. The Forest Conservation Act, the Wildlife Protection Act, the Environment Protection Act (including its specific notifications protecting coastal areas and ecologically sensitive areas) . . . all these would become constitutionally invalid, since they all pertain to "land" issues including forest land."[5]

The tribal world is watching.

As the previous chapter attests many human disturbances, perhaps most, have a negative effect on ecological health and biodiversity. But ethnoecology and other new sciences are discovering that there are positive human disturbances, agricultural, grazing and gathering practices that enhance biological diversity and protect ecosystems from natural damage.

10

Disturbances

To live and die with the land is to know its rules.
—Kent Redford, Wildlife Conservation Society

Before *Man and Nature* was sent to press, its author, George Perkins Marsh, wanted to release it under a more misanthropic title—*Man the Disturber of Nature's Harmonies*. His editor thought it was awkward and too negative. He talked him out of it. But the message remained in the text of that classic of early American environmental thought. Human beings are destined to disturb nature, Marsh said. Our mission is to do so as stewards, not vandals.

Wildlife biologists, ecologists, ethnobiologists, and anthropologists concerned about our disturbances of nature have, since the publication of *Man and Nature* in 1864, spent untold effort trying to differentiate between the negative and positive ecological disturbances of humankind. It's no easy task. Most geographers, ecologists, botanists, and anthropologists agree that both exist, but sorting them out is difficult and subject to ongoing debate. They also agree that more species than once was believed rely for their survival on disturbances, human and other, that agitate and revitalize their habitats.

There is no disagreement in conservation science that many human activities have a negative effect on ecosystems, and that too much activity can drive other species to extinction. And there are field-based conservation biologists who are convinced that even minimal human disturbance leads inexorably to a decline of flora and fauna. However, a closer examination of some traditional practices, such as the cultivation of selective perennials, methodic grazing of livestock, and the deliberate setting of grass and forest fires, suggests that human interference can, if practiced wisely, enhance eco-complexity and species diversity.

A 1997 study conducted by Krishna Ghimire of the UN Research Institute for Social Development and Michel Pimbert, agricultural ecologist at the International Institute for Environment and Development, found the biological diversity of the Serengeti grasslands was being enhanced by the grazing and migration practices of the Maasai, which tend to mimic the grazing habits of local wildlife.

Maasai cattle, which have been grazed from the Rift Valley to the Serengeti for somewhere between six thousand and eight thousand years, and rely on the same grasses as the topi, zebra, gazelle, impala, and other grazing animals, prevent thorny scrubs and woodland species from overgrowing, which in turn allows for more grazing opportunities for wildlife. In fact, many recent studies of rangeland ecology indicate a positive symbiosis between wild and domestic ungulates grazing together. Shared grazing can, if properly managed, create a landscape that supports both wild and domestic species better than if they were apart.[1] Other studies indicate that if disturbances are either too rare or too mild, "competitive exclusion" can result in the reduction of biological diversity, in some occasions to a single species.

Here Fikret Berkes describes the resilience in grasslands created by indigenous cattle herders: "African herders behave like a pulse disturbance by following the migratory cycles from one area to another. Pulses of herbivore grazing contribute to the capacity of the semiarid grasslands to function under a wide range of climatic conditions. If this ability of the ecosystem to deal with pulses is reduced, it could flip the grassland into a relatively unproductive state, dominated and controlled by woody plants for several decades."[2]

The whole notion that carefully managed rotational cattle-grazing methods can enhance biotic health is widely accepted by experts in both traditional and contemporary modern agriculture. "Most traditional pastoral management can now be seen to be environmentally benign," according to Ian Scoones, research fellow at the Institute of Development Studies in Sussex. "Indeed customary institutions for land management are potential models for the future." Wildlife conservationists remain skeptical. In fact, many of those who question the positive disturbance theory attack just such studies in their critiques.

Allan Savory, founder of Holistic Management International and creator of highly productive rotational grazing systems, goes a step beyond the advocates of constructive grazing by encouraging conservationists to consider the deliberate introduction of domestic ungulates into areas threatened by desertification. "No tool is known to science that can reverse desertification better than livestock properly handled until such time wild herbivore and predator populations are sufficiently recovered to maintain grasslands," Savory asserts. "If national parks in such grasslands are to be regenerated it would [thus] be wise to consider working with pastoralists so that their animals, properly grazed, can restore wildlife habitat and water sources."[3]

Although some conservationists also question the value of fire, there is less argument that periodic fires in coniferous forests, whether deliberately set or natural, open serotinous cones and canopy gaps, both of which encourage an increase of endemic species. And extensive research indicates that pastoralist burning of rangeland cover encourages the new growth of nutritious grasses that are attractive to wildlife and livestock alike.

One study of Maasai rangeland practices, in fact, found that "by forbidding controlled grazing regimes, national parks encourage the growth of grass species that are less palatable and nutritious for grazing wildlife. . . . Attempts to protect savanna[h] against damage or to reduce heterogeneity may damage resilience [and] protection against fire renders the range vulnerable to much more severe fire damage through the buildup of dry matter."[4] It still remains hard for many conservationists to accept the fact that extreme events and disturbances—even anthrogenic shocks like fire that push ecosystems rapidly from one equilibrium to another—can be of real value. This despite ample, well-documented examples such as the long-term "adaptive management" practiced by natives of the Camas Prairie in Oregon's Willamette Valley.

The edible roots of the camas plant (also known as the "Indian potato") were for centuries a staple of native peoples throughout the American Northwest. Camas thrived in vast meadows alongside wildflowers and native grasses. The meadows, which were also grazing grounds for Roosevelt elk and other ungulates, were periodically burned off in late summer after the camas had released their seeds into the soil. Upon regrowth the meadows provided a ready source of free and natural carbohydrates and protein. When the burning was ceased to make way for settling ranchers, the meadows were soon overtaken with shrubs and conifers and seeded with exotic grasses. The camas died off with a host of other meadow-dependent species, and so did an ancient culture.[5]

Perhaps the most controversial human disturbance is swidden agriculture (aka rotational farming, shifting cultivation, *chitemene, jhum,* or, when disapproval is intended, "slash and burn"). Of course rotational agriculture is a method of farming that is not always practiced well. In some cases it can be devastating to forest systems, particularly in areas of growing population or when it is accompanied by other extractions, such a logging, or when milpas are not given an adequate opportunity to regenerate. And some forest ecosystems respond better than others to rotational clearing. But if practiced as it has been for thousands of years in some parts of the planet, in appropriate arboreal systems, clearing and burning small patches of a forest, planting and rotating food crops for as many years as the soil will support them, then clearing out a new area, allowing the old one to go fallow and slowly return to forest, can enhance the health of the larger ecosystem.

One of the indigenous communities that conservationists are most incensed about in this regard are the Mayans. Swidden agriculture practiced in the Mayan areas of Guatemala, Belize, Honduras, and Mexico does, for an extended period, create a rather unsightly mess. In the summer of 2006 I hiked alongside a recently created clearing outside the Mayan village of Conejo in Belize, en route to an unmapped, trail-less section of the recently created Sarstoon-Temash National Park. I tried to imagine John Muir or John Terborgh's horror upon seeing uprooted trees and stumps lying in deep mud, their sun-bleached branches overgrown with a kudzu-like vine.

However, as unappealing as it may have seemed at the time, and it was not a pretty sight, rotational clearings in that biome create a regular disturbance pattern where patches of young vegetation more resistant to the frequent hurricanes and fire enrich the highly valued mahogany groves that surround them. Community-based natural resource managers call the process "shifting mosaic." It is a common form of contemporary forestry, widely preferred to frontier-type clearings and massive clearcutting.

Studies performed by the U.S. Forest Service (USFS) station in Puerto Rico conclude that mahogany populations in some forests actually flourish under shifting mosaic management. In fact, in Mesoamerican forests the USFS concluded that mahogany would simply not survive without the disturbances. Concurrent anthropological studies show that the Mayan people practicing rotational agriculture in those areas have been doing so for centuries. Moreover, anthropologist David Bray found that a region of logged community forests had the lowest rates of deforestation in southeastern Mexico, lower than regions that contained protected areas.[6]

Similar studies conducted in Sarawak, Malaysia, and Thailand showed that traditional shifting cultivation produced much lower erosion rates than other systems of tillage and clearing. In fact, if practiced with care, swidden agriculture has a smaller ecological footprint than any other system used in the tropics.

Observing the immediate and undeniable beauty of the lush tropical rainforest bordering that slash pile in Belize, accompanied by the roar of howler monkeys and an occasional jaguar, I could understand anyone being bothered by the practice of rotational cultivation. In that setting it would be hard not to call it slash and burn, particularly immediately after a burn. And without realizing the positive long-term consequence of swidden agriculture along the Atlantic seaboard of Central America, one might be moved to support the eviction of people who practice it. Fortunately, the environment ministries of the region have learned from extensive research the value of positive human disturbance.

Conservationists have described the Bantu tradition of shifting cultivation, which has been adopted by some Pygmies in central Africa, as a forest destroyer. However, Stéphanie Carrière, an ecologist from the Institute de Recherche pour le Dévelopement, who studied rotational systems used by the Ntumu on the Cameroon-Guinea border, found that farmers do not cut all the trees when they clear a parcel, and that the remaining "orphans" become a base for regeneration. In some places she found that biodiversity can even be stimulated by the practice.

The Kayapo in Brazil's Para have for centuries cultivated small rotational gardens on forest patches they call *Apêtês*. Conservation biologists, even some with serious misgivings about slash and burn agriculture, believe that the Kayapo's particular methods are beneficial to forest conservation.

The creation of an Apêtê begins with a small, natural mound of vegetation, about three to six feet in diameter. The mound is an abandoned ant nest rich in organic material and tunneled in such a way that it will retain moisture. Seeds or seedlings are planted in each mound during the first part of the rainy season.

Garden tenders will often cut down a few trees to let light into the Apêtê. Palms are then planted in their place, alongside vines that produce drinkable water. After a few years of cultivation, Apêtês grow to look so natural that visiting biologists fail to recognize them as human artifacts.

Observed the late legendary ethnoecologist Darell Posey, who lived among the Kayopo for twenty-five years:

The Kayapo are aware that some species develop more vigorously when planted together. They frequently speak of plants that are "good friends" or "good neighbours." One of the first of these "neighbour complexes" I was able to discover was the "tyrutiombiqua," or "banana neighbours." Among the two dozen varieties of edible tubers and numerous medicinal plants that thrive near bananas are some of the mekrakeldja ("child want not") plants, which are very important in regulating fertility among the Kayapo.

Other managed plant communities are concentrated around papaya, genipapo (Genipa americana L.) and urucu (Bixa orellana L.) which produce their own unique microzones for planting. The Kayapo characterize such synergistic plant groups in terms of "plant energy." These groups can include dozens of species and require complex patterns of cultivation. Thus a Kayapo garden is created by carefully combining different "plant energies" just as an artist blends colours to produce a work of art. Indian fields thrive on diversity within the plots. This diversity is quite ordered to the Indian eye, with careful matchings between plant varieties and microenvironmental conditions. What appears to us to be random field plantings turns out to have five more or less concentric zones, each with preferred varieties of cultivars and different cultivation strategies.

The Kayapo exploit the properties of fields in transition between new and old, but also show how microenvironmental planting zones are created to modify effects of secondary forest growth. Equally significant is the indigenous conceptualisation of plant communities, rather than individual species, as the basis for ecological management."

Like so many native cultures in the world, the Kayapo do not distinguish between cultivated and natural environments. It's all natural, or as they prefer to say "cultivated wilderness." And what we called second-growth forest, they call "old fields."

The scientific lesson learned from the shifting mosaic practices of the Kayapo, the Mayans, and others, according to University of Arizona geographer Paul Robbins, suggests that humans "can maintain biodiversity by ensuring that within a given ecosystem, disturbance is sufficiently patchy and sporadic to create a landscape mosaic in which plant communities at multiple stages of recovery coexist."[7] In other words, a landscape where plantations, fallow areas, primary vegetation, pastures, household gardens with a wide variety of crops (no mono-cropping), and bodies of water comprise a unified production system can provide a healthy disturbance of nature. Studies currently are underway in protected areas where mild conservation rule breaking, such as controlled burns or the harvesting of wild fruit, grasses, bark, honey, or an occasional tree, appears to be enhancing biodiversity.

"Once conservationists start to devise strategies for conservation where people actually live," says conservation historian William Adams, "they have to face the fact that 'nature' is usually profoundly influenced by human action." That's not necessarily a bad thing; in fact, as some of the preceding examples show, it could be a good thing.

And there are times when the banning of an indigenous lifeway, perceived as a negative disturbance, can have the opposite of the desired effect. After all grazing was ceased in the Keoladeo National Park in Rajasthan, India, for example, paspalum grass grew so thick without cattle to keep it back that shallow bodies of water in the wetlands were choked off and wintering waterfowl lost their nesting grounds. The illegal reintroduction of cattle into the area improved the situation. In fact, the deliberate breaking of conservations rules and regulations has been found to maintain, even enhance, floral diversity at various settings around the world. Not much research has been done on this phenomenon, but some is under way.

Even without conclusive science, it is not surprising that a deliberate human disturbance mimicking a natural disturbance, if timed correctly, would quite likely have the same effect on an ecosystem as the natural disturbance would. But timing is everything. Knowing precisely when to light that fire or clear that patch is a deeply complex aspect of traditional ecological knowledge. So is knowing and understanding exactly why some people break conservation rules. Is their motive survival? Corruption? Or is it rebellion against a conservation regime the rule-breakers can neither see nor understand, or a project operating under a rubric such as "co-management" when in fact it is administered from a faraway national capital by a foreign NGO under contract with a government, bank, or international agency that barely recognizes the rights or existence of indigenous communities?

The story of Botswana's Bushmen, the Basarwa or San peoples, might not have been noticed by the world, or even included as a chapter in this book, had they not won a major legal victory in their country's supreme court. The court-ordered return of the Basarwa to their ancient homeland in the Kalahari has inspired displaced indigenous people around the world to never give up their struggle for justice or their quest to live sustainably, as the Basarwa did for millennia, on their own land.

11

Basarwa

We have great respect for the sovereign governments of Africa.
—Paul Schindler, conservationist

New Xade is a fetid, disease-ridden refugee settlement built on arid, barren land by the government of Botswana. One of three camps of its kind, New Xade is perversely named after Xade (pronounced Ka Day), the ancestral homeland of the earliest inhabitants of the African subcontinent, a people of many names—"Basarwa," "Khwe," "Gana," and "San "—many of whom just call themselves "Bushmen." New Xade is home to about fifteen hundred Basarwa. The government's stated purposes for creating the camps was "wildlife conservation" and the "human development"—in other words, the assimilation—of the primitive Bushman into modern Botswana society. The Bushmen, some of whom call New Xade a "concentration camp," believe that securing access to diamonds on their homeland was the government's ulterior motive. The government denies this.

Diamonds were suspected because they generate 64 percent of the Botswana's gross domestic product (GDP). They are the country's largest export, generating about 70 percent of Botswana's foreign exchange and about 50 percent of government revenue. Debswana Diamond Company (Pty) Ltd. is a partnership jointly owned by DeBeers and the government of Botswana. Many government ministers are also on the Debswana board of directors. In 2001 Debswana sold $2.3 billion of diamonds (almost 30 percent of the world market). However, because diamonds are so widely associated with gunrunning, bloodshed, and genocide, the government may have chosen to publicize a more respectable motive for relocating the Bushmen—wildlife conservation.

It would not be the first time conservation was used by a national government as a fig leaf to cover questionable economic activities. Nor would it be the first time that international conservation NGOs active in the country would be willing to play along, providing additional respectability to the eviction and incarceration of indigenous peoples. The Republic of Botswana, Africa's longest-standing multiparty democracy, has always been a favored nation for wildlife conservationists. Its president, Seretse Ian Khama, is a member of the Conservation International board. As vice president, Khama oversaw the demarcation of 17 percent of Botswana's total surface area for national parks and game reserves. Another 34 percent is zoned as "Wildlife Management Areas." Half of the country's land is set aside for some form of wildlife protection, compared to 4.7 percent of the entire African continent. International conservationists like to cite Botswana as an exemplar for Africa—even, some claim, for the world.

The government of Botswana has declared that all residents of the country are indigenous and does not accept the term *First People*. The government has also chosen not to target assistance to particular ethnic groups. Some development funds are provided for "Remote Area Dwellers," defined as people living outside villages. The number of Remote Area Dwellers in Botswana varies depending on the source of information. Estimates range from sixty thousand to one hundred thousand, about fifty thousand of them Basarwa.

Bushmen have hunted and gathered in Southern Africa for an estimated thirty thousand years. Central Kalahari Game Reserve (CKGR) was originally set aside in 1961 by colonial authorities to protect Bushman lifeways and culture. Approximately the size of Wales, CKGR is the second-largest game reserve in all Africa, whereas the New Xade camp is about the size of an average Texas trailer court. Inside the fenced encampment, at the center of a dry, dusty plain, live Basarwa displaced from the CKGR. Roy Sesana is one of their leaders. He is a very bitter man who detests his new home. Until recently he was in prison for protesting his fate.

Sesana describes returning from an extended hunting trip one day to find that government officials had razed his entire village, destroyed his water source, and forced his nine children and two wives into trucks, transporting them like cattle to New Xade. He had no other option but to follow his family, which took him three days on foot.

"Being here is like being a prisoner of war," Sesana says. "If I'd had my way, I would have physically resisted the eviction and would not be here at all." He truly believes " they would have killed me had I stayed put."[1]

Amid New Xade's crowded rows of makeshift shacks and huts, the government tapped some wells and built a school, a clinic, and a bar, outside of which some of the world's best trackers and hunters while their lives away building pyramids of empty beer cans. The purpose of New Xade is clearly assimilation. While the government rejects the Bushmen's First People designation, it nevertheless believes that the primitive people it has dubbed Remote Area Dwellers should be dragged into the money economy.

"We have an obligation to integrate Bushmen into 'modernity,'" asserts James Kilo, the Botswana government's representative in New Xade, "and they should be thankful. I don't see how anyone can argue that it's better to live in the wilderness with animals than being here." Kilo's attitude reflects that of former president of Botswana Festus Mogae, who publicly asked: "How can we continue to have Stone Age creatures in an age of computers?"

Nare Gaoboene seems to prefer the Stone Age life. After his home was destroyed and his eleven children and three wives forcibly moved to New Xade, he stayed behind and slept in trees until he could build a new hut to protect himself from predators. About 140 diehard Bushmen remained with Gaoboene inside the Kalahari reserve, some having escaped from the alcoholism and despair of New Xade and returned to the bush. To drive them out, the government repeatedly cut off their water supply. Gaoboene would occasionally sneak into New Xade to visit his family. On one trip he ran into Basildon Peta, a *London Independent* reporter who was there to interview Sesana. "I met Nare only because he was visiting his family," recalls Peta. "It was only the second time he had set foot in New Xade since his family was evicted two years ago."

Gaoboene told Peta: "I have come to tell my wives and children that I have finished building new huts and they should come back to join me if they wish that I remain their father, otherwise I am not coming to visit here ever again." It's a four-day trek back to the new homestead he had built for his family, and he knew that game wardens would try to stop them. But he said he knew a safe route.

Returning to the CKGR had become a high-stake gamble because the government treats anyone found hunting there as a poacher. Botswana President (then Vice President) Ian Khama told *National Geographic* writer Douglas Lee that "no country can ignore armed men crossing its borders. . . . We took on the poachers aggressively—we actually shot a few of them."

Box 11.1

The First "First People"

They call themselves Khwe Khoe, Gana, Basarwa, or San. But San means "vagabond" in Nama, the language from which it derives, and the word has been used by racists throughout southern Africa much the way "negro" is used in America. So while some members of one of the oldest living cultures on Earth still call themselves San, most of the aboriginal people of the Kalahari prefer Basarwa, Khwe, or Bushman. However, some despise the latter name as well and identify themselves with a tribal or clan name, or simple call themselves "First Peoples of the Kalahari."

Ancestral DNA markers that turn up frequently among the San people suggest that they are closely related to the ancestry of all humans. We may all be Bushmen.

The Bushman's homeland once ranged from what is now South Africa through Namibia and deep into Botswana and into Angola, Zambia, and Zimbabwe. Bushmen currently number about ninety thousand, and speak an assortment of dialects characterized by click consonants. Their language family is called !Ui. Archaeological data indicate that Bushmen once had a fairly advanced culture dating back over ten thousand years, when early ancestors from the Botswana region migrated to the Waterberg Massif.* Rock paintings at Lapala and Goudriver record a life in close harmony with rhinoceros, elephants, and a variety of antelope species resembling the impala, kudu, and eland, all of which still remain in the Kalahari.

Until quite recently most Bushmen were hunter-gatherers living in rough wood-and-thatch shelters. As their formerly open homelands were expropriated for game preserves or cattle ranches during the colonial era, their access to wild foods became restricted. That didn't bother colonials or the governments they had created in southern Africa.

Some colonials regarded Bushmen as human, some did not. "We look upon them as the fauna of the country," wrote Colonel Denys Reitz, South African minister of native affairs in 1941. While Reitz recommended allowing the Bushmen to remain in the Kalahari Gemsbock National Park "and to hunt with bows and arrows," South African and Namibian policy toward the San bordered on genocide. The last permit to hunt a Bushman was issued by the South African government in 1936. But the killing didn't end. Any Bushman who hunted the quarry of white hunters was fair game himself. There is no record of anyone being convicted of murdering a Bushman in South Africa, Namibia, or Botswana before 1962.

In 1965, a fence was raised along the Namibia-Botswana border dividing the forage lands of Bushmen and closing their migratory routes. Some abandoned their nomadic life to raise loaned cattle in migrant villages. Like so many pastoral nomadics around the world, Bushmen have gradually been forced into sedentary lives in makeshift towns and villages set up near rare water sources. Domestic animals, sugar, garden produce, and porridge of ground maize they call "mealie-meal" became their major foods.

The Central Kalahari Game Reserve (CKGR) was originally created in 1961 to protect about five thousand Bushmen in the area, who were being persecuted by farmers and cattle-rearing tribes. They have no voice in political processes and are not recognized as an official tribe by the constitution of Botswana. The Bushmen of South Africa have been officially absorbed into the "coloured" population.

The Bushman kinship system is based on an "age rule" and a "name rule." The age rule resolves confusion arising around kinship, because the older of two people always decides what to call the younger. According to the name rule, if any two people have the same name, for example an old man and a young man both named Twi, each family uses the same kin term to refer to them: Young Twi's mother could call Old Twi "son," Old Twi would address young Twi's sister as his own, Young Twi would call Old Twi's wife "wife," and Old Twi's daughter would be strictly forbidden to Young Twi as a potential bride. Since relatively few names circulate, and each child is named for a grandparent or other relative, Bushmen are guaranteed an enormous family group with whom they are welcome to travel. They generally settle together with four or five other families in settlements of twenty-five to fifty people.

Traditional gathering gear was a hide sling called a kaross. It is still used to carry foodstuffs, firewood, or young children, smaller bags, and a digging stick.

The few remaining traditional villages range in size from temporary rain shelters built in the warm spring, when people moved constantly in search of budding greens, to formalized rings built in the dry season around permanent waterholes. Early spring is hot and dry, and generally the hardest season, as autumn nuts are exhausted and most plants dead or dormant.

Government harassment of the Bushmen in the Central Kalihari Game Reserve began in 1986. The first forced evictions were in 1997. Those who remained faced drastic restrictions in hunting rights and continued harassment, even torture. In early 2002, these abuses intensified, accompanied by the destruction of water pumps, draining of existing water supplies into the desert, and banning of hunting and gathering.

There are today only about three thousand Bushmen who depend partly on their traditional lifestyle of hunting and gathering. They move about the Kalahari without chiefs or leaders, in family bands of ten to fifteen individuals in search of food, water resources, and migratory game. Their temporary shelters, made from branches tied together in a semicircle with grass tufts on top, blend into the bush. The men hunt with bows and arrows tipped with poison, the women gather. The hunt is an elaborate, laborious, and highly skilled exercise, which often lasts a full day or more. The kill is always shared. Gathering has less social significance than hunting, but generally provides up to 80 percent of the family band's food.

The Bushmen's hunting skills have made them popular with various armies, which have used them to track guerillas and even map out mine fields. Farmers also hire Bushmen to chase down poachers and rustlers. And conservationists are training a few to be parataxonomists—to count wildlife on a handheld device that automatically records the geolocation of each animal.

---

* Spencer Wells, *The Journey of Man* (2003), pp. 56–58.

As the government continued to sell claims and concessions in the Kalahari reserve to diamond prospectors, it also continued to deny that diamonds had anything to do with the relocation of Bushmen. "It is necessary for them to relocate so they could be helped to lead sustainable, self-reliant livelihoods," Foreign Ministry spokesman Clifford Maribe told my colleague Tom Price. They had, Maribe said, outgrown their traditional lifestyle and were killing off the reserve's animals. That assertion is contradicted by a Botswana Department of Wildlife and National Parks study, which reports that the population of all hunted species has doubled over the past decade.

The First People of the Kalahari (FPK) organization was formed by the Bushmen to champion their rights, led by Roy Sesana. "If I thought you were primitive and in need of help, would I visit you in Johannesburg or London and destroy your home, expel your wife and children, and leave them without food or a roof over their heads?" asked FPK's coordinator, Jumanda Gakelebone. "Do I have to strip you of your dignity just because I believe you need help?"

In 2004 FPK filed suit against the Botswana government, citing a constitutional provision guaranteeing protection of Bushmen in all parts of the country, and petitioned to have the evicted Bushmen returned to their homeland in the Central Kalahari Game Reserve. When the government realized that the Bushmen might have the national constitution on their side, a bill was introduced in Parliament to repeal the pertinent clause. However, before the bill passed, a judge of the High Court dismissed the case. But the FPK appealed and on December 12, 2006, the court ruled two to one that the San had been "wrongfully deprived of their possessions," their eviction from the CKGR was unlawful and unconstitutional, and they had the right to return to their former settlements in the reserve and to hunt there for their food. "Today is the happiest day for us Bushmen," FPK leader Sesana told the *Washington Post*. "We have been crying for so long, but today we are crying with happiness. Finally we have been set free."

"This landmark case sends a signal to the world that indigenous peoples have ownership rights to land and other assets, even if they are desirable for conservation purposes," declared Rebecca Adamson, a Cherokee American whose Virginia-based organization First Peoples Worldwide helped finance the San's litigation. "And in Africa a precedent has been established whereby indigenous people are entitled to protection of the law." This was a heartening outcome for all tribal people throughout the continent who hoped one day to return to homelands lost to conservation.

Family by family, the San have slowly returned to the Kalahari and rebuilt their homes. However, the government continues to deny them the right to hunt or to use the water boreholes they drilled before their eviction. It's a condition that one High Court justice described as "tantamount to condemning the residents of CKGR to death by starvation." Yet despite such judicial comments, dozens of San have been arrested by the government for hunting in what they regard as their ancestral homeland.

Native Stewards

The right to be let alone is the beginning of all freedom.
—William O. Douglas

The problem facing all indigenous peoples in southern Africa is that the process of turning informal common property rights into nationally recognized legal rights is difficult, if not impossible. In fact, the only way Bushmen have been able to obtain legal title to land in Botswana is through purchase of freehold land by an NGO. But it has been difficult for Bushmen or any "native stewards" to buy or obtain rights over blocks of land that correspond to their traditional ancestral territories.

As a way to recover use rights over former homelands, the San of bordering Botswana and South Africa attempted to take part in community-based natural resource management programs. The !Khomani San of South Africa, for example, sought land rights in what is now the northern Cape region of the country. They were forced out of that area in the 1930s, when the Kalahari Gemsbok Park was created to conserve what the South African government felt was a unique set of habitats and resources in the southern Kalahari Desert. The !Khomani dispersed to farms, small towns, urban areas, and mining communities and their culture all but dissolved. In 1999, when the park became southern Africa's first transfrontier park (or "Peace Park" as they are sometimes known), the !Khomani submitted a claim to the government of South Africa under the Restitution of Land Rights Act of 1994. Jakob Malas, a !Khomani hunter whose lands were enveloped by the Kalahari Gemsbok Park, testified that "The Kalahari is like a big farmyard. It is not a wilderness to us. We know every plant, animal, and insect, and know how to use them. No other people could ever know and love this farm like us."

The out-of-court settlement was a small victory for Malas and the !Khomani, who received some land and cash compensation and now have extensive resource-use rights in the southern portion of the park, from which they also collect some tourism revenue. Community-based conservation clearly doesn't work everywhere, but it seems to in the Gemsbok Peace Park. The lesson here appears to be that the most effective means of promoting conservation and development together is one that allows indigenous people to benefit from both a protected area and its natural resources.

Box 11.2

Roy Sesana Speaks

In December 2005, Bushman elder and founder of First Peoples of the Kalihari Roy Sesana (also known as Tobee Tconi) was given the Right Livelihood Award before the parliament of Sweden in Stockholm. His acceptance speech follows.

My name is Roy Sesana; I am a G//ana Bushman from the Kalahari in what is now called Botswana. In my language, my name is "Tobee" and our land is "T//amm." We have been there longer than any people have been anywhere.

When I was young, I went to work in a mine. I put off my skins and wore clothes. But I went home after a while. Does that make me less Bushman? I don't think so.

I am a leader. When I was a boy we did not need leaders and we lived well. Now we need them because our land is being stolen and we must struggle to survive. It doesn't mean I tell people what to do, it's the other way around: they tell me what I have to do to help them.

I cannot read. You wanted me to write this speech, so my friends helped, but I cannot read words—I'm sorry! But I do know how to read the land and the animals. All our children could. If they didn't, they would have all died long ago.

I know many who can read words and many, like me, who can only read the land. Both are important. We are not backward or less intelligent: we live in exactly the same up-to-date year as you. I was going to say we all live under the same stars, but no, they're different, and there are many more in the Kalahari. The sun and moon are the same.

I grew up a hunter. All our boys and men were hunters. Hunting is going and talking to the animals. You don't steal. You go and ask. You set a trap or go with bow or spear. It can take days. You track the antelope. He knows you are there, he knows he has to give you his strength. But he runs and you have to run. As you run, you become like him. It can last hours and exhaust you both. You talk to him and look into his eyes. And then he knows he must give you his strength so your children can live.

When I first hunted, I was not allowed to eat. Pieces of the steenbok were burnt with some roots and spread on my body. This is how I learned. It's not the same way you learn, but it works well.

The farmer says he is more advanced than the backward hunter, but I don't believe him. His herds give no more food than ours. The antelope are not our slaves, they do not wear bells on their necks, and they can run faster than the lazy cow or the herder. We run through life together.

When I wear the antelope horns, it helps me talk to my ancestors and they help me. The ancestors are so important: we would not be alive without them. Everyone knows this in their heart, but some have forgotten. Would any of us be here without our ancestors? I don't think so.

I was trained as a healer. You have to read the plants and the sand. You have to dig the roots and become fit. You put some of the root back for tomorrow, so one day your grandchildren can find it and eat. You learn what the land tells you.

When the old die, we bury them and they become ancestors. When there is sickness, we dance and we talk to them; they speak through my blood. I touch the sick person and can find the illness and heal it.

We are the ancestors of our grandchildren's children. We look after them, just as our ancestors look after us. We aren't here for ourselves. We are here for each other and for the children of our grandchildren.

Why am I here? Because my people love their land, and without it we are dying. Many years ago, the president of Botswana said we could live on our ancestral land forever. We never needed anyone to tell us that. Of course we can live where God created us! But the next president said we must move and began forcing us away.

They said we were killing too many animals: but that's not true. They say many things which aren't true. They said we had to move so the government could develop us. The president says unless we change we will perish like the dodo. I didn't know what a dodo was. But I found out: it was a bird which was wiped out by settlers. The president was right. They are killing us by forcing us off our land. We have been tortured and shot at. They arrested me and beat me.

Thank you for the Right Livelihood Award. It is global recognition of our struggle and will raise our voice throughout the world. When I heard I had won I had just been let out of prison. They say I am a criminal, as I stand here today.

I say what kind of development is it when the people live shorter lives than before? They catch HIV/AIDS. Our children are beaten in school and won't go there. Some become prostitutes. They are not allowed to hunt. They fight because they are bored and get drunk. They are starting to commit suicide. We never saw that before. It hurts to say this. Is this "development"?

We are not primitive. We live differently to you, but we do not live exactly like our grandparents did, nor do you. Were your ancestors "primitive"? I don't think so. We respect our ancestors. We love our children. This is the same for all people.

> We now have to stop the government stealing our land: without it we will die. If anyone has read a lot of books and thinks I am primitive because I have not read even one, then he should throw away those books and get one which says we are all brothers and sisters under God and we too have a right to live.
>
> That is all. Thank you.

Many of the issues facing the San and other indigenous peoples are a consequence of economic and cultural globalization. As they have been forced into the international community, people who rarely left their isolated homelands have sought to redress injustices and basic human rights through international institutions. Sometimes they have undertaken passive resistance. They have also resorted to demonstrations, strikes, boycotts, and other forms of civil disobedience. In protest against exclusionary conservation they have blockaded entrances to national parks, as the Penan of Malaysia did in 1980 and the San did in Namibia in 1997. But they have also sought to reassert their rights to traditional homelands and to protect their cultures through national courts and international law.

In aggressive lawsuits native peoples have challenged colonial powers and national constitutions that resulted in their dispossession of their homelands. In a few countries they have won impressive concessions. In Canada, for example, the 1982 Constitution Act formally recognized "the aboriginal rights of first nations," which led to a Supreme Court decision affirming native title to vast expanses of northern land that had previously been assumed by the Crown. In Australia, the 1992 High Court decision in *Eddie Mabo and Others v. The State of Queensland* gave Aboriginals and Torres Strait Islanders title to ancestral lands and compensation for past losses.

Indigenous peoples of Africa and many parts of Asia have not fared so well because the nation-states that enveloped their traditional homelands either do not recognize them as indigenous, or as citizens deserving equal protection under laws that govern the management of natural resources, wildlife, and forests. Thus millions who lost their rights to land and resources upon which they depended for generations, like the

Basarwa, continue to protest and file suits against governments, some of which barely acknowledge their existence. And they bring their complaints to the fora of transnational conservation. As chapter 12 indicates, progress has been real but slow.

Despite the widest possible diversity of cultures and languages, indigenous peoples have, over the past few decades, organized themselves into an impressive global force for land and civil rights. In their stories, pleas, and petitions their leaders and representatives frequently invoke Yosemite, and few are unaware of the name Tenaya. And millions of evictees, squatting in hovels on the borders of national parks that were once their ancestral hunting grounds, rather bitterly refer to themselves as conservation refugees, a term that has been translated, in some form or another, into a thousand or more dialects.

12

Fighting Back

It has been a strategic error for conservation organizations to fall into open conflict with indigenous peoples.
—David Barton Bray, Florida International University

There are over 370 million self-described "indigenous peoples" alive today—about four thousand five hundred distinct cultures speaking as many different languages and dialects. They account for 80 to 90 percent of the world's cultural diversity. While only comprising 5 percent of the world's total population, indigenous people occupy about 20 percent of the planet's surface area. They reside within and across the borders of 75 of the world's 184 recognized countries. They thrive in tropical forests, boreal forests, deserts, tundra, savannahs, prairies, islands, and mountains; and they occupy every remaining complex biotic community ("biome") on the planet. Many of them regard their ancestral territories as a "nation" and would draw a very different map of the world than those found in most atlases. Instead of two hundred countries, their map would demarcate four thousand five hundred nations.

Although for most of the thousands of years they have survived they knew little of each other's languages, cultures, or lifeways, indigenous people have somehow managed during the last seventy-five years to organize one of the most impressive worldwide social movements in human history. It began in 1923, when a Mohawk chief named Deska-heh led a small delegation of American Indians to Geneva, Switzerland. There they called upon the recently formed League of Nations to defend the rights of their people to live under their own laws, on their own land, and according to their own faith. The delegation was turned away at the gate, but the event is still remembered by indigenous peoples worldwide as the first foray into what would become the most unexpected social movement of modern times.

In the decades that followed Deskaheh's futile venture, millions of very poor, almost illiterate people, living in thousands of small communities, without electricity or communication infrastructure, and speaking thousands of different languages, have managed to organize a global protest for land and human rights that has literally changed the way the world regards property, the commons, and human rights.

As the world shrank and transportation accelerated, inhabitants of the most remote villages began to discover that they were not alone. There were others like them on almost every continent—people with unique dialects, diets, cultures, and cosmologies who were at best misunderstood, at worst oppressed by the dominant nationalities that surrounded them. These indigenous groups began to communicate with one another and to meet, and through interpreters they learned of ways that aboriginals in other societies had succeeded in protecting their cultures and recovering their sovereignty, independence, and homelands lost to colonization. They began to resist assimilation and to petition for recognition of territorial rights. And coming to their aid in the "developed" world were people who valued cultural diversity as much as biological diversity—anthropologists in particular, as well as human rights lawyers, social activists, and members of organizations like Cultural Survival, Survival International, EcoTerra, the Forest Peoples Programme, and First Peoples Worldwide. Members of this growing social movement established links, formed networks, and founded new NGOs, from the Arctic to the Kalahari, from Micronesia to the Amazon Basin, some with fewer than a hundred members, others with millions.

By the 1960s, indigenous peoples and their organizations were formally petitioning national courts and governments, international bodies, and the World Bank for recognition of their civil, economic, and cultural rights. They began to confront directly transnational extractive industries that were treating their homelands as if they were part of a global commons available to anyone who sought the resources above and below the ground. Local uprisings against economic exploitation and resource extraction were refocused to confront northern conservationists who, despite claims to the contrary, were perceived to be in league with the extractors.

As the 1960s unfolded, a decade remembered for its strife and protest, indigenous activists tested new and somewhat less polite tactics—nonviolent direct action, passive resistance, labor strikes, public demonstrations, and boycotts. As a protest against conservation displacements, they blockaded national park entrances. It was an era of civil disobedience, when the vibrant force of native people joined the worldwide resistance of minorities to oppression and injustice. While their agenda included a broad spectrum of issues and demands, conservation, as practiced by European and American NGOs, became a major target of protests and action, and eventually stimulated a powerful mini-movement within the larger struggle for justice.

In 1974, indigenous leaders from North America, Latin America, Australia, and New Zealand established the World Council of Indigenous Peoples. WCIP was immediately granted consultative status by the United Nations, which in 2003 established the UN Forum on Indigenous Issues.

Under mounting pressure from native people, who began attending their quadannual conventions in the mid-1970s, both the World Conservation Union (IUCN) and World Parks Congress have voted by wide majorities their approval of statements like the Kinshasa Resolution and the Zaire Declaration on the Protection of Traditional Ways of Life. These declarations recognize the rights of indigenous peoples and the need to accommodate those rights in the creation and management of protected areas. They call on governments and conservation organizations to value indigenous traditions and devise ways for indigenous peoples to bring their lands into conservation areas without having to relinquish their rights or be displaced. Unfortunately, many of the protected areas established since 1975 have violated those rights.

In 1977, American Indians petitioned the Decolonization Committee of the United Nations for recognition of their sovereign right to self-determination, full ownership of their communal lands, control of their natural wealth and resources, cultural freedom, informed consent prior to any activity on their lands, self-representation through their own institutions, and the freedom to exercise their customary laws. Like the

League of Nations fifty years beforehand, that committee ignored their petition and denied them access.

In the years that followed, indigenous peoples continued to challenge all the assumptions and mechanisms that resulted in the dispossession of their lands. They have been more successful in some countries than others. In 1973, the Canadian Supreme Court in *Calder et al v. Attorney General of British Columbia* challenged the way Canada structured aboriginal rights. Then in 1982, as noted in chapter 11, the Constitution Act was enacted that recognized the inherent aboriginal rights of "First Nations," paving the way to another Supreme Court decision confirming first natives' original title to the land; and a decade later in Australia, on June 3, 1992, the High Court in *Eddie Mabo and Others v. The State of Queensland* affirmed ancestral land title to Aboriginals and Torres Strait Islanders, who were also compensated for the losses they incurred when all land in the new colony of Australia was declared terra nullius (unoccupied) and therefore state property of the government.

In Africa and Asia, particularly in countries like Kenya, Tanzania, the Congo, Botswana, India, Malaysia, and Indonesia, where all land unoccupied by colonial settlers became "state lands," indigenous peoples have not fared as well; in some countries because colonial governments did not recognize them as indigenous, in others, like Botswana, because all inhabitants were declared to be "indigenous" no matter how long they had been living in a particular area or territory. In all those countries, laws that govern the management of wildlife and forests have led to people losing access to land and resources on which they had depended for generations.

At the 1982 World National Parks Congress in Bali, Indonesia, the rights of traditional societies to "social, economic, cultural and spiritual self-determination and "to participate in decisions affecting the land and natural resources on which they depend" were affirmed. While indigenous delegates at the Congress were disappointed that political self-determination was explicitly excluded from their proposed resolution, they were not surprised, as they knew from bitter experience that almost all national governments regard indigenous rights to own and control specific territory as a prelude to secession. Therefore, delegates instead supported "the implementation of joint management arrangements between societies which have traditionally managed resources and protected area authorities."

That same year, the World Bank issued Operational Manual Statement (OMS) 2.34 entitled "Tribal People in Bank Financed Projects." OMS 2.34 sought to recognize the bank's need to protect indigenous peoples from potentially adverse effects of development projects. The statement applied to "ethnic groups typically with stable, low energy, sustained yield economic systems as exemplified by hunter-gatherers, shifting and semipermanent farmers, herders or fishermen." Two years later, in 1984, the World Bank issued guidelines to all its officers not to fund conservation projects that would lead to the displacement of indigenous peoples. And in 1991 bank policy was realigned to recognize emerging international thinking on indigenous peoples, and to provide "detailed provisions on consultation and participation of indigenous peoples" in all bank projects, including conservation initiatives.[1]

By 1992, international conservationists had begun to notice that most of the areas they were mapping and targeting for protection were inhabited, and all too frequently by people who had been there for centuries or longer. At the World Congress on Protected Areas held in Caracas that year, conducted under the title "Parks for Life," members addressed the issue of occupancy and formally recognized that the denial of indigenous rights in protected areas was not only unrealistic but also counterproductive. In his keynote address, IUCN president Sir Sridath Ramphal advised his fellow members to seek ways to improve the welfare of all people, indigenous and local, living near parks. As for why, he noted, "Quite simply, if local people do not support protected areas, then protected areas cannot last."[2]

These were not hollow words. Ample evidence by then had accumulated from around the world documenting that the removal of people from protected area was undermining biodiversity. The problem has worsened since that 1992 gathering. Embittered hunter-gathers forced into sedentary cultivation in Gabon, for example, are reentering their former hunting grounds in Korup National Park and killing wildlife for the bush meat trade. At the same time, their cultivation is causing serious soil erosion. This is not an isolated case: similar threats to biodiversity are happening all through Central Africa, where an estimated three hundred thousand displaced people are living on the perimeter of national parks.[3]

Later in the 1992 IUCN proceedings it was politely suggested that the union reconsider its stated definition of a national park as a place "where the highest competent authority of the country (the state) has taken steps to prevent or eliminate as soon as possible exploitation or occupation of the whole area." After the World Congress, IUCN released a policy statement entitled "Indigenous and Traditional Peoples and Protected Areas," acknowledging the needs and rights of people in and around future protected areas.

Box 12.1

Recommendation 5.24

At the Fifth World Parks Congress, held September 8–17, 2003, in Durban, South Africa, thirty-two recommendations were introduced for discussion and approval. Eleven of those recommendations dealt with the relationship between protected areas and indigenous peoples. At the heart of those proposals was recommendation 5.24, which was approved by a majority of the congress.

Recommendation 5.24: Indigenous Peoples and Protected Areas

Indigenous peoples, their lands, waters and other resources have made a substantial contribution to the conservation of global ecosystems. For this trend to continue, where appropriate, protected areas, future and present, should take into account the principle of collaborative management attending to the interests and needs of indigenous peoples.

Many protected areas of the world encroach and are found within and overlap with lands, territories and resources of indigenous and traditional peoples. In many cases the establishment of these protected areas has affected the rights, interests and livelihoods of indigenous peoples and traditional peoples and subsequently resulted in persistent conflicts.

Effective and sustainable conservation can be better achieved if the objectives of protected areas do not violate the rights of indigenous peoples living in and around them.

It is widely acknowledged that successful implementation of conservation programmes can only be guaranteed on long term basis when there is consent for and approval by indigenous peoples among others, because their cultures, knowledge and territories contribute to the building of comprehensive protected areas. There is often commonality of objectives between protected areas and the need of indigenous peoples to protect their lands, territories and resources from external threats.

In addition to the benefits to conservation, it is also necessary to acknowledge that indigenous peoples have suffered human rights abuses in connection with protected areas in the past and in some cases continue to suffer abuses today.

Resolution WCC 1.53 Indigenous Peoples and Protected Areas, adopted by IUCN members at the 1st World Conservation Congress (Montreal, 1996), promotes a policy based on the principles of:

1. Recognition of the rights of indigenous peoples with regard to their lands or territories and resources that fall within protected areas;
2. Recognition of the necessity of reaching agreements with indigenous peoples prior to the establishment of protected areas in their lands or territories; and
3. Recognition of the rights of the indigenous peoples concerned to participate effectively in the management of the protected areas established on their lands or territories, and to be consulted on the adoption of any decision that affects their rights and interests over those lands or territories. At the request of the World Commission on Protected Areas (WCPA), IUCN's Council endorsed in 1999 "Principles and Guidelines on Indigenous Peoples and Protected Areas," in response to actions called for in Resolution WCC 1.53. In addition, several inter-governmental bodies and international agreements, as well as international conservation organizations, have adopted and promote policies that support recognition of the rights and interests of indigenous peoples in the context of biodiversity conservation and protection of the environment.

Therefore, PARTICIPANTS in the Cross-Cutting Theme on Communities and Equity and in the Stream on Governance at the [Fifth] World Parks Congress, in Durban, South Africa (8–17 September 2003) stressing that the following recommendations shall be conducted in full partnership with the freely chosen representatives of indigenous peoples:

1. RECOMMEND governments, inter-governmental organizations, NGOs, local communities and civil societies to:
a. ENSURE that existing and future protected areas respect the rights of indigenous peoples;
b. CEASE all involuntary resettlement and expulsions of indigenous peoples from their lands in connection with protected areas, as well as involuntary sedentarization of mobile indigenous peoples;
c. ENSURE the establishment of protected areas is based on the free, prior informed consent of indigenous peoples, and of prior social, economic, cultural and environmental impact assessment, undertaken with the full participation of indigenous peoples;

d. Further ELABORATE and APPLY, in coordination with indigenous peoples, the IUCN-WWF Principles and Guidelines on Indigenous and Traditional Peoples and Protected Areas (available at http://www.iucn. org/themes/wcpa/pubs/pdfs/ Indig_people.pdf), as well as principles that build on IUCN Resolution WCC 1.53 and which fully respect the rights, interests, and aspirations of indigenous peoples;

e. RECOGNISE the value and importance of protected areas designated by indigenous peoples as a sound basis for securing and extending the protected areas network;

f. ESTABLISH and ENFORCE appropriate laws and policies to protect the intellectual property of indigenous peoples with regards to their traditional knowledge, innovation systems and cultural and biological resources and penalise all biopiracy activities;

g. ENACT laws and policies that recognise and guarantee indigenous peoples' rights over their ancestral lands and waters;

h. ESTABLISH and implement mechanisms to address any historical injustices caused through the establishment of protected areas, with special attention given to land and water tenure rights and historical/traditional rights to access natural resources and sacred sites within protected areas;

i. ESTABLISH participatory mechanisms for the restitution of indigenous peoples' lands, territories and resources that have been taken over by protected areas without their free, prior informed consent, and for providing prompt and fair compensation, agreed upon in a fully transparent and culturally appropriate manner;

j. ESTABLISH a high level, independent Commission on Truth and Reconciliation on Indigenous Peoples and Protected Areas;

k. ENSURE respect for indigenous peoples' decision-making authority and SUPPORT their local, sustainable management and conservation of natural resources in protected areas, recognising the central role of traditional authorities, wherever appropriate, and institutions and representative organizations;

l. REQUIRE protected area managers to actively support indigenous peoples' initiatives aimed at the revitalization and application, where appropriate, of traditional knowledge and practices in land, water, and resource management within protected areas;

m. UNDERTAKE a review of all existing biodiversity conservation laws and policies that impact on indigenous peoples and ensure that all parties work in a coordinated manner to ensure effective involvement and participation of indigenous peoples;

n. DEVELOP and promote incentives to support indigenous peoples' self-declared and self-managed protected areas and other conservation initiatives to protect the lands, waters, territories and resources from external threats and exploitation;

o. ENSURE open and transparent processes for genuine negotiation with indigenous peoples in relation to any plans to establish or expand protected area systems, so that their lands, waters, territories and natural resources are preserved and decisions affecting them are taken in mutually agreed terms;

p. INTEGRATE indigenous knowledge and education systems in interpretation of and education about natural, cultural and spiritual values of protected areas; and

q. ENSURE that protected areas are geared towards poverty alleviation and improve the living standards of the communities around and within the parks through effective and agreeable benefit sharing mechanisms;

2. RECOMMEND IUCN and WCPA to:

a. FORMULATE and CARRY OUT a programme of work, with the full participation of indigenous peoples, to support their initiatives and interests regarding protected areas, and to actively involve indigenous peoples' representative authorities, institutions and organizations in its development and implementation;

b. PROVIDE support and funding to indigenous peoples for community conserved, co-managed and indigenous owned and managed protected areas;

c. ENCOURAGE international conservation agencies and organizations to adopt clear policies on indigenous peoples and conservation and establish mechanisms for the redress of grievances; and

d. CONDUCT an implementation review of the World Conservation Congress Resolution 1.53 Indigenous Peoples and Protected Areas and the IUCN-WWF Principles and Guidelines on Indigenous and Traditional Peoples and Protected Areas; and

3. RECOMMEND IUCN Members to consider the establishment of an IUCN Commission on Indigenous Peoples and Protected Areas at its next World Conservation Congress.

Two years later, with pressure mounting inside the IUCN from one of its six major task forces, the Commission on Environmental, Economic and Social Policy (CEESP),[4] and an intercommission working group formed by CEESP and the World Commission on Protected Areas (WCPA) named the Theme on Indigenous and Local Communities, Equity, and Protected Areas (TILCEPA), the IUCN adopted some new categories of protected areas where indigenous peoples may own and manage the area. Also in 1996 at the first IUCN World Conservation Congress held in Montreal Canada, members passed six new resolutions:

• Recognizing the rights of indigenous peoples to their lands and territories;

• Recognizing their rights to manage their natural resources in protected areas either on their own or jointly with others;

• Endorsing the principles enshrined in International Labor Organization's Convention 169, agenda 21, the 1992 Convention of Biological Diversity (CBD)[5] and the Draft Declaration on the Rights of Indigenous Peoples;

• Urging member countries to adopt International Labor Organization (ILO) Convention 169 (only fourteen have signed and ratified the convention);

• Recognizing the right of indigenous peoples to participate in decision making related to the implementation of the CBD; and

• Recognizing the need for joint agreements with indigenous peoples for the management of protected areas and their right to effective participation and to be consulted in decisions related to natural resource management.

All of these reforms reflected changes taking places in countries like Canada and Australia regarding the land rights of indigenous peoples. In both countries national parks had already been created and communities in them resettled—200 households from the Forillon National Park in Quebec, 228 from Kouchibouguac Park in New Brunswick. Following intensive protests during the 1987 creation of Gros Morne National Park in Newfoundland, the Canadian government reconsidered its policy of eviction and allowed seven indigenous villages to remain in the park. The following year the Canadian National Parks Act was amended to allow selective animal trapping and controlled woodcutting in the parks.

In 1983 a special meeting on indigenous peoples was convened by the United Nations Human Rights Commission and a process set in motion that has since allowed indigenous peoples to press the UN General Assembly for a recognition of their rights. Ten years later, the UN General Assembly declared 1993 "The International Year of the World's Indigenous Peoples." After the dedication, Erica-Irene Daes, chair of the indigenous delegation, complained that the event was "about to become the poorest and smallest of its kind in the history of the United Nations." She didn't stop there: "It continues to be a matter of great disappointment to indigenous peoples, and to me, that some Member States cannot yet agree to include them in the family of nations. In an age which has overcome racism, racial discrimination and colonialism in so many fields, there are Member States that still perpetuate a myth as old as the European colonization of the Americas that indigenous peoples are legally unequal to other peoples."[6]

The following year, the Forty-eighth Session of the UN General Assembly proclaimed the next ten years the "International Decade of the World's Indigenous Peoples," established a permanent forum for indigenous peoples, and began the process of drafting a declaration on the rights of indigenous peoples. Eleven years after the first draft, the declaration was finally approved by the UN Human Rights Commission in Geneva in 2007 and sent to the General Assembly for a final vote (see appendix C for the full text of the United Nations Declaration on the Rights of Indigenous Peoples). Meanwhile, the permanent forum continued to gather every year with little attention or support provided by member nations. Ted Moses, ambassador from the Grand Council of Crees in Quebec, describes the forum as "an orphan within the UN system . . . barely recognized or acknowledged. . . . And appears not to affect the work of the United Nations."[7]

While they awaited approval of the declaration during those eleven years, indigenous peoples pressed other international bodies such as the Interamerican Court of Human Rights, ILO, CBD, Organization of American States (OAS), and Organization of African States, all of which have passed some form of declaration supporting indigenous peoples' rights to:

- Self-determination;
- Ownership control and use of communal lands;
- Free disposition of their natural wealth and resources;
- No deprivation of their means of subsistence;
- Free enjoyment of their own culture and traditional way of life;
- Informed consent prior to activities being conducted on their lands;
- Self-representation through their own institutions;
- Free exercise of customary laws; and
- Restitution of and compensation for land already lost.

The CBD, which was adopted at the Earth Summit of Rio de Janeiro in 1992, specifically imposes obligations on signatory governments to respect, preserve, and maintain indigenous "knowledge, innovations and practices and to protect and encourage their customary use of natural resources." It was at the same gathering that the global conservation community committed itself to placing 10 percent of the planet under protection.

Although none of the ILO, CBD, or OAS declarations are truly enforceable, despite their inclusion in treaties, they are often regarded as a body of international law protecting indigenous rights, and both the IUCN and its WCPA have recognized these advances and called upon governments to comply with them. In 1994, as previously noted, the IUCN revised its categories of protected areas to allow indigenous peoples to own and manage protected areas. Five years later, the WCPA adopted guidelines for putting these new conservation principles into practice by placing emphasis on indigenous co-management of protected areas.

In 1989 *La Coordinadora de Organizationes Indegenas de la Cuenca Amazonia* (COICA), a group founded in 1984 by Indians from Colombia, Ecuador, Peru, Bolivia, and Brazil, complained that "conservationists have left us out of their vision of the Amazon Biosphere." This, they argued, was leading to a massive failure of conservation initiatives. They appealed to "the community of concerned environmentalists" to form an alliance with them "in defense of our Amazon homeland" and to "work directly with our organizations on all your programs and campaigns."

At the close of the meeting, COICA released the following declaration: "We, the Indigenous Peoples, have been an integral part of the Amazon Biosphere for millennia. We have used and cared for the resources of that biosphere with a great deal of respect, because it is our home, and because we know that our survival and that of our future generations depends on it. Our accumulated knowledge about the ecology of our home, our models for living with the peculiarities of the Amazon [b]iosphere, our reverence and respect for the tropical forest and its inhabitants, both plant and animal, are the keys to guaranteeing the future of the Amazon Basin, not only for our people, but also for all humanity."[8]

In May of the following year, COICA hosted a summit with environmentalists in the isolated Peruvian river city of Iquitos. Conservation International and the Worldwide Fund for Nature (WWF) were there alongside delegates from the Sierra Club, Friends of the Earth, Greenpeace, National Wildlife Federation, Rainforest Action Network, and the World Resources Institute. All in attendance signed the The Declaration of Iquitos. The full text follows:

Having met in the city of Iquitos from May 9 to 11, 1990 between the Coordinating Body for Indigenous Peoples' Organizations of the Amazon Basin (COICA) and environmental and conservationist organizations to analyze the serious deterioration of the Amazon biosphere and look for joint alternatives.

We consider that the recognition of territories for indigenous peoples, to develop programs of management and conservation, is an essential alternative for the future of the Amazon.

We recognize that we must look for adequate mechanisms to reach this objective, [which] include ways to channel international, technical, and financial resources.

We recognize the importance of indigenous peoples' own proposals for the management and conservation of the Amazon.

We recognize the need for actions of diffusion, studies, or projects to advance the territorial and societal rights of the indigenous peoples and the recognition of the value of their culture, according to the proposals of COICA and according to the particular objectives of each environmental and conservationist organization.

We conclude that in order that these considerations be put into practice, it is necessary to continue working as an Indigenous and Environmentalist Alliance for an Amazon for Humanity.

We decide to make this joint work concrete through the formation of a provisional Coordinating Committee of the environmentalists that are present and COICA, which will meet in September, 1990, in the city of Washington, DC, to continue analyzing and designing the best strategies for the defense of the indigenous Amazon.

While this was not the first declaration of indigenous territorial or civil rights, it was the first to be signed by representatives of international conservation organizations. It is thus regarded as a seminal document for a new conservation paradigm that would eventually treat indigenous peoples as equal partners in the creation and management of protected areas, at least in theory.

In 1992, the IUCN held their Fourth World Congress on National Parks and Protected Areas in Caracas, Venezuela. During the meeting,

WWF International, headquartered like IUCN in Gland, Switzerland, proposed a set of principles recognizing the value of traditional ecological knowledge (TEK) and the need to respect indigenous cultures and institutions. For the next four years, a draft proposal was passed around the vast IUCN and WWF communities. On May 22, 1996, a declaration that had grown to thirty-two principles was released in Gland. "Indigenous peoples inhabit nearly 20 percent of the planet," the foreword began, "mainly in areas where they have lived for thousands of years. Compared with protected area managers, who control about 6 percent of the world's land mass, indigenous peoples are the earth's most important stewards." That was a stunning admission for any conservation NGO, and particularly encouraging, coming as it did from the largest of them all, WWF.

"The Principles and Guidelines in Indigenous and Traditional Peoples and Protected Areas" acknowledged that native people had "made significant contributions to the earth's most fragile ecosystems" and should thus "be recognized as rightful, equal partners in the development and implementation of conservation strategies that affect their lands, territories, waters, coastal seas and other resources, and particularly in the establishment and management of protected areas" (for the full text see appendix A).

As the 1996 World Conservation Congress approached, indigenous leaders and their advocates pushed the IUCN to expand the agenda to include discussions of ways to implement conservation without exacerbating poverty. A call went out for a sort of Hippocratic compromise that would apply a first-do-no-harm standard for all new protected areas. According to such compromise, however a new park or reserve is mapped, structured, and regulated must be done with no harm to local human communities. The principle was hotly debated at the 1996 conference held in Montreal, and has been ever since. Traditional conservationists say it's too restrictive, that it's simply impossible in some locations to protect biological diversity without some social disruption. Indigenous peoples and their advocates say it doesn't go far enough, that poverty reduction can be and should be a primary goal of land conservation. Strict conservationists argue back that poverty and conservation are and should remain separate policy realms, which should be addressed by separate agencies. Anthropologists and social advocates retort that the two can't be separated because poverty is a critical constraint on conservation, and conservation should never compromise poverty reduction, which in rural environments depends entirely on the use of living resources.

Here again was the age-old conflict of two arguments, one that said areas needed to be set aside to protect wildlife from a growing population of people with no understanding or respect for conservation biology, the other asserting that the creation of protected areas too often impoverished people native to those areas and turned traditional hunter-gatherers into wildlife poachers, fuel-wood thieves, and other "trespassers."

As the Montreal conference proceeded, indigenous leaders caucused to prepare a series of resolutions to be debated and voted on at the Congress. The following passed with majority votes from the full IUCN membership:

• Resolution 1.49 calls upon members "to consider the adoption and implementation of the objectives of" ILO Convention 169 and the CBD, "and comply with the spirit of" the UN Draft Declaration on the Rights of Indigenous Peoples.

• A resolution on "Indigenous Peoples, Intellectual Property and Biological Diversity" recognizes "the rights of indigenous peoples to their lands and territories and natural resources, as well as their role in management, use and conservation, as a requirement for the effective implementation" of the CBD.

• Resolution 1.53 calls for the "recognition of the rights of indigenous peoples to their lands or territories and resources which fall within protected areas."

Publication of those resolutions and release of the WWF Principles sparked a host of new initiatives in the global conservation movement, and as many funding proposals to foundations, international banks, and transnational corporations. And new buzzwords appeared to describe a new level of collaboration—"community-based natural resource management (CBNRM)," "community-based conservation," "integrated conservation and development," and, of course, the mantra that launched a thousand conferences: "sustainable development."

The most popular and widely attempted of these initiatives were the Integrated Conservation and Development Programs (ICDPs), first discussed in chapter 3. As the name implies, ICDPs were efforts to combine conservation and economic development into a single program created and managed by a conservation group. Conservation and development are mutual goals. Typically, an indigenous community is given a set of management tasks and asked to avoid destructive practices in a protected area. In return they are given access to natural resources. It was hoped that providing even a modest economic base for communities in or near protected areas would lessen their dependence on vital natural resources. ICDPs grew in popularity as more funding for small-scale economic enterprise became available from the UN Development Program, USAID, and the international banking community.

With a few exceptions ICDPs failed to meet one or both goals, leaving a residue of mutual cynicism in the minds of both conservation and indigenous communities. Conservationists openly attacked what they called the "seductive appeal" of community-based conservation, arguing that eco-friendly native communities were a myth, while indigenous communities felt that their economic opportunities were limited rather than advanced by the projects, too many of which they complained were managed by conservation NGOs. Thus ICDPs are one of the few conservation experiments that all sides seem to accept as a major disappointment, if not an outright failure.

One problem facing antipoverty advocates is the way poverty is quantified. Personal income is the benchmark. It seems impossible for economists to understand that people living in the complete absence of money can be far wealthier than their neighbors in close proximity who live at the edge of the local (and global) economy. Indigenous people earning zero dollars per year, but with balanced, protein-rich diets, clean water, protection from the elements, traditional medicines, and strong cultures, should probably not be placed on a regional, national, or global poverty scale beneath or even on par with people earning a few dollars a week from menial labor but who have short life spans, bad health, undernourishment, no medicines, and a brutish culture.

The sad fact is that very few of the lofty resolutions and principles ever filtered down to ground level in Africa, South America, or Southeast

Asia, where indigenous peoples are still marginalized. While they fill their brochures, newsletters, and websites with passionate statements of support for native land rights and cultural integrity, transnational conservation groups still hide behind nation-states' deep reluctance to grant land rights, and there remains a deep mistrust between people working to protect the biota and those working to protect human cultures.

"Conservationists feel that their job is to protect nature," says Dorothy Jackson, coordinator of the Forest Peoples Programme (FPP) in Africa. "There is a strong feeling that wildlife and people are not compatible. They do recognize the social aspect of their work but say it's unfair to put the onus on them. National legislation itself often ignores indigenous people's rights and conservationists argue that it is the state's job to define areas and protect people." Even if that is so, Jackson adds, conservationists, who tend to have money and influence with governments, could push far harder to protect indigenous people.

"The trend to promote sustainable use of resources as a means to protect these resources, while politically expedient and intellectually appealing is not well grounded in biological knowledge," wrote three prominent American conservationists, Katrina Brandon, Kent Redford, and Steven Sanderson, in a widely read critique of ICDPs and sustainable development. "Not all things can be preserved through use," they said. "Not all places should be open to use. Without an understanding of broader ecosystem dynamics at specific sites, strategies promoting sustainable use will lead to substantial losses of biodiversity."[9]

The debate that followed would lead slowly toward a new model for conservation that placed native communities in the role of initiator, owner, and primary manager of new protected areas. IR (Indigenous Reserve) and IPPA (Indigenous Peoples Protected Area) would replace CBNRM and ICDP on the list of acronyms defining local participation. In form, the new models often looked much like their predecessors, the only difference being the ownership and primary governance of indigenous peoples. Fortress conservationists would resist this approach to conservation, as they had resisted its predecessors, even when some of the earlier methods produced undeniably superior results (see chapter 18 for more on conservation's resistance to indigenous management of protected areas).

At the 1992 Earth Summit in Rio de Janiero, indigenous peoples were recognized for the first time as a "Major Group" that should participate in sustainable development. Agenda 21, which was approved by all parties to the summit, devotes a whole chapter (no. 26) to the subject. It reads: "Indigenous peoples and their communities and other local communities have a vital role in environmental management and development because of their knowledge and traditional practices. States should recognize and duly support their identity, culture and interests and enable their effective participation in the achievement of sustainable development."

At the summit, the Convention on Biological Diversity (CBD), a legally binding international agreement, enjoined all parties to the convention to endorse section 8j, which reads: "Subject to its national legislation, [to] respect, preserve and maintain knowledge, innovations and practices of indigenous and local communities embodying traditional lifestyles relevant for the conservation and sustainable use of biological resources."

In 1999, the World Commission on Protected Areas, an IUCN task force, adopted guidelines for putting the principles contained in these six resolutions into practice. The guidelines placed emphasis on co-management of protected areas, on agreements between indigenous peoples and conservation NGOs, on indigenous participation, and on recognition of indigenous peoples' rights to "sustainable, traditional use" of their lands and territories. Thus collaboration was being adopted as a form of self-defense.

But as anthropologist Marcus Colchester has observed, "Putting new principles into practice is easier said than done, particularly when conservation initiatives take place within the same constraints as other 'development' activities. They have to deal with the same competing enterprises and vested interests that confront local communities everywhere." (For more on Colchester, see chapter 6) Add to that the deep and intractable prejudices held by so much of the world against native peoples whose lifeways are regarded as "backward," "dirty," or "subhuman."

At a series of regional conferences organized by small NGOs—such as Colchester's Forest People's Programme, the International Work

Group for Indigenous Affairs and the Inter-Ethnic Association of the Development of the Peruvian Amazon, the Asia Indigenous Peoples Pact and Partners of Community Organizations, and the Communaute des Autocthones Rwandaises, in out-of-the-way locations such as Pucallpa, Peru; Sabah, Malaysia; and Kigali, Rwanda—it was agreed that while sincere efforts were being made in each region to apply new standards to conservation, the new collaborative paradigm was not yet widely used. In fact, local conservation efforts were more likely to be tied to parallel development schemes. Indigenous people were beginning to realize that, as practiced, conservation and development were really two sides of the same coin. "Both are impositions on indigenous territories, which overrule their rights and authority," observed the FPP's Marcus Colchester.

There have also been triumphs, few and small indeed, but potential models indicating that restitution of traditional homelands and recognition of indigenous rights are not incompatible with effective conservation. Some examples:

• In the Annapurna Sanctuary of Nepal, village communities are given an opportunity to gain an income from trekkers who come through the sanctuary.

• In Zimbabwe, local participants in the CAMPFIRE program manage wildlife reserves and collect revenue from controlled hunting and protein from wildlife culls.

• In Indonesia, where national law does not recognize indigenous rights to land, parks authorities have nevertheless granted de facto land rights and involve communities in park management.

• In South Africa, the Khomani San, a branch of the San (Basarwa),once expelled from their lands and scattered to the winds—and who were thought to have become extinct—have not only recuperated their language and revived their settlements but have also had their land restituted. They are now being progressively granted rights of access and use in large sectors of their former territory. (For more on the San in Botswana see chapter 11.)

• In Australia, several protected areas have been returned to their original owners. For example, what is known as Ayer's Rock—Uluru to the

Aboriginals—is now recognized as being owned by indigenous people who co-manage the area as a national Park. And Mt. Cook has been returned to its Maori owners.

What these stories have taught both conservationists and indigenous peoples is that in order for collaborative conservation to work it must advance beyond the shopworn buzzwords of partnership—"capacity building," "stakeholder," "participation," and "conflict management"—and allow real transfers of power and economic benefits to local communities, as well as recognition of indigenous land rights.

September 2003 was a historically significant month for both the global environment movement and indigenous peoples. There were indications that they could, at least on some issues, work together.

In that month, the World Trade Organization hosted global trade talks in Cancun, Mexico. Environmental and indigenous organizations held massive protests against unregulated markets and inequitable trade. Talks broke down and the meeting was regarded by all involved as a massive failure.

Also in September, the Food and Agriculture Organization of the UN convened the World Forestry Congress in Quebec City. Again both conservationists and indigenous peoples attending targeted the social and environmental consequences of the prevailing forestry model of industrial-scale logging and tree monoculture, which is destroying both forests and forest peoples' cultures. Protesters from both movements jointly offered a more socially equitable and environmentally friendly approach called "community forest management."

During the same month, the World Parks Congress was held in Durban, South Africa. While there was less gloom about the socially and environmentally destructive impositions of the neoliberal agenda, there was also more tension between conservationists and about a hundred and twenty indigenous peoples from almost every country in the world were national parks have been created. The focus of the congress was on "Benefits Beyond Boundaries"—implying that conservationists were seeking to imagine parks that provided benefits to, rather than only impose restrictions on, local people. That process would be encouraged and aided by the Theme of Indigenous and Local Communities, Equity and Protected Areas (TILCEPA), a recently formed IUCN task force.

Although they were invited to be part of the opening plenary and to sit on a host of panels and workshops, indigenous leaders came to the conference with serious doubts about the conservationists' sincerity. Did IUCN and its powerful member organizations really stand, as they claimed in their proclamations, for ecological justice and indigenous rights, or were they engaged in a pact with the devil, cutting deals with transnational corporations and development banks? Would they stand up against mining in protected areas, rainforests, and indigenous territories? Did conservationists really oppose an unfair globalization process, or were they crafting "win-win scenarios" whereby the profits of "free trade" would be channeled into their growing empire of protected areas, while restive locals would be bought off with short-term "community development" and "co-management" projects? Would the end result of this Faustian pact be a planet where 10 percent of the land is set aside as "wilderness," while the other 90 percent is sacrificed to the neoliberal agenda? Were parks and development just two sides of the same coin? In short, were the BINGOs part of the problem or part of the solution?

"If the World Parks Congress is to be judged a success by the environmental movement these doubts must be convincingly allayed," read a preconference bulletin of the World Rainforest Movement. "The Congress must come out with a vision, and a strategy to match, which recognizes that parks are for people, where rights are respected, where indigenous peoples regain control of their territories and destinies, which are no-go areas for extractive industries. No more stitch ups with the corporations that are driving the world to ruin. No more colonial deals trading other peoples' territories and destinies for land use plans, which include parks, logging, oil-pipelines and plantations." It was an overt and clear challenge to the global conservation movement.

Also present and recognized for the first time, as a vital part of the world's native community, were thirty representatives of mobile indigenous peoples—pastoral nomadic tribes like the remarkable Todas of Nilgiri, the Saharan Tuareg, the Banjara of Rajesthan, the Kuhi of Persia, and, of course, the Maasai of Eastern Africa. At the close of the conference they presented their own set of recommendations calling for recognition and respect for self-determination, equitable benefits, collective rights, transboundary mobility through traditional corridors, traditional knowledge, crosscultural dialogue, and their customary laws. It was a general reiteration of the Dana Declaration on Mobile Peoples and Conservation passed a year earlier at an international meeting of social and natural scientists and NGOs in the Wadi Dana Nature Reserve in Jordan.

At the close of the congress, the indigenous delegates issues the following statement:

The declaration of protected areas on indigenous territories without our consent and engagement has resulted in the violation of our rights, the displacement and impoverishment of our peoples, the loss of our sacred sites and the slow but continuous destruction of our cultures. It is thus difficult to talk about "benefits" for Indigenous Peoples when protected areas are being declared on our territories without consent. First we were dispossessed in the name of kings and emperors, later in the name of State development and now in the name of conservation.

To overcome this history of exclusion and violence we propose the establishment of a high level, independent Truth and Reconciliation Commission to investigate and respond impartially to each instance of abuse and to promote the restitution of our lands.

A Truth and Reconciliation Commission has yet to be formed, but millions of stolen acres have since been returned to native people. It's a beginning.

Box 12.2

The Kinshasa Resolution (1975)

Protection of Traditional Ways of Life:

Recognizing the value and importance of traditional ways of life and the skills of the people which enable them to live in harmony with their environment;
Recognizing also the vulnerability of indigenous people and the great significance they attach to land ownership
The 12th General Assembly of IUCN meeting in Kinshasa, Zaire, in September 1975:

Recommends:

(1) That governments maintain and encourage traditional methods of living and customs which enable communities, both rural and urban, to live in harmony with their environment;

(2) That educational systems be oriented to emphasize environmental and ecological principles and conservation objectives derived from local cultures and traditions, and that these principles and objectives be given wide publicity;

(3) That governments devise means by which indigenous people may bring their lands into conservation areas without relinquishing their ownership, use and tenure rights;

(4) That the governments of countries still inhabited by people belonging to separate indigenous cultures recognize the rights of these people to live on the lands they have traditionally occupied, and take account of their viewpoints;

(5) That in the creation of national parks or reserves indigenous peoples should not normally be displaced from their traditional lands, nor should such reserves anywhere be proclaimed without adequate consultation with the indigenous peoples most likely to be directly affected by such proclamation.

Five months after the Durban World Parks Congress, the Seventh Conference of Parties (COP) of the CBD met in Kuala Lumpur, Malaysia. Previous COP meetings, attended almost exclusively by conservationists, had dealt almost exclusively with conservation issues. Largely in response to the eleven recommendations passed in Durban, COP-7 was a departure from its predecessors. For the first time indigenous peoples were present and participated fully in marathon sessions that drafted a new "Programme of Work on Protected Areas." As a consequence, terms were included in the program calling for increased benefits of protected areas for indigenous and local communities, and enhancing the involvement of those communities in "the establishment, management and monitoring of protected areas" in a manner that afforded "full respect for the rights of indigenous and local communities consistent with national law and applicable international obligations." Also following the example of Durban, "community reserved areas" initiated by indigenous peoples were recognized as legitimate protected areas.

The BINGOs Respond

They threw off colonialism. One day they will throw off eco-colonialism.
—Raymond Bonner, *New York Times*

When indigenous criticism of international conservation began to focus on the work and policies of its organizations, and the world took notice, the BINGOs responded with a spate of supportive declarations. The Nature Conservancy issued a "core value" statement that read in part: "We respect the needs of local communities by developing ways to conserve biological diversity while at the same time enabling humans to live productively and sustainably on the landscape."[10]

One important lesson indigenous people have learned for themselves and taught the world is that nature and culture are not the only forces at work in conservation. Politics is a big factor. The political stability of nation-states hosting protected areas is vital to the long-term ecological health of a region. What is to stop some future government of Bolivia—to choose a country at random—from abrogating by fiat all agreements, contracts, concessions, use rights, and treaties that created national parks or communal reserves?

Communal reserves in Brazil are created by presidential decree and can be rescinded by the next president, or for that matter by the very president who created the reserve. And that same president can grant a mining concession in a protected area without consent of its inhabitants, as happened in Suriname, where large-scale bauxite mining takes place in the Wane Kreek Reserve, homeland of the Kalina and Lokono peoples. One large check from Shell Oil could prompt a similar concession to drill for oil or gas. The only thing that can stop this kind of corruption is the political force of the people most affected by it. In Ecuador, that force was great enough in 1993, when millions of indigenous people, in a protest sparked by oppression, flooded into the major cities of the country and brought the economy to a standstill until they got their lands back.

The following year, in Chiapas, Mexico, the Zapatistas protested an amendment of the Mexican constitution that, to conform with the North American Free Trade Agreement, would allow the public sale of former *ejidos* that had been communally owned by Mayan communities. A subtext of the protests was a complaint about the alleged collaboration of Conservation International with the Mexican government.

In 2000, in Bolivia, the Coalition for the Defense of Water and Life mounted a national protest against the government's willingness to sell the nation's water-delivery system to Bechtel Corporation. At the same time, the U'wa people in Colombia were successfully demonstrating against an Occidental Petroleum pipeline through their territory.

Then, in 2004, the Second Continental Summit of Indigenous Peoples and Nationalities was held in Quito, Ecuador. Eight hundred people gathered from sixty-four indigenous "nations" in twenty-five countries. Two powerful indigenous groups—the Confederation of Indigenous Nationalities of Ecuador (CONAIE) and the Coordination of Indigenous Organizations of the Amazonian Basin (COICA) organized the meeting. The agenda addressed the age-old list of complaints heard from native people the world over—subversion of sovereignty, theft of land, privatization of natural resources, expropriation of traditional knowledge and genetic material, foreign-based ecotourism, undermining of international law, and conservation-related evictions. The conference issued a strong call for the direct participation of indigenous peoples in international forums, such as the World Trade Organization and the UN Conference on Trade and Development, where decisions regarding indigenous rights and knowledge are affected.

Seeming like a direct response to that call, the Eighth World Wilderness Congress, held the following year in Anchorage, Alaska, had a strong native theme. Over thirty indigenous groups from five continents were invited to participate. The walls of the plenary were lined with flags of Alaska's native peoples—Inupiaq, Yupic, Cupik, Alutug, Aleut, Haida, Tsinshai, Eyak, Tinglit, and Athabascan—and the congress opened with a vast traditional ceremony.

In an interview, the congress's organizer, Vance Martin, told me that the Wild Foundation, of which he is president, was actually the first wilderness organization ever to invite indigenous peoples to its meetings. "In fact, the first World Wilderness Congress was held in Durban, South Africa, and blacks were invited in defiance of apartheid laws. The congress," he said, "was promoting 'traditional knowledge' before the term existed."

"The World Wilderness Congress has since Durban always integrated indigenous participation into its sessions," he continued, "so in this respect the eighth session is no different. But what is different this time is the scale. Native lands management is critical to conservation efforts, and we will do everything we can this week to ensure that indigenous groups are full partners at the table during the congress, and that their knowledge and centuries-old expertise as land stewards is recognized."

At the Anchorage congress, which ran for almost two weeks, there was a Native Lands and Wilderness Council meeting that ran concurrently throughout the entire congress. A few carefully selected tribal people were invited to address plenary sessions, but were encouraged to describe how they managed wilderness on their reservations and not to advocate for territorial rights. While Peter Seligmann and Russell Mittermeier, CEO and president, respectively, of Conservation International, gave rousing plenary speeches to political and corporate leaders, and Cemex Corporation, one of the world's largest cement producers, announced the creation of a new, cross-boundary "Peace Park" on the U.S.-Mexican border, the Native Lands and Wilderness Council presented and discussed their lives and aspirations in a windowless room in the convention center basement. There were many times during the congress when I was the only white person in that room.

Toward the end of the third day, indigenous people from every continent began to realize that they were relating their stories and sharing their traditional knowledge with people who already knew them, and that their agenda was carefully controlled by people upstairs. Frustration began to accumulate in the room until Francois Paulette, a Dene from northern Canada, spoke from the floor: "We have been marginalized again. We are a sideshow to this convention."

After that the agenda began to shift. Territorial rights were openly discussed (although not in plenary sessions) and plans presented to reclaim parks and other protected areas that had been removed from native homelands and hunting grounds in the interest of preserving wilderness for the enchantment of the folks upstairs.

Inviting so many indigenous peoples to gather in one place and discuss what wilderness meant to them was definitely a giant step in the right direction, for which Vance Martin and his supporters should be commended. Perhaps the Ninth World Wilderness Congress will be hosted by the Native Lands Council, in a venue less splendid and compartmentalized than a vast convention center with catered food and other amenities surrounded by branch offices of global oil.

A Small but Significant Triumph

On September 13, 2007, after more than two decades of heated international debate, the United Nations General Assembly finally got around to voting on the Declaration on the Rights of Indigenous Peoples. One hundred and forty nations were in favor, eleven abstained, and four—Australia, New Zealand, Canada, and the United States—voted against the measure.

Although the declaration is nonbinding, it does affirm "that indigenous peoples are equal to all other peoples," it articulates the individual and collective rights of 370 million indigenous people, and it endorses their self-determination of culture, identity, language, and political status, emphasizing their right to remain distinct, pursue their own visions of social development, maintain and strengthen their own institutions and traditions, and pursue the economic systems of their choice.

The Declaration on the Rights of Indigenous Peoples also prohibits all discrimination, and in a section that is of particular interest to native people contending with international conservation actions, the declaration advocates their full participation in all matters concerning them. It also guarantees their right to participate, if they choose to, in the political, economic, social, and cultural life of the state or states that annexed or enveloped their homeland.

While the text of the declaration says nothing about conservation per se, it offers the following protections:

• Article 4 guarantees "autonomy, or self government in matter relating to internal and local affairs."

• Article 8 protects indigenous peoples from "dispossession their lands, territories or resources."

• Article 10: "Indigenous peoples shall not be forcibly removed from their lands or territories. No relocation shall take place without the free, prior and informed consent of the indigenous peoples concerned and after agreement on just and fair compensation and, where possible, with the option of return."

• Article 18: "Indigenous peoples have the right to participate in decision-making in matters which would affect their rights, through representatives chosen by themselves in accordance with their own procedures, as well as to maintain and develop their own indigenous decision-making institutions."

• Article 19: "States shall consult and cooperate in good faith with the indigenous peoples concerned through their own representative institutions in order to obtain their free, prior and informed consent before adopting and implementing legislative or administrative measures that may affect them."

• Article 26: "1. Indigenous peoples have the right to the lands, territories and resources, which they have traditionally owned, occupied or otherwise used or acquired. 2. Indigenous peoples have the right to own, use, develop and control the lands, territories and resources that they possess by reason of traditional ownership or other traditional occupation or use, as well as those which they have otherwise acquired. 3. States shall give legal recognition and protection to these lands, territories and resources. Such recognition shall be conducted with due respect to the customs, traditions and land tenure systems of the indigenous peoples concerned."

All of these articles protect native homelands and native people from being marginalized in negotiations between conservation NGOs and national governments.

General Assembly President Sheikha Haya Rashed Al Kalifa described the passage of the Declaration on the Rights of Indigenous Peoples as another "major step toward the promise and protection of human rights and fundamental freedom for all." However, she warned, "even with this progress, indigenous people will still face marginalization, extreme poverty, and other human rights violations." And she predicts that they will still be "dragged into conflicts and land disputes that threaten their way of life and very survival."[11]

San Bushman Jumanda Gakelebone called from the office of First Peoples of the Kalahari in Botswana to say how "happy and thrilled" he was "to hear about the adoption of this declaration, which," he says, "recognizes that governments can no longer treat us as second-class citizens and throw us off our lands like they did."

Ogiek leader Kiplangat Cheruiot believes that if signatories abide by the declaration, it will place "the lives of [millions of] indigenous peoples on an equal footing with the rest of the world's citizens."

This declaration was a long time coming. It reflects years of hard work, perseverance, and negotiation on the part of indigenous people and their supporters. It was a triumphant accomplishment, and in the history of this remarkable social movement will long be remembered by native people the world over, as will the date it became official: September 13, 2007.

Despite the enormous progress made on behalf of indigenous peoples over the past century, there are still private and nonprofit conservationist forces and institutions in the world that regard themselves above international law and treaty and even duty-bound to ignore the rights of some native people in their quest to protect wildlife and biodiversity. The experience of the Ogiek in Kenya gives witness to this ongoing and unfortunate abuse of basic human rights.

13
Ogiek

But how can one poach one's own game on one's own ancestral land?
—Guy Yeoman, explorer and author

Kenya has lost 90 percent of its closed canopy forest. One of the few surviving stands of original forest in the country is the 393,000-acre (159,000-hectare) Mau Forest, situated 125 miles northwest of Nairobi. The Mau, largest of all Kenyan forests, is nicknamed "the water tower" because its nine major rivers flow through a catchment area that supplies water to almost twenty million East Africans.

An ecosystem assessment of the Mau Forest released in 1999 by Kenya's Permanent Presidential Commission on Soil Conservation and Afforestation concluded that the forest was under severe ecological stress, mostly as a consequence of excessive logging and agriculture. Although gazetted as a national forest in 1957, the Mau remained an essentially unprotected area, where conservation was frequently mentioned but rarely practiced. The forest also became a catchment area for squatters and large-scale landowners who were sold titles to the land or granted them by presidential fiat.

Under the severely corrupt administration of former president Daniel arap Moi (1978–2002), land titles and logging concessions went to Moi family and cronies who logged and farmed in the forest at their pleasure. Moi himself held title to 2,300 acres of the escarpment. If the Mau Forest was to survive something had to be done. An ad hoc conservation organization called Friends of the Mau claimed that human activities were endangering the forest and called for a complete evacuation. From a strict conservation standpoint it was a wise suggestion. The water supply of East Africa was at stake.

No one knows for sure how many people have since been evicted from the Mau Forest. Estimates range wildly from seventeen thousand to one hundred thousand. What is clear from remaining evidence is that thousands of homes and over one hundred schools were razed—one school burned to the ground as horrified teachers and students looked on.

Rounded up with powerless land owners, lumberjacks, and squatters were a few Maasai and a remote tribe of forest people who have lived in the Mau Forest on and off for centuries. Some anthropologists believe that the Ogiek are East Africa's aboriginals and thereby Kenya's first people. They were certainly in the Rift Valley before the Bantus and the now-dominant Kikuyu migrated there, and long before the colonialists who from 1903 to independence in 1963 made the lives of the Ogiek miserable.

When Ogiek leaders complained about the evictions and the conservation rhetoric that seemed disingenuous in the face of rampant logging, they were simply told that the trees in the Mau Forest (with the exception of one hundred they had been given nine years earlier) were the government's property to sell to whomever it pleased. The consequences were devastating to both the forest and the Ogiek people.

Honey Hunters

Biodiversity won't feed our children.
—Ogiek chief

The Ogiek are hunter-gatherers who, when the need arises, also grow beans, potatoes, and cabbage. The Kenyan nickname for them is "Dorobo," derived from the Maasai word *il torobo*, which means "poor people who cannot afford cattle." Some are insulted by the name and by the allegations made by government evictors that they are not good stewards of the forest. They in fact strive to be the best imaginable conservators of land. No one who knows them well contests that.

First, they only hunt animals with buoyant populations such as the warthog and tree hyrax. The larger ungulates and more charismatic species are regarded as totems, which the animist Ogiek believe were sent

to them by divine forces to protect. The animals they do kill are only for their own domestic use. They do not sell to the active and lucrative bush meat market. When they notice that the species they rely on are in short supply, they practice self-imposed conservation by curtailing the hunt and raising sheep and goats for protein.

Wild honey is the most important item in Ogiek diet and culture. It is why they live in the forest, where the location of every hive is known and guarded. The Mau Forest is home to many breeds of bee. Thus it is regarded not only as ancestral home, nation, pharmacy, food supply, and sacred place.

British veterinarian and adventurer Guy Yeoman, who lived among the Ogiek on his travels up and down the Great Rift Valley, describes them as "capable of being totally and comfortably self-sufficient on the natural products of the forest, with the exception of what little iron they need for making their arrow heads, knives and spears."

He remembers them as "a shy and diffident people, of engaging gentleness and charm, considerable intelligence, of quite astonishing technical expertise in their special arts of hunting and bee-keeping, and having a most unusual sensibility in relation to their forests and the creatures which inhabit them." The Ogiek he says "are not gregarious and are happiest in situation of isolation, the trees and animals providing them with psychological support."[1]

This would not be the first attempt to remove the Ogiek from their forest homeland. As far back as 1903, British settlers attempted to clear the Mau Forest of its original inhabitants to make way for tea planters. But the Ogiek were not people who were easy to push around. According to Guy Yeoman, "to European administrators, the Ogiek represented a tiresome problem. They were an elusive, apparently (but not truly) nomadic, uncountable people lacking a recognizable hierarchical structure, and were resistant to tidy organization."

The Kenya Land Commission, created by British colonials in 1937, deprived the Ogiek of tribal status and denied them any claim to ancestral land. The Ogiek were forcibly moved, either onto the tribal reservations of other dispossessed communities, particularly the Maasai, or to Forestry Department labor camps. However, no sooner had colonial forces turned their backs than the Ogiek abandoned the reserves and returned to their Mau Forest homes, where they were regarded by nearby colonial settlers and the government as "squatters" and "poachers."

Invoking the Forest Act of 1957 and the Wildlife Conservation Act of 1977, postcolonial governments have repeatedly displaced Ogiek settlements to "conserve" the forests. On several occasions they were moved to conifer plantations, which the Ogiek described as "totally sterile, unproductive, and useless for either bees or wild animals."[2] Ogiek settlements were later evicted from the Mt. Elgon Game Reserve in western Kenya throughout the 1980s, a process that was completed in 1992 when Mt. Elgon became a national park. Once again the Ogiek were homeless. Poverty, illiteracy, and sickness continued to plague them. Their life expectancy dropped from almost sixty to forty-six years.

In a memorandum written to members of Kenya's parliament, the Ogieks lamented the continued loss of their land: "Our ancestral land has been turned into private property. We commit trespass when we go to our homes. Most of the men in our community are employed as manual laborers and saw millers earning as little as 30 shillings a day. We have been driven out of three forests—the Sururu, Likia and the Teret. A part of our homeland has been allocated to 'foreigners.' We are forced to live in Njoro in abject poverty. We are, as it were, in exile." To which Ogiek elder Joseph Kariangei adds this: "Our entire lifestyle has been criminalized, we are refugees in our own country."

In June 2005, a High Court order was issued to stop the evictions. Defying the order, Kenyan Lands Minister Amos Kimunya ordered the evictions to continue. He said the entire cabinet endorsed his decision. Not entirely true: Wangari Maathai, winner of the 2004 Nobel Peace Prize and later minister of environment for Kenya, defended the Ogiek and argued that their exceptional lifeways qualified them to return to the Mau. "The Ogiek are a class of their own," she said. "We should realize that they are different from other communities in the Mau Forest."

In early October 2005, Kenyan President Mwai Kibaki announced his intention to issue twelve thousand title deeds in the Mau Forest to Ogiek people who had been evicted. Again the High Court responded, this time barring issuance of the deeds.

Advocates for the Ogiek had argued that Tinet, a small forest inside the larger Mau Forest, was the ancestral land of the community; that nine years ago the government had agreed that they should remain there and granted them each a five-acre plot; and that depriving them of access to the forest and its products infringed their right to life and livelihood. Supporters had written from all over the world on their behalf.

But the court dismissed the Ogiek's case, saying the people had no right to continue living in Tinet. According to witnesses, the tone of the judgment was harsh and contemptuous. The judges seemed determined not only to deny the title to the Tinet Ogiek, but also to frighten off any other group of native people who might try to make a similar claim.

In response to one petition, a judge invited the vicar of a Christian church to testify on the Ogiek's behalf. When the vicar turned up, the judge used his presence and testimony as proof that the Ogiek had adopted modernity and thereby lost their authenticity as an ancient culture—petition denied.

The final judgment climaxed in an outburst of environmental rhetoric clearly aimed at enlisting the support of conservationists: "The eviction is for the purpose of saving the whole of Kenya from a possible environmental disaster." The Ogiek, the judges alleged, had engaged in "massive developments" (scattered wooden schoolhouses and little one-room stores), which disqualify them from living in the forest.

Nothing was said about the real threats—the huge logging operations that are still destroying other parts of the Mau Forest in defiance of the logging ban recently imposed by the government, tea plantations owned by a company belonging to former President Moi, or the intensive cultivation of flowers for export. There was no mention, either, of the large estate and mansion in the forest owned by Zakayo Cheruiyot, permanent secretary for provincial administration and internal security in the Office of the President.

Once again the government ignored the court. On October 15, 2005, President Kibaki handed out the deeds. Opponents accused him of pandering for votes even though the Ogiek announced they would vote against his proposed constitution. And conservationists, still reeling from Kibaki's earlier decision to cede control of the Amboseli National Park back to the Maasai, were outraged. Kibaki denied buying votes, stating that he was merely correcting "historical injustices." Not many Kenyans take that claim seriously, particularly as Kibaki has allowed three large logging companies—Pan African Paper Mills, Raiply Timber, and Timsales Ltd.—to remain in the Mau Forest. Among them those three companies employ thirty thousand Kenyans; and the government owns shares in Pan African Paper Mills.

At issue here is the International Covenant on Civil and Political Rights (ICCPR), a legally binding UN covenant to which Kenya is a signatory. Article 27 of the covenant states: "In those States in which ethnic, religious or linguistic minorities exists, persons belonging to such minorities shall not be denied the right in community with the other members of their group, to enjoy their own culture, to profess and practice their own religion, or to use their own language." Having ratified the convention, the Kenyan government is obliged to ensure that all individuals under its jurisdiction enjoy their rights and this may require specific action to correct inequalities to which minorities are subjected. Ogiek leaders and lawyers are asking the UN to enforce the convention on their behalf.

And ecologists and hydrologists are telling the Kenyan government what the Ogiek have known for millennia: Kenya needs forests to catch water for the nation. The recommended forest cover for a secure and healthy national water supply is 10 percent of landmass. Kenya is down to 1.7 percent—and falling. It would seem wise then to regard traditional keepers of the forest as essential to the nation's water supply. And thus it would make sense to resettle a shy and gentle people whose industrious beekeeping pollinates and regenerates the forest, who only hunt small and plentiful game for their own kitchens, who use the forest as their apothecary, and who consider the Mau a sacred place.

The fate of the Ogiek remains uncertain. They don't give up easily and may yet return to their land. In the meantime, they will continue to be regarded by cultural survivalists as prime examples of a people who for generations practiced sustainable livelihood in a forest threatened by all other occupants.

In October 2007 African cartographer Julius Muchemi took me to visit the Ogiek village of Nessuit about two hundred kilometers north of Nairobi. All of the structures in the settlement seemed temporary except for a former school building where eight Ogiek elders greeted me, each representing a different clan of the ancient tribe. They had something to show me, something that gave them great pride.

In the center of the schoolroom was a five-by-five meter three-dimensional map of their former homeland. Muchemi had helped them create the map over the previous two years. It showed the detailed topography of the escarpment that caught fresh water for twenty million Kenyans, and demarked the standing forests next to the clear-cuts, the former villages, the clan borders, the trails, springs, honey-gathering sites, and the sacred places.

"This map keeps our emotional attachment to this land alive," one of the elders told me. "It's the only way now that we can see our place in the world." I suspected that it was also giving them a sense of power, some hope for a better future than the refugee life they were living on the border of the forest they knew and loved.

14

The Science of Princes

As much as guns and warships, maps have been the weapons of imperialism.
—J. Brian Harley, historian

More indigenous territory can be reclaimed and defended by maps than by guns.
—Bernard Neitschmann, University of California

Dr. Peter Poole is a cartographer—a "mapper"—and a very skilled one, but unlike most in his trade, Poole works exclusively for indigenous communities. On every continent there are remote native villages using the maps he made for them to rename and reclaim their lands.[1] He does so because he understands better than most the value of a professionally created, scientifically accurate, officially approved map to any community attempting to establish land rights by virtue of origin or tenure, and to secure what he describes as "recognition of their rights to self-determination and the collective ownership and control of their territories."

"Maps are power," he is fond of saying. Bernard Neitschmann, quoted in the chapter epigraph, is right: more indigenous territory has been claimed by maps than by guns. And, Poole believes, more yet can be reclaimed and defended by maps.

I traveled with Poole through the remote southern reaches of Belize while he and an Indian geomatics expert named Sujoy Chauduri planned a training exercise for Mayan and Garifuna peoples living in small villages scattered though the area.

In 1994 the government of Belize, quietly and without warning or local advice, created a new national park north of the Sarstoon River along the border between Belize and Guatemala. In 1997 Mayan and

Garifuna people living in six remote villages in southern Belize were informed by the government of Belize that they were living on the border of the Sarstoon-Temash National Park, which would soon be put off limits for hunting and fishing. Their protest was loud and immediate. This would bring an end to their livelihood as most of their food, fodder, and fiber came from the forest. They were almost unanimously opposed to the park.

A compromise was reached at a community meeting attended by village leaders and government representatives, held on February 22, 1997, in the Garifuna village of Barranco. The local communities would approve and support creation of the park if they could manage it and continue to hunt, fish, and gather from its border areas as they had for countless generations. Some species would be placed off limits and only line fishing (no nets) would be allowed. Before the deal could be finalized, a map of traditional Mayan and Garifuna hunting and fishing grounds would be produced.

"The most urgent challenge facing those people," Poole says, "is to get others to respect their land rights." The first strategy, he believes, is for the people most familiar with an area to generate hand-drawn maps that "articulate traditional knowledge and express ancient patterns of occupancy," then combine those maps with high-tech geomatics. He explains: "The use of global positioning satellite (GPS) receivers converts detailed information into cartographic forms which relevant government agencies find digestible—or less difficult to dismiss."[2]

I traveled again with Poole through the South Pacific. This time he was working more as a circuit rider for a new organization called First Peoples Worldwide. Together we searched for small island communities that intended to create their own protected area. We called them Indigenous Peoples Protected Areas (IPPAs). But the people of the South Pacific didn't like the term *protected area*. "It represents bad memories for so many people we have met around the world who have been evicted from so-called protected areas. Can't you please find a better term?" asked Alifereti Tawake, a Fijian marine biologist. "How about 'indigenous stewardship area'?" It sounded a bit awkward, but it certainly said what it is. So *indigenous stewardship area* (ISA) became our term of use. And it was greatly appreciated by the communities we visited.

Mapping is often called "the science of princes" because it has been used to establish so many domains of wealth, to consolidate power, and to protect the authority of nations and colonies. Here is the observation of J. Brian Harley, the cartographer quoted in the chapter epigraph:

Insofar as maps were used in colonial promotion, and lands claimed on paper before they were effectively occupied, maps anticipated empire. Surveyors marched alongside soldiers, initially mapping for reconnaissance, then for general information, and eventually as tools of pacification, civilization, and exploitation in the defined colonies. But there is more to this than the drawing of boundaries for the practical, political, or military containment of subject populations. Maps were used to legitimize the reality of conquest and empire. They helped create myths which would assist in the maintenance of the territorial status quo. As communicators of an imperial message, they have been used as an aggressive complement to the rhetoric of speeches, newspapers, and written texts, or to the histories and popular songs extolling the virtues of empire.[3]

In other words, maps reflect the interests of those who draw them. Conservation maps delineate watersheds and highlight features such as forest density, soil quality, migratory routes, ocean and wind currents, and species distribution. Deforestation, erosion, and visible pollution might also be indicted. Human settlements that are spotted from satellites or airplanes are marked with dots, some named, some not. Tribal identity, human activities, hunting grounds, cultural artifacts, plantations, cemeteries, and sacred sites are rarely indicated; thus the need for indigenous tenure mapping.

Box 14.1

Mapping for Power

The Tapajos National Forest is located near Santarem in the central Brazilian Amazon. There are eighteen villages scattered along banks of Tapajos River, which winds through the heart of the forest. The villagers have a long history of conflict with IBAMA, the federal agency that manages Brazil's national forests. In 1995, with the assistance of a small Brazilian NGO called the Institute of Forest and Agricultural Certification and Management (IMAFLORA), the villagers initiated a participatory mapping project.

The resource maps showed that the ancestral rights of each community extended over an even larger area than they had previously claimed. While the maps, which were meticulously prepared by village participants and professionally produced by IMAFLORA, were validated by independent observers from various institutions, IBAMA refused to recognize the territorial rights of the villagers over forest lands. IBAMA prepared its own maps, without community participation, and used them to deny land tenure. Nevertheless the community maps were used to develop a zoning plan that empowered tribal leaders by placing them on a *Grupo Gestor* (Board of Directors) for the Tapajos National Forest.

While the outcome of this particular case of participatory mapping did not produce all the desired results, it did protect the interests of people who might otherwise have been evicted or surrounded by stumps.

In the nineteenth century, European leaders took the map of Africa and divided it up into "possessions." Most of that mapping was done in European capitals, not in Africa, and the indigenous peoples of Africa had no input whatsoever. It wouldn't be until individual empires were carved up for timber, mining, oil exploration, and wildlife reserves that the mapping art would be applied in Africa itself, but even then mapping would remain a colonial function.

Although mapping has clearly been most accessible to people with economic, military, and political power, the availability of inexpensive Geographic Information Systems (GIS) technologies and the commitment of people like Peter Poole have made the technology available to the powerless, for whom it has become a source of pride, a means of conflict resolution, and a protector of traditional homelands from the spurious claims of outsiders. In the early 1970s, however, the new field of cartography that Poole is part of—tenure mapping—emerged to gain legal recognition of ancestral territory. It was first used by the Inuit and Cree in northern Canada, and led eventually to the creation of Nunavut, a vast, autonomous region of the country owned and governed completely by Canada's first natives.

Once established as an effective tool for the preservation of indigenous homelands, tenure mapping was expanded to include new data and factors. Poole calls the newer form "culture mapping" because it goes so far beyond classic cartographic coverage to include "anthropological, sociological, archaeological, genealogical, linguistic, botanical, and musicological" entries. While tenure maps often look quite like culture maps, their purposes differ. While the main use of cultural maps is the revitalization of cultural identity, tenure maps are primarily used to protect and restore indigenous lands and territories or, as it was for the Saramaka community with which Poole worked in Suriname, to enforce respect for treaties that guaranteed tenure.

Despite the appearance and periodic success of tenure and culture mapping, University of California Professor of Environmental Science Nancy Lee Peluso believes that cartography is "unlikely to ever become a 'science of the masses' simply because of the level of investment required by the kind of mapping with the potential to challenge the authority of other maps."[4] It is Peter Poole's intention to challenge that very authority, not only of maps created to define the boundaries of timber, mining, and petroleum concessions, but also national parks and other protected areas that intersect or overlap the territories of indigenous peoples.

What Poole and others like him are doing "is a truly revolutionary use of mapping," according to anthropologist Mac Chapin, who for years has worked on similar mapping projects along the Atlantic coast of Central America, and more recently in Papua New Guinea.[5]

Until quite recently, official maps of much of the eastern shorelines of Honduras, Nicaragua, and Panama, except for a few small ports, were blank, suggesting that no one lived there, that it was wild, open space. There are in fact about six million indigenous peoples encompassing forty-three distinct ethnic and linguistic groups along the eastern shores of Mesoamerica, among them the Mayan, Miskitu, Pech, Tawahka, Bribri, Teribe, Creole, Kuna, Rama, Sumu, and Garifuna, residing in hundreds of settlements up and down the region. They know the borders of their territories, one from another. But these boundaries were never mapped. So loggers, miners, cattle ranchers, and land speculators from western Mesoamerica simply helped themselves to land and untouched natural resources they believed was unowned—terra nullius—because the only maps available showed no villages, no residents, no boundaries, no owners.

In 1993 a Washington-based organization created by Chapin called Native Lands took it upon itself to map as much as possible of the entire region. Indigenous people up and down the coast were trained in basic surveying and GIS skills, and each community mapped, as best it could, the boundaries and key geographical, cultural, and sacred sites in its domain. The maps not only became a means of defending territory, fostering local planning, and conserving the last remaining forests in Central America, they also were an enormous source of community pride, and remain so today.

Beginning with meticulous handmade drawings of creeks and river systems, symbols were devised for houses, churches, schools, barnyards, wells, cemeteries, fences, animal habitats, hunting and fishing grounds, sources of natural medicines, and sacred sites (which some tribes like the Kuna had been mapping independently for years.) Sometimes sacred sites are deliberately omitted from a map, particularly those of archeological value. The most important features on most indigenous maps depict land usages and their effects on the biota. Maps that include arboreal types and densities, for example, alongside active logging and mining concessions give communities an immediate sense of the impact of extraction on the forest.

Locally produced maps are then combined or overlaid with aerial photographs, base maps, and satellite images keyed to measure forest taxa; canopy depth; and ground, air, and water temperatures. These features add a strong scientific component to community maps, providing highly detailed and accurate data that government officials and conservationists are far more likely to respect than a simple map hand-drawn by local citizens.

The important thing to keep in mind about mapping projects, Mac Chapin tells fellow cartographers whenever he has a chance, is that they are "community-based projects that just happen to have a technical component, [not] technical projects that are set in communities. . . . Villagers and the leaders must be at the helm of these projects, if they are going to produce maps they can call their own."

Although not as common as in Latin America and Southeast Asia, several displaced communities throughout the African continent have begun mapping their former territories. The San of South Africa and

Namibia, for example, have used maps to recover some of their former homeland in and outside Kgalagadi Transfrontier Park and Etosha National Park. In Kenya, the Ogiek have been mapping their former territories in the Mau Forest, as have the Sengwer to their east. The Baka and Bagyeli in Cameroon have obtained GIS technology and have begun a mapping project with hopes of regaining access to land they tended for thousands of years before it became the Lobeke and Boumba National Parks.

Box 14.2

An Object Lesson

One of the most remarkable, if not completely successful examples of empowerment achieved through participatory mapping occurred in Guyana in the mid-1990s. Most Guyanan Indians have no legal land title, despite residing in what is now known as the Guyana shield a thousand years or more before Guyana existed. Some possess tenuous deeds covering a fraction of their homeland. And those titles can be revoked unilaterally by a government that has repeatedly promised more "state land" to indigenous people, all the while granting mining, timber, gold, and diamond concessions on land already occupied by the Wapishan, Wai Wai, Akawaioi, and Macusi tribes.

By 1991, 35 percent of the country was under gold and diamond concessions. Guyanan Indians reacted by forming the Amerindian Peoples Association (APA), a coalition of over eighty communities representing the nine indigenous tribes of Guyana. Local APA outposts are linked through a radio system run from a headquarter in Georgetown, which keeps constant pressure on the government to honor the rights of tribal people and informs members in the field about government decisions that effect them.

In 1994, an APA delegation from the Upper Mazaruni region of Guyana met with the country's president to press for full title on their land. The president raised doubts that the Akawaioi and Arekuna people had really been living on the land they claimed, reliant as they said they were on its natural resources. When they returned to their communities the Indians decided the only way to convincingly demonstrate their right to and knowledge of their homeland was to map it. With the help of Peter Poole and others, the Indians produced maps of the Upper Mazaruni, which to this day are used to defend the traditional rights of the APA tribes.

There have been some unintended negative consequences of rural mapping—boundary conflicts between indigenous communities and the unwanted privatization of common land—and some communities have voted against having their territories mapped because mapping makes invisible settlements visible. Some isolated communities prefer to remain invisible. A tribe I visited in Papua New Guinea ceremoniously burns maps that show the whereabouts of their villages.

But the overall effect of mapping has been positive for indigenous peoples. Maps remain instruments of power, and are becoming even more so for the least powerful people on the planet, who often have no other document to protect their interests than a well-produced map of their territories. Brought to a negotiating table at the right moment, a well-produced map can swing a decision, change a park boundary, or even better, stop an eviction. Maps, therefore, are threatening not only to government authorities but to extractive corporations, colonial land titles, and, yes, at times to conservationists.

They are so threatening, in fact, that it is illegal to produce one without government permission in Indonesia or to buy a topographical map without a permit in India. And in Sarawak, Malaysia, an indigenous person can be arrested and imprisoned for simply possessing a map. States like Chad and Cameroon have proactively unmapped vast areas of their counties, most often at the behest of transnational logging companies wishing to draft their own maps, free of indigenous settlements they know very well are in the forests they seek to harvest. And there are maps of Gabon that show no one living in some of the thirteen national parks recently created there; anthropologists familiar with the areas in question are able to point to the sites of many permanent settlements of forest dwellers on the maps.

The clear strategy, which is no secret to anyone seeking control over a particular area of land, is to produce the first credible map of the area. To be "credible" to most governments a map must be created by professional cartographers using approved technologies. An accurate hand-drawn map of an indigenous homeland produced by natives of the area, even longtime natives, is less likely to impress a government eager for oil, timber, mineral, and gas royalties or a generous loan from the World Bank, than a map produced by ESRI for Exxon Mobil or even by Conservation International, which has its own in-house mapping team.

So the race is on. And if people like the Mayans and Garifuna in southern Belize are going to retain any of the rights they have held over the past millennium, and save their fragile hunting and fishing grounds from the loud and obtrusive seismic explosions of oil exploration companies measuring the reserves under the Sarstoon-Temash National Park, they need their own map of the area. So Peter Poole and Sujoy Chauduri returned to Belize in November 2005 to transfer the power of mapping to the people of the six villages bordering the new park, who hope to document centuries of occupancy and fight the imminent expropriation of their homelands and hunting grounds.

What must be understood about the future of land rights in the world is that most of the Earth's remaining natural resources and most of its high biodiversity ecosystems are currently occupied by people, most of whom are indigenous. So whether the ultimate quarry is gold, oil, timber, tin, or tigers, human inhabitants are going to be placed in conflict with other interests. And to them it doesn't really matter much whether the conflict is with an extractive transnational, the World Bank, a BINGO, or the Brazilian military; the end result is pretty much the same—loss of livelihood, food security, freedom, and culture. The Kayapo of Brazil offer an inspiring example to native people anywhere in the world who are struggling to preserve their land and culture.

15
Kayapo

Kayapo culture holds beauty that our world cannot afford to live without.
—Ava Goodale, Cornell University

Fly from any direction on a clear day over the Central Plateau of Brazil, from any altitude, and the most dominant geographical feature visible will be a vast, lush green "island" in the heart of the state of Para surrounded on all sides by heavily deforested, overcultivated, and mine-stained land. Intact forests are becoming an exception in the Amazon Basin, where forest loss is now measured in "Belgiums." The entire basin now hosts four Belgiums of deforestation. That's 47,120 square miles (30 million acres) of high-biodiversity rainforests, an area equal to the entire state of North Carolina, lost to mines, soy farms, and cattle ranches.

That 28.4-million-acre green island in Para is the *Area Indigena Kayapo* (AIK), one of the largest single expanses of closed-canopy rainforest in the world, a territory almost as large as Austria. Beneath the canopy there are about seven thousand Kayapo Indians living in nine sparsely distributed wheel-shaped villages ranging in population from one hundred to one thousand people.

The mysterious and fiercely independent Kayapo lead a rich ceremonial life, based on a complex cosmology that defines them as traditional stewards and guardians of the rainforest. In 1988, a new Brazilian constitution changed them from "orphans of the state," according to the old constitution, with the political status of children and the mentally ill, to full citizens with all rights to the land they had occupied for millennia. Then in 1992, the Kayapo became partners in one of the most intriguing of all collaborations between Western conservationists and indigenous peoples—an arrangement forged in crisis that would become the most frequently cited model for a new conservation paradigm whereby indigenous people not only control and manage a protected area, but also serve as the impetus for its establishment.

The Kayapo are rare survivors of a long era in South American history when the entire Amazon Basin was occupied by millions more people than it supports today, some in elaborate city-states with complex infrastructures and social systems, others in neotropical cultures intimately dependent for survival on their immediate ecosystems. Most of those millions of people died from diseases brought from Europe by Spanish settlers, but many like the Cintas Largas were killed in a protracted campaign of extermination that completely annihilated at least fifty-seven separate cultures that were once as large and prosperous as the Kayapo. Only the most isolated tribes and the most militant defenders of their homelands survived the death squads that roamed the Amazon Basin from the early to mid-twentieth century, slaughtering Indians at the behest of Euro-Brazilian rubber barons, timbermen, and transnational oil executives, often with direct complicity of Brazil's Service for the Protection of Indians (SPI).

The Kayapo have always been low-impact occupants of ecologically supersensitive landscapes along the upper reaches of the Iriri, Bacaia, and Fresco rivers, as well as along both banks of the much larger Xingu River. They hunt small game and fish and forage fruit and honey. They also cultivate gardens using biological pest control in rotational forest patches they call *Apêtês*. They domesticate insects for that purpose and for food. Each village has its own specialist in plants, animals, soils, crops, and medicines, and every ecosystem represents a different complex in interactions among flora, fauna, soil, and, of course, the Kayapo themselves.

Traditional lifeways and construction practices produce minimal disturbance of the rainforest, which is why it's almost impossible to spot many of their communities from the air, and why there remain many species of wild plants and animals, among them the tapir, white-lipped peccary, collared peccary, brown capuchin monkey, and the bearded saki, which have been driven to near extinction in the nearby Matto Grasso.

The Kayapo have also been ferocious defenders of their territory. Until the late 1980s, encroaching soy farmers, cattle ranchers, and gold miners were often killed. Even the Brazilian military was put on notice that they entered the AIK at their peril. Conservation biologists and anthropologists developed a healthy respect for these militantly independent people.

However, in the early 1980s a trickle of disturbing rumors flowed out of the region. A handful of Kayapo leaders, it was whispered, were negotiating secret contracts with logging and mining companies, granting them concessions to operate on Kayapo lands in return for a percentage of the proceeds. Some of the rumors had Kayapo leaders using the income from these contracts to maintain lavish personal life styles in Brazilian towns far from the reserve. There were stories of townhouses, servants, and bodyguards, cars, airplanes, and mistresses; all this while 99 percent of the Kayapo population remained in their villages, in relative poverty. One of the leaders, Paiaka (also spelled Payakan) was reportedly living this lifestyle in direct contradiction of his legendary worldwide reputation as an ecowarrior.

While the rumors of lavish lifestyles may have been exaggerated, as such rumors often are, what turned out to be true is that some Kayapo men were taking bribes and kickbacks from logging and mining companies and allowing them into the AIK. By 1988 the estimated annual take, just from mahogany, had reached an astounding $33 million. International conservationists feared that the Kayapo were becoming collaborators in the destruction of their own forests and rivers, all for the sake of short-term monetary gain. And anthropologists, who had marveled for years at the survival of this remarkable culture, bemoaned the decay of an egalitarian social structure under the weight of material luxuries from the modern world.

In January 1988, Paiaka and a fellow Kayapo leader named Kube'i were invited to a Miami conference on rainforest conservation. Of particular interest to the Amazon-based conservationists who organized the conference was the Altamira-Xingu River Complex, a $10.6 billion World Bank dam project that would inundate almost twenty million acres of land along the Xingu River, and create the world's largest manmade lake. About 85 percent of the land to be flooded belonged to indigenous peoples, including the Kayapo. Though they came to the conference largely unaware of the project, Paiaka and Kube'i left determined to stop it. Their next stop was Washington, DC, where American ethnoecologist Darrell Posey, who lived among the Kayapo for twenty-five years, arranged meetings at the U.S. Treasury Department, the Senate Appropriations Committee, and the World Bank.

The Kayapo leaders' visit made headlines in the United States and Brazil. Brazilian officials were not amused and, upon their return, the government detained the chiefs and Posey. When they were released, the Kayapo chiefs set out on a world tour of Europe, Japan, and North America.

In early 1989 the Kayapo organized a rally at Altamira, near the site of the proposed dam. About six hundred Kayapos joined by contingents from forty other indigenous tribes of Amazonia, as well as Sting, the world-famous British rock star who had embraced the Kayapo as his cause celebre, drew over four hundred representatives of the Brazilian and world news media, documentary filmmakers, photographers, and NGO executives. The Brazilian government and World Bank executives were reluctant to accept the Kayapo's invitation. Only when it became clear that Sting and other opinion leaders would attend did President Sarney agree to send a personal representative. Also present was the chief engineer of Electronorte, the Brazilian state power company that would own and manage the dam. He presented his case for the project to a polite but thoroughly unconvinced audience. Global pressure was too intense, even for the powerful World Bank, and the project was stopped, at least for the time being. It's not entirely dead and the Kayapo know it. They are determined that it will never happen.

Among the other conservationists Paiaka met in Washington was a Canadian ecologist named Barbara Zimmerman, who had recently been working with WWF. He invited her to A'ukre, his village in the AIK. When, to his surprise, she arrived a few days later, Paiaka asked her to help him create a preservation zone inside the AIK where hunting and fishing would be prohibited and where a biological research station could be established—an ecologist's dream. In 1992, with funds from the Suzuki Foundation and Conservation International (CI), Zimmerman and Paiaka mapped and established the Pinkaiti Reserve and Ecological Station.

To reverse the plunder of AIK resources, CI funded the construction of sixteen guard posts around the border of the area. They also provided motorboats, fuel, GPS systems, and radios for each post and training for ecoguards. The number of surveillance posts has since increased to twenty-two. All management decisions are made by the Kayapo at three-day meetings held at various places in the AIK.

The stopping of a $10 billion dam project is an undeniable triumph for the Kayapo, and the relationship subsequently formed with CI is a triumph for both. The Kayapo are CI's poster children. It's almost impossible to find a CI report, brochure, or newsletter that doesn't mention them. Larger-than-life photos of Kayapo chiefs and warriors adorn the CI information booth at conservation conferences, and Barbara Zimmerman travels far and wide with Kayapo delegates to share the story of their remarkable coalition, how together they have kept the extractive industries at bay, and created an island of ecological sanity in the barren waste of the Brazilian frontier.

What is often left out of the CI-Kayapo story, particularly as it is projected from CI's Washington headquarters, is perhaps the most vital ingredient of this collaborative success: the undying ferocity of the Kayapo. They will not be intimidated by private or public armies, nor will they come to a negotiating table as "stakeholders." They regard themselves as "rights holders"—the outright owners of land guaranteed to them by virtue of origin and backed up by Brazilian and international law. And thus they expect to be seated as equals at any meeting involving government or conservation NGOs. The truth is that CI and the Brazilian government really had no choice but to give the Kayapo what they wanted.

University of Maryland anthropologist Janet Chernela draws an interesting conclusion from watching Barbara Zimmerman work with the Kayapo. "Much lip service is given by environmental NGOs to 'listening' to the voices of indigenous peoples. Yet listening requires a degree of attentiveness and engagement in which most NGOs invest few resources. Zimmerman, the mediator between CI and the Kayapo, as a counter-example, has invested over ten years working among them. She speaks Kayapo and maintains 'fictive' familial relationships with a Kayapo extended family through whom she is related to others and by whom she is addressed as 'daughter,' 'sister,' or 'aunt.' In A'ukre many new-borns are given the names of Pinkaiti researchers."[1] As an example in the other direction, in 2007, CI invited Kayapo chief Megaron Txuccara-mae to join its board. He accepted and became the first-ever indigenous representative on a BINGO board.

As we have seen, CI has made some serious blunders with other indig-enous communities in the Amazon Basin, most notably the Ashaninka in the Vilcabamba region of Peru and the Wapishana people of Guyana. And as the next chapter attests, CI has blundered elsewhere in the world. But thanks to the patience and sensitivity of Barbara Zimmerman, and the earlier work of Darrell Posey, CI representatives appear to have struck a positive chord with the Kayapo, who certainly deserve as much credit for the collaboration's success as CI or the Brazilian government, both of whom claim it. And all partners know, from bitter experience, how short-lived any conservation initiative's success can be in a world that is force-feeding industrial development and modern values to ancient cultures. One anthropologist, Janis Alcorn, predicts that by 2050 even the most remote cultures will be drawn completely into the modern economy, resulting in a total loss of cultural diversity. It's a depressing scenario, and one that the Kayapo, of all people, are most likely to dis-prove, as they are one of the few native peoples that have learned to work with the West while maintaining the integrity and traditions of their ancient culture.

Inspired by the Kayapo's story, indigenous communities around the world are increasingly asserting their rights to territory and its natural resources. And they are observing that ferocity can be a valuable asset. When displayed at the right moment, it can protect a small animal from being killed and devoured by a much larger animal, or a small country by a larger country, or a tribe of natives by its host nation. This is the lesson that the Kayapo will share if you visit them in their homeland, quite different from the Brazilian government's story or the spin pro-jected from Conservation International headquarters in Washington.

In sharp contrast to the militant ferocity of the Kayapo is the submissive, gentle nature of South Pacific islanders. Had the people in and around

Milne Bay in Papua New Guinea known the Kayapo story or observed their leaders in negotiation with Conservation International and the Brazilian government, things might have turned out very differently than they did for the islanders in 2006.

CI's experience with the Kayapo in Brazil and with the islanders of Milne Bay, which I describe in the next chapter, indicates that the same organization is capable of practicing conservation well in one place and badly in another. While it may seem I am unfairly focusing on CI, I am not. This inconsistency is true of all BINGOs, and it illustrates the folly of placing so much wealth and influence in the hands of three or four extremely large international organizations.

16

Fiasco

If conservation strategies distress human populations, especially those who are less powerful, politically marginalized, and poor, little that conservationists argue on behalf of biodiversity makes sense.
—Arun Agrawal and Kent Redford, Wildlife Conservation Society

Late one morning in September 2002, the luxury megayacht *Reef Encounter* cruised slowly into the tiny Milne Bay harbor of Kwaraiwa. There were twenty-one passengers and a crew of nine aboard. Each passenger occupied a private suite with bath. After days of scuba diving in resplendent coral and visiting enchanting tribal villages, the passengers, all of them American, met on board with their peers for cocktails, a catered dinner, and a PowerPoint presentation about the state of the area's ecosystems.

Milne Bay, a large archipelago off the southeast coast of Papua New Guinea, they learned, possesses some of the most impressive and bountiful coral reefs in Melanesia. While biodiversity remains high in the region, the impending collapse of about 8 percent of the area's coral and early signs of "habitat degradation" have raised the concern of some local citizens and the international conservation establishment, a few key members of which were aboard the *Reef Encounter*. Like the first battle of Milne Bay, their mission was preemptive: to stop the archipelago's decline in biodiversity before it became irreversible.

Along the shoreline of Kwaraiwa islanders gathered to greet the passengers, among whom were rumored to be actor Harrison Ford and director/actor Clint Eastwood. But first to come ashore was someone the people of Kwaraiwa didn't recognize—Peter Seligmann, CEO and chairman of the board of Conservation International. CI, based in Washington, DC, is the largest international conservation organization in the world ($117 million revenue in 2006) and Seligmann, its cofounder, had come to explore the ecosystems of Milne Bay, and perhaps restore some lost biological diversity to its shoreline.

Clint Eastwood, as it turned out, was not on board, nor was Harrison Ford. Ford might have been, though, as he is a loyal member of the CI board, its "celebrity" poster boy, and a generous donor to the organization. Eastwood would have been along for the ride. World-renowned oceanographer Sylvia Earle was there by Seligmann's side, as was Stone Gossard, rhythm guitarist for Pearl Jam, who with his girlfriend was hoping to explore ways, through support of CI's work, to offset the 5,700-ton carbon footprint he was about to create with his band's world tour.

The major "targeted" donor aboard, and there is almost always at least one on such voyages, was H. Fisk Johnson, CEO of S. C. Johnson Co. of Racine, Wisconsin (maker of Pledge, Drano, Ziploc, Raid, Glade, and Windex). Fisk is number 215 on the Forbes 400 list of richest Americans, and known by Seligmann to be a generous supporter of conservation. Seligmann is a legendary fundraiser in conservation circles. He has to be. Aside from funding enormous conservation projects around the world, he must meet a payroll for over eight hundred people, pay rent in twenty-seven countries, subcontract with hundreds of other organizations, and maintain a fleet of boats, planes, and other vehicles around the world.

To court high-rollers like Fisk Johnson, Seligmann created an internal department called CI Sojourns. It was that office that leased the $25,000 a day *Reef Encounter* and made all the arrangements for its expedition into Milne Bay. The trip was a moderate success for CI Sojourns. Pearl Jam did not come through with a carbon offset, but Fisk Johnson is now on the CI board, an honor he shares with Harrison Ford; Queen Noor of Jordan; Lewis Coleman of DreamWorks; IAC Chairman Barry Diller, Wal-Mart CEO Ron Walton; former World Bank President James Wolfensohn; Gordon Moore, founder of Intel; and Lt General S. K. I. Khama, who ascended to the presidency of Botswana in April 2008.

There were also four guests of Gordon Moore's foundation, who flew in from San Francisco on a chartered jet and sojourned at the plush

($500/night) Karawari Lodge while they waited for Seligmann and the *Reef Encounter* to arrive from Cairns, Australia. The Gordon and Betty Moore Foundation was about midway through a ten-year, $280-million commitment to CI, the largest single grant to a conservation NGO in foundation history. So a substantial portion of CI's future support was aboard the *Reef Encounter* that day, an impressive array of wealth and generosity. However, the islanders had no interest in CI's large donors; it was the mere mention of Dirty Harry and Indiana Jones that drew them to the beach that day and gave Seligmann the rapt audience he sought for his clear and simple message.

"Five years ago we dove in these waters and saw tuna and other large fish everywhere," Seligmann told the citizens of Kwaraiwa. "This week we have been diving wherever we could on our way to your island and the big fish are gone. Our scientists tell us that the biological diversity, health, and productivity of your marine systems are eroding rapidly. We want to restore biodiversity to your reefs and fisheries and believe that with sound science, enough money, and your help we can do it in ten years." In a part of the world where fish is food and food security is a constant worry, this was a welcome message, particularly when spiced with promises of debt reduction, new school houses, water systems, clinics, and community centers, some of which would never be delivered.

"Peter told the island councilor to come up with a list of what the community needed, to be given in a week, and he would deliver in three months," recalls David Mitchell, a CI staffer familiar with the risks of trading modern goods, known in the region as "cargo," for conservation. "When I heard this I advised the councilor to put together a small list of mostly urgently required items and not to be greedy. I also told him that Peter was really looking for conservation and that this list should not be tied to it." To tide the village over while they awaited Seligmann's promised cargo, Sylvia Earle signed one of her magnificent marine atlases and donated it to the school.

For the next two weeks the *Reef Encounter* continued to cruise between dive spots, dropping anchor at islands with names like Nuakata, Iaban, and Pahilele and calling on the villages of Guga, Huhuna, Iapoa, Keia, and Porotona. The big fish message was repeated, ecosystem collapse forewarned, and more promises of cargo proffered. When the voyage ended on October 1, passengers were driven to Alotau, the capital of Milne Bay province, where they caught chartered flights to Australia and beyond. Five stayed on to dive in Indonesia's lush and remote Rajah Amphat islands, a targeted CI conservation site.

Imperial Conservation

While proof of conservation success is ultimately biological, conservation itself is a social and political process.
—Janis Alcorn, Worldwide Fund for Nature

What followed the voyage of the Reef Encounter was four years of what seems certain to become one of the most dazzling worldwide examples of botched conservation. By November of 2006, when I arrived in Milne Bay, the $6,443,022 provided to the Milne Bay Community-Based Coastal and Marine Conservation Project (MBCP) by the World Bank's Global Environmental Facility, the United Nations, the governments of Japan and Australia, and the Moore Foundation had been spent two years earlier than budgeted, on high-salaried scientists and expatriate staff, a fleet of sports utility vehicles, fast boats, plush offices, first-class air travel, complex marine monitoring technologies, and a 10 percent management fee paid to CI. Somewhere between $800,000 and $1.2 million (U.S.) was still unaccounted for and the UN didn't know whether CI had ever contributed the $1.65 million it committed to the project.

There was also very little in the way of conservation to show for this massive investment of public and private funds. Moreover, the Milne Bay governor wanted CI out of his province immediately and was calling for a forensic audit of what he called "the grossly misnomered" MBCP. "These large NGOs . . . believe they are above the law," Governor Tim Neville told Papua New Guinea's parliament the following week, "and can simply do and say as they please, without respecting the people of the countries where they work."

The day I left Alotau, Neville threatened to confiscate all of CI's equipment, evict its last two staffers from their offices, seal the doors, and ask the country's prime minister, Sir Michael Somare, to expel CI entirely from Papua New Guinea (PNG). Somare is the longest-serving national leader in Melanesia, and is highly regarded among his peers in the region. An expulsion from PNG might have spawned a domino effect of evictions of CI throughout the South Pacific. And CI has grand ambitions in the South Pacific.

So Seligmann fought back with all the PR muscle and diplomacy he could muster. A global reputation was at stake, and scores of supporting foundations, banks, national governments, development agencies, and corporations were watching. CI admits that the Milne Bay project faltered, but blames the outcome on "insurmountable political and institutional issues, that, despite our best efforts, we were unable to resolve." That institutional phrasing is code for "Tim Neville," who, when he realized that his people were to be "tricked into embracing conservation" made a frontal attack on CI in Papua New Guinea. Seligmann also denied any financial impropriety and invites the audit that Neville threatened. And he predicted that once the storm settled from their first foray into Milne Bay, phase two would commence and CI would be back in action.

Not one of the CI regional staffers I interviewed in PNG, some of them serving out their last days on the CI payroll, held that assessment. They, the United Nations, the Global Environmental Facility, and the Milne Bay project's three independent evaluators all placed blame for the entire fiasco squarely on the shoulders of Seligmann and CI's leadership, who they say ran the "community-based" project with minimal concern for or understanding of the culture, historical practices, or traditional ecological knowledge of the islanders.

Cargo Conservation

When you visit a community, walk in, don't fly.
—Papuan proverb

Until Christian missionaries flooded the South Pacific with bibles and rosaries in the late nineteenth century, cargo cults were common. These bizarre sects literally worshipped the goods that were unloaded from the shiny boats and airplanes that floated and flew mysteriously into their world as global trade expanded. Cargo was manna from heaven, and the white men who brought it were revered as demigods. When missionaries gave the islanders something more powerful to worship than cargo, most though not all of the cults disappeared. What has not completely dissolved in Melanesia, however, is cargo mentality, a residual desire for Western material goods that makes it easy for a superwealthy organization like CI to get attention by promising schools, clinics, boats, and community centers—cargo—in return for compliance to a conservation agenda designed in and imposed from Washington. And that, to the horror of CI's regional staff, is precisely what Peter Seligmann did as he and his boatload of demigods cruised through the islands of Milne Bay.

At Nuakata, Seligmann and his fellow travelers displayed their wealth by purchasing its small fleet of rustic but well-crafted outrigger canoes, which were loaded on the *Reef Encounter*'s upper deck and shipped back to America to adorn the homes and offices of CI and its donors. The $50 price per canoe was a steal by American standards, but a windfall to a people who have only recently seen the face of Ulysses S Grant. Although his own local staff repeatedly warned him that trading cargo for conservation would never work, Seligmann persisted.

Long before the *Reef Encounter* arrived, both the islanders and the national government of PNG were aware that the 210-island archipelago of Milne Bay was ecologically imperiled and in need of conservation. Local long-line fishermen and some from faraway ports were depleting vital fish stocks and had killed thousands of endangered sea turtles in the process. Aggressive harvesting of shark fins and bêche-de-mer (sea cucumbers) for the booming, delicacy-obsessed Chinese culinary market was threatening those species, while rotational agriculture and a growing human population stressed shoreline ecosystems.

Seligmann had heard or read all this from preliminary research conducted by CI social and biological scientists for two years before he set sail. But like so many leaders of global, science-based conservation, he tended to pay more attention to ecological findings than the advice that came from sociologists and others who had studied and knew the traditions and cultures of Melanesian islanders—people like anthropologist Jeff Kinch, who repeatedly warned Seligmann and others at CI headquarters in Washington about the hazards of cargo conservation. In short, Kinch knew, and told them frequently, it would backfire. "Peter [Seligmann] could not have picked a worse place to make promises," he told Bruce Beehler, CI's Washington-based overseer of Melanesia. "These promises will now spread throughout the other islands in the area and people will have their hands out, opening the way for 'conservation blackmail.'"

Kinch is an Australian. He is married to a Papuan woman and has three children. He has lived in PNG and plied the waters of Milne Bay for ten years and knows many of its community leaders by their first names. For the two years prior to the Milne Bay project's start-up, he researched and coauthored two studies for CI and sent voluminous reports to Port Moresby (PNG's capital) and Washington on the ecological and social conditions of the islands in Milne Bay. Many, both in and outside CI, believed Kinch would have made an ideal chief technical advisor (CTA), the project's top management position in the field, which would be filled as soon as the funds arrived from the GEF and other funders.

The main problem with cargo conservation, Kinch warned in his communications, is that when practiced, the local incentive to conserve natural resources shifts from food security to cargo. So when promised goods are not delivered, as was the case in many parts of Milne Bay, the conservation motive disappears, contractual "use agreements" are torn up, no-catch *tabus* are lifted, and embittered islanders return to overfishing sharks and beche-de-mer for export to China. And some of their leaders begin putting a hand out for more cargo, this time from commercial fishing companies and other exploiters of the reef.

While making my way to PNG I visited scores of coastal villages from Fiji through Vanuatu to the Solomon Islands. In many I was shown new community centers built with international conservation NGO money as an incentive to conserve. As I toured the new facilities, local conservationists were telling me, sotto voce, that the same village was violating the very *tabu* it had exchanged for cargo. Cargo conservation was clearly failing, even when the cargo was delivered. Where conservation worked was in villages that had clear title to their land and the power to protect the offshore waters that provided their protein. This was a message that was lost on the man CI hired to run the Milne Bay project instead of Jeff Kinch.

When project funding arrived for the project in January 2004, CI imported another Australian to be CTA. Peter McKay could not be more different in style or philosophy than Jeff Kinch. McKay had an impressive resume of experience managing large projects. He was a high-powered, systems oriented micromanager who had run a large UNDP project in the Red Sea but knew next to nothing about Milne Bay islanders and the complex ownership systems or local conservation practices they had developed over the centuries, things Kinch already knew.

In the weeks before the *Reef Encounter* dropped anchor at Kwaraiwa, carefully selected "Village Engagement Teams" (VETs) comprised mostly of PNG nationals, had toured the islands to inquire into the state of their fisheries, appraise inhabitants of the impending CI project, and begin resource and social mapping in each village. The aim was to ascertain resource use and access rights and make local communities comfortable with the project. The VETS were to be the heart of a unique conservation initiative that emphasized the words "Community Based" in its title. Their message was simple and consistent: "We are not a company, we are not a bank, we are not here to give you things, we are here to teach each other, to help each other." They were promoting self-reliance and conservation to local communities.

"But McKay did not want to hear 'local,'" recalls Mikkel Christensen, the community development specialist who worked on the project. "In fact, in one meeting he declared that the term *Locally Managed Marine Area* (LMMA), the prominent model of island conservation throughout the South Pacific would be replaced with *Marine Protected Area* (MPA). LMMAs, McKay said, lacked institutional framework, scientific rigor, and were difficult to regulate. And the boundaries for large MPAs, which would envelop as many as six or more previous LMMAs, McKay insisted, would be set by him, in consultation with CI headquarters in Washington.

This order flew in the face of all previous planning for the Milne Bay project, which recommended "not only that local communities be fully involved, but also that the decision making authority remain with local communities." That sentence was written by Jeff Kinch, who resigned in

2003 shortly before Peter McKay came on board. It would not have been well received by McKay. In fact, some say he would have fired Kinch just for saying it.

"Peter McKay was a bully," recalls CI's PNG director Guy Kula, a PNG citizen who says he tried but failed to rein him in. "It's amazing how much damage one man can do." But CI leadership in Washington kept McKay on and persisted in trading promises of cargo for conservation agreements. And things grew worse in Milne Bay as cargo enticement evolved into a form of conservation blackmail, as predicted by Kinch. In the end, Kula says, "money killed conservation."

In the months that followed, the "grossly misnomered" Milne Bay *Community Based* Marine Conservation Project (emphasis added) descended into complete disarray. Morale collapsed, money was squandered on useless and unnecessary overhead charges, and funders began to have second thoughts about CI's choice of a project manager. CI, which had created so many promising and generous jobs for so many scientists and local leaders, some of whom told me it was the best job they ever had, was becoming the bête noir of Milne Bay, but worse by far, of the conservation-funding community. The MacArthur Foundation, one of the largest marine conservation grantmakers in the world, announced that it was cutting CI off everywhere in the South Pacific.

In their assessment of the project, completed in July 2006, independent evaluators Peter Johnston, John Duguman, and Graham Baines described a gradual decline of staff morale and deep community frustration in the Milne Bay area caused by a combination of overbearing control, bad communications, slipshod management, lack of transparency, project debts, cultural insensitivity, and a long string of broken promises. In their two-month review the three evaluators interviewed 109 project staffers, village and civic leaders, government officials, and church leaders. The most common response from local citizens was characterized as: "Big cars, fancy office, lots of talk but nothing to show for it." One CI staffer predicted that "the only thing that will save this project is the forgiving nature of the Milne Bay people."

"Project management by CI has been extremely poor, indeed negligent" reads the evaluation, "with poor reporting, excessive charges for overhead expenses, a poor relationship with provincial government officials and little or no effective oversight or control of project activities. . . . There are records from early 2005 expressing serious concerns. . . . Yet CI Washington made no effort to investigate and resolve the issues. Had CI intervened at that time the project could have delivered good results." The authors of that harsh judgment told funders and local Milne Bayans that in comprising their final report they had restrained their negative opinions of CI.

To be fair, the Milne Bay project was not a total failure. CI did manage to get a restraining order against a Nuakata-based bêche de mer harvester, and the biodiversity assessment the regional staff produced between 1997 and 2002 is still of use. While CI's behavior painted an unfortunate and unproductive picture of international conservation, conservation remains part of the daily conversation in Papua New Guinea's island communities, and several grass-root efforts have emerged since CI left the area.

And to be fair to Peter Seligmann, one must keep in mind the true nature of his job. Supporting huge staffs and infrastructure demands that the CEOs of enormous, quasicorporate entities like Conservation International keep fundraising high on their agenda—goal number one, in fact. When you have to raise $100 million a year just to keep your organization afloat there isn't time to think about much else.

Box 16.1

Bioprospecting

Recent developments in biotechnology, world trade rules, and intellectual property regimes that permit the legal enclosure of genetic material have prompted a worldwide interest in genetic and biochemical resources. Of particular interest are those found in the high-biodiversity areas of the gene-rich Southern Hemisphere, many occupied by people who for centuries have extracted their pharmacopoeia from those very resources. Having carefully studied the ancient science of traditional medicine, phytochemists from Northern pharmaceutical and agriculture companies now have a better sense of where to prospect for the raw materials and gene sequences that will lead to the creation of new drugs and food crops.

While there were only vague rumors of bioprospecting being carried out during Conservation International's rapid biological assessment of the Milne Bay region, all of them denied, CI makes no secret of its enthusiasm for the practice and what it considers bioprospecting's positive conservation effect. All of the BINGOs broker bioprospecting deals. They regard them as a unique way to bring some economic benefit to conservation, both for indigenous peoples and themselves.

Although bioprospecting is high on the list of indigenous complaints about the economic forces that are exploiting their resources, conservationists claim to have found a way to partner with pharmaceutical companies so that everyone, including the rightful owners of, say, an herbal remedy, benefits from the process of turning traditional genetic knowledge into profitable world-market drugs and agricultural products.

No matter what they say, most indigenous communities I visited that had participated in a "benefit sharing" bioprospecting agreement, and seen the overall economics of the deal, considered it, in retrospect, a beads-and-trinkets transaction. The true beneficiaries of most conservation-based bioprospecting appear to be the private prospectors, the government of the source country, and the conservation organization that brokered the deal.

Conservation International, which has a sizeable office in Washington, DC, with the exclusive mission of "ecologically guided bioprospecting" has partnered with many firms, among them the U.S.-based International Cooperative Biodiversity Group (ICBG), Monsanto, Novartis, Bristol Myers Squibb, and Dow AgroSciences.

CI also has a comprehensive bioprospecting partnership with a California-based genomic sequencing firm called Hyseq, in which CI actually prescreens floral and faunal samples, for which Hyseq pays CI an annual fee.

In most cases, however, a BINGO's role is simply to garner permission to prospect from the source country, win the trust of indigenous communities and healers, and then broker the so-called benefit-sharing agreement. Every bioprospecting contract is different, but in most the host country receives a flat fee up front. The indigenous communities I found that had been party to such agreements had been offered 2 to 4 percent of any royalties, which many of them did not expect to see for years because royalties generally are based on revenues from a finished product. In every case I found the prospecting company had applied for and won a patent on both the genetic material and the final product. ICBG holds patents on more than fifty active compounds isolated from Suriname alone, many with a major assist from CI.

As the global commons has been subjected to a battle over genetic material, gene-rich developing countries have become aware of the enormous economic imbalance created by aggressive bioprospecting and unfair trade treaties. Many have taken action to protect their interests. Over a dozen countries have passed laws restricting access to their genetic resources, with similar legislation pending in many more. And indigenous organizations the world over have issued charters, declarations, and statements supporting the intellectual property rights of a genetic resources first-discoverer and "the equitable sharing of the benefits resulting from the use of genetic resources."*

The only argument supporting bioprospecting that seems to make sense, from a conservation standpoint, is that its success in creating new food crops and medicines supports the value of preserving biological diversity. Of course, the same thing can be said for cultural diversity, for it is aboriginal cultures, with their longstanding dependence on ambient vegetation, that first discovered the healing powers of medicinal plants like hoodia, yew bark, and rosy periwinkle, as well as the extraordinary nutritional value of wild grains like amaranth, kamut, spelt, and quinoa.

---

* Third goal of the Convention on Biological Diversity.

By most accounts, the Milne Bay area's marine health is pretty much as it was before 2002. The large pelagics are back. If they left at all it was only for a while, perhaps drawn eastward by El Niño, the warm-water current that appears every three to seven years in the eastern Pacific and throws the whole oceanic food chain into temporary disarray. When I first interviewed Seligmann I asked if he knew that 2002 was an El Niño year. He refused to answer the question. He also refused to say whether CI would ever account for the $800,000 to $1.2 million that UNDP says is still unaccounted for. Later, through his media director, he asserted that CI had every intention of returning to Milne Bay to complete its mission there. Then, shortly before we went to press, I received replies to my questions in writing. Seligmann admitted he had known it was an El Niño year and claimed that "an independent audit of the project found no financial irregularities." He did not say who had performed or paid for the audit, or provide any documentation of its existence.

If Milne Bay's new governor, John Luc Critten, opens his arms to CI, its staff will still be returning to a very different and wary community. As a somewhat embittered Modi Pontio, community engagement coordinator for the project told me the day before I left, "We don't need scientists who we don't know coming back in here to tell us how to manage our ecosystems."

"We were used and it will be hard to face some of the people we worked with in the future," remarked local Program Manager Bena Seta the same day.

"It's going to be difficult to achieve conservation in Milne Bay in light of all the broken promises," said Geoff Callister, an anthropologist on the project, who when I spoke with him last November was still suing CI for six months' back pay. "WWF is good here and so is TNC, but they and all foreign conservationists have been tarred by the CI brush. It's hard for any of us who worked on the project to find work here." Fortunately for the international conservation establishment, The Nature Conservancy (TNC) and World Fund for Nature (WWF) both maintain respectable footholds in Papua New Guinea, staffed largely by Papua New Guineans who respect and understand the hundreds of complex cultures that comprise their country.

While failures of this magnitude are rare in transnational conservation, the Milne Bay fiasco is not a unique episode, nor is CI the lone culprit in the insensitive treatment of local peoples. Nor do they always fail, as earlier chapters attest. TNC, WWF, the African Wildlife Foundation, and the Wildlife Conservation Society all share CI's worldwide reputation for imperious behavior and also have failures on their project lists. But the Milne Bay story best illustrates the folly of cargo conservation and the arrogance so often projected by extremely well-endowed Northern environmental NGOs in the global South.

What is ironic about this project, and unjust in a way, is that a people who have been living sustainably in a relatively healthy environment for thousands of years were in effect being blamed for its recent decline in ecological health by people and organizations whose support comes directly from the economic surplus of the civilization that is doing the real, long-term damage to coral reefs and oceanic marine ecosystems, in fact to the entire planet international conservation seeks to protect. One lesson to be learned from the Milne Bay fiasco is that the people who will help you most in conservation are those who depend on the environment for their livelihood. Another lesson from an old Papuan aphorism: "When you visit a community, walk in, don't fly."

A relatively new institution has appeared in transnational conservation—the national park managing contractor. The African Parks Foundation, a public-private hybrid based in the Netherlands, is one of the new arrivals in this field. If APF's behavior in Ethiopia is a fair indication of its principles, the tribal people of Africa may be in for another rude awakening.

17

Mursi

We bring people and parks together—pragmatically and effectively.
—African Parks Foundation Web site

Parks must become virtual companies.
—Paul van Vlissingen, founder, African Parks Foundation

"The Omo Valley is virtually free of human habitation but is rich in paleo-anthropological remains," reads the Web site for Omo National Park in Southwestern Ethiopia. Tell that to the eight thousand thriving Mursi people in the valley, whose ancestral artifacts date them as its first human residents, or the twenty-eight thousand Suri, Nyangatom, Dizi, Kwegu, Bodi, and Me'en. The Omo Valley is, in fact, teeming with human life . . . and wildlife—eland, oryx, zebra, hartebeest, buffalo, giraffe, elephant, waterbuck, kudu, lion, leopard, cheetah, and 306 species of birds. However, change is in the wind. Some of the humans living in the valley may soon be replaced by rhinos imported from a breeding farm in South Africa, all to enhance the tourist value of a privately managed national park, which until recently was to be privately managed by a Dutch foundation.

The Mursi, one of the oldest tribes in Africa, are pastoralists who combine nomadic cattle herding with flood retreat cultivation. They are also proficient botanists, able to identify and name every plant in their habitat. And they love public debate.

The Mursi do kill some wildlife, buffalo mostly, but only for their own use and mostly in times of severe hunger. Mursi women make the buffalo hides into clothing. What is left from that enterprise is bartered for medicine, grain, and vegetables. And they will kill hyenas that have attacked their cattle. A semi-arid environment and uncertain rainfall force most members of the population to remain mobile, although they generally migrate fairly short distances within the valley and stay as long as possible at water sources and cultivation sites. The prize land for grass and water is what is now Omo National Park.

There is a "Tragedy of the Commons" myth that has been held by foreign conservationists in East Africa for over a century. It says that pastoralists are bad land managers, don't understand sustainable range management, and are destroying the habitat of wildlife. It is this belief that has motivated the creation of most East African parks and protected areas. In truth, tribes like the Mursi, Suri, and Maasai are among the best cattlemen in the world, having kept their ranges productive and biologically diverse for centuries, even as their populations and herds grew in size. It has been misguided grazing regulations and wildlife conservation projects that have affected the fertility of pastoral ranges, not the ancient herdsmen. Northern conservationists seem to forget that when they first "discovered" the Omo Valley in the early nineteenth century, the Mursi were already there, living sustainably alongside abundant wildlife. In fact, lip plates of the kind still worn by Mursi women have been found along the Omo River and carbon dated to five thousand years ago.

The Omo National Park was established in 1966 on the recommendation of Julian Huxley, who led a UNESCO mission there three years earlier. At that time the Mursi were allowed to stay. The first recommendation to evict them from their most productive land can be found in two 1978 reports, one prepared by a Japanese park planning team, the other by two European scientists working for the Ethiopian Wildlife Conservation Department. The authors' main concern is protecting the wildlife of greatest interest to tourists in "the country's last unspoiled wilderness," an area that has "retained its primeval character from ages past."[1] They recommended merging the Omo National Park with the nearby Mago National Park, which were both at the time mere paper parks. "The Omo and the Mago will lose their value as national parks if vested human interests are permitted to exist between them," the European report read. The Mursi, who moved between both the parks, were regarded as threats to conservation that should be removed and resettled. The authors estimated that the parks merger would displace about seventeen hundred people. The parks were not merged, but foreign preservationist sentiments did not disappear.

In 1993 a second European-sponsored report was issued on the Mago-Omo situation, this time for the Southern Ethiopia Wildlife Conservation Project, which, after the study was completed, was renamed the Southern National Parks Rehabilitation Project (SNPRP). After a week of helicopter flyovers, a wildlife biologist, a civil engineer, and an economist concluded that "it is almost certainly in the socio-cultural area that the greatest long term threats to project sustainability lie." The authors went on to recommend an "increase [in] the tangible economic benefits that rural people get from land used for wildlife conservation [by] introducing revenue sharing with rural communities [and] giving priority to local people in opportunities for employment."

The subtext of this recommendation, of course, was to move the indigenous agriculturists and cattle herders as rapidly as possible into the money economy, using financial "goodwill" to keep them out of the loop in park and resource management. This is a common conservation-as-development solution posited by Northern conservationists working for international NGOs, and the consequences have almost always been devastating to traditional communities and cultures that lack the knowledge or skills to survive in a market-based society, or to rise above the bottom rung of a local labor market. In fact, many of the "squatters" and "poachers" that conservation authorities complain about, and seek to control, are evicted former residents of the park or protected area in question.

David Turton, a British anthropologist with over thirty-five years of experience working among the Mursi, who formerly directed the Center for Refugee Studies at Oxford, was alarmed by the SNPRP scheme. "The willingness this shows to spend huge amounts of money on such a complex and far reaching environmental project . . . without taking virtually any notice of human ecology, environmental knowledge capacities or the rights of the local population is staggering." Turton is also livid about the European study's authors' claim of "serious environmental degradation" as a consequence of people "who have settled in the park"—an assumption made without a shed of evidence of degradation that can be linked to the people who "settled" the Omo Valley so long ago that their record is studied by archeologists.

That sort of unsubstantiated, Africa-in-crisis alarmism so frequently heard from conservation NGOs has more to do with "getting donors to release funds," Turton reminds us, "than with the actual situation in the area." But not long after he made that observation, Turton shifted his attention to a new European organization interested in the Omo Valley.

In November 2005, African Parks Foundation (APF), a Netherlands-based organization—founded by Dutch retailing and oil drilling billionaire Paul Fentener van Vlissingen and generously supported by Walmart Chairman Rob Walton, USAID, and Conservation International—signed a twenty-five-year contract with the Ethiopian government to lease and manage the recently gazetted Omo National Park. APF has been managing another Ethiopian national park, Nech Sar, since February 2005, and has similar contracts in South Africa, Sudan, Malawi, Zambia, and the Republic of Congo. APF's stated goal is to privatize as many national parks in Africa as possible.

The 1500-square-mile Omo Park was established in 1966, but like so many others around the world, it remained a "paper park" until APF took an interest in managing it and the ecotourism industry saw an enticing opportunity. At that point the Ethiopian government planned to have it gazetted. At a demarcation ceremony held in March 2005, a few randomly selected, illiterate Mursi elders were asked to place their thumbprints on a document describing the park boundaries and policies. Government officials later told them that by signing the document they had given "prior consent" to be moved out of the park. Their "signatures" had in effect made them illegal squatters on their own land.

For the Mursi to see what was in store for them, they needed to look no further than the nearby Nech Sar National Park. When the Nech Sar agreement was signed, in February 2004, it was understood by APF that the Kore peasant farmers and Guji-Oromo cattle herders living in and utilizing the park would be resettled before APF took over its management. APF wanted nothing to do with the eviction per se; they just didn't want any natives there when they took over management of the park. And so, as so often happens during the creation of new parks, a conservation organization looked the other way while police and soldiers arrested and trucked indigenous people to resettlement camps outside the park.

In February 2004, around a thousand Kore families were resettled to an area about eight miles south of Nech Sar National Park. Resettling the Guji-Oromo was more challenging. They refused to move. So on November 25, 2004, police and park authorities torched 463 Guji houses situated in the park.

According to a report posted on the website of Refugees International in April 2005:

The Guji-Oromo were previously expelled by the government of Mengistu Haile Mariam in the 1980s but came back and reestablished themselves in five villages. Facing expulsion again they filed six appeals to the Federal and Regional governments to allow them to remain in the park. However, the regional government then ordered the Guji-Oromo to visit and choose one of two resettlement sites.

It was during the visit of their leaders to the second site when their houses were burned without warning. Some of the houses were occupied at the time; others were temporarily abandoned as the Guji-Oromo typically migrate with their herds and return to their houses during the rainy season. No compensation has been paid for the property destroyed during the house burning.

More recent reports say that around five thousand Guji have been allowed back into two crowded villages in a corner of the park, but their access to grazing land in the park has been severely restricted.

In an August 2005 interview in *New Scientist* magazine, Paul van Vlissingen said this about the Nech Sar incident: "We said [to the government] that we could work with people in the park, as we do in Zambia, but they said no. We didn't want to be involved in the resettlement, so I put a clause in the contract that said we wouldn't take over the park until the resettlement was completed."

Furthermore, van Vlissingen said, APF "has never been and will never be involved in questions of a political nature, such as the resettlement of people . . . resettlement is not a matter for our organization as governments are sovereign in these matters in every country." That, in so many words, is the most common excuse used by international conservation NGOs for not stepping in to stop evictions of indigenous peoples from protected areas. And when it's a fait accompli the sound bite is: "Don't blame us, it's the government."

To his credit, van Vlissingen did sit down with Mursi and Nyangatom elders in September 2005. The elders' main concern was their loss of access to agricultural and grazing land within the Omo National Park. In response, van Vlissingen said that APF was powerless on that issue: "We are not the government."

The Mursi remained doubtful. Here is the recollection of an elder who attended the meeting: "Mr. Paul was telling us everything and told us he would not move any Mursi, but he would let the Mursi live in the park, but doesn't want people to kill animals. He said this but maybe later he will trick us. I think he is a very nice man, very friendly, but we see only the outside not the inside. He said not to worry since 'no one will move you.' He said 'I want your help and we will help each other.' He said he doesn't know about government plans. He said he wants to train local people to be scouts. He said APF are not allowed to move people, but I don't believe it. I read about the Guji and Kore people, and he said the government did that, and not APF, but now he took over that place."

After the meeting van Vlissingen reiterated APF's position in a letter to Mursi elders, in which he said: "As we manage State Assets we can not be seen by any government as interfering." Despite endless rhetoric about "co-management" and "collaboration," van Vlissingen and APF in fact disempowered those it wished to collaborate with by denying them legal rights to their land or a realistic chance of engaging on equal terms in discussions about future management of the park. Once again, indigenous people were invited to negotiate over the use and occupancy of land they have tilled and grazed for thousands of years as minor stakeholders rather than equal-rights holders.

According to Ulikoro, a Mursi leader, government officials told his people last March that they should "go to live in the Maganto area, plus their cattle too—the government say that four wells in the Elma River will supply all the water needed."

If this happens, the Mursi will be confined to one small part of their present territory that lies outside the park boundaries. This would severely disrupt their lives, depriving them of their most fertile agricultural land along the banks of the Omo River. They would also lose their main areas of dry-season grazing, which, as David Turton puts it, "would render the economy of the Mursi totally unviable."[2] Their worst fear is becoming permanently dependent on food aid.

At issue here is ILO Convention 169 on Indigenous and Tribal Peoples, article 14 of which states: "The rights of ownership and possession of the peoples concerned over the lands which they traditionally occupy shall be recognized. In addition, measures shall be taken in appropriate cases to safeguard the right of the peoples concerned to use lands not exclusively occupied by them, but to which they have traditionally had access for their subsistence and traditional activities. Particular attention shall be paid to the situation of nomadic peoples and shifting cultivators in this respect." Ethiopia has refused to ratify this convention, but the Netherlands, where van Vlissingen was a citizen, before he died in 2006, and whereAPF is a registered foundation, has done so.

Due to international outrage over treatment of the Guji-Oromo, the Mursi may not be tossed into trucks and shipped out of Omo National Park, watching their homes burn to the ground. But if history repeats itself they are almost certain to be denied access to vital subsistence resources without compensation. This is what indigenous people have come to call "soft eviction," a limiting of local resource use that is tantamount to displacement. In fact, the World Bank, USAID, and other multilateral donors now equate them, as official resettlement policy, because they know from direct experience that both forms of eviction inevitably force adults into intractable poverty, alcoholism, and prostitution, leaving their children with malnutrition, death, and disease.

After the contract had been signed between APF and the Ethiopian government, David Turton intervened to ask whether it would be possible for an addendum to be signed, guaranteeing the land rights of local people. The response, he says, was threefold. "First, I was told, this would not be *possible*, because the government would not agree. Second, it would not be *worth it* because, even if such a clause were added, the government would not consider itself bound by it. And third, it would not be *necessary* because the rights of 'pastoralists' to their land are already guaranteed by the Ethiopian constitution (Article 40, subsection 5). There is no need to point out the contradictions here. As for the Ethiopian constitution, most informed observers of the Ethiopian political scene would surely acknowledge that the government still has a long way to go to bring political practice into line with constitutional theory" (emphasis in original).

Not only did APF fail to sign any agreements protecting the land rights of the Mursi, but it also appears to have no intention of doing so in the future. Furthermore, the foundation only recently made available to local people the contracts it has signed with the federal and regional governments. Nor were the Mursi given copies of the documents their leaders had signed with their thumbprints. APF has thereby denied local people the right to seek and obtain independent legal advice about two contracts that will have enormous consequences for their own and their children's futures, one of which was agreed to and signed without their knowledge or consent, the other without their knowledge of what it said. When Turton asked a national park official why those who signed these papers were not given copies of them, he was told: "because they would not have been able to read them." "This," according to Turton, "is the very reason why they *should* have been given copies, so that they could get independent legal advice about the implications of what they had been asked to sign" (emphasis in original).

According to Turton, APF may have claimed to have no intention of displacing people from their land, but "unless it is prepared to enter into legally binding agreements to back up its claims, it cannot expect them to be taken seriously. One can safely assume that those who are nevertheless prepared to take its words at face value would not be so willing to do so if their own property, their own livelihoods and their own children's futures were at stake."

APF representatives later agreed that they would not interfere with agriculture on the west bank of the Omo River, but would not allow any new riverbank areas to be cleared. That ban indicates a gross misunderstanding of flood retreat agriculture by which, after an extensive flood, new land that has not been used for years is cleared and cultivated. The ban also illuminates the almost unconscious imperious tendencies of northern conservationists. Who is APF, a Netherlands-based foundation, to be telling Ethiopian citizens where to cultivate their food? The Mursi have practiced flood retreat cultivation on the west bank of the Omo for five thousand years. While APF did permit cattle grazing in the park, it completely outlawed hunting, and refused to offer food assistance during drought periods when the Mursi are traditonally forced to resort to hunting.

APF also claimed that at a meeting in September 2006 the Mursi gave the foundation all of the land west of the Omo River. The Mursi say that the translation of the meeting's minutes were deliberately distorted by APF, to whom they only "gave" a small area around park headquaters. APF again refused to provide the previously mentioned documents the Mursi were coerced to sign with thumbprints in 2005.

However, APF did promise to create a "Community Fund," with a $5,000 annual contribution to go toward whatever the Mursi community needs—schools, clinics, and so on. Five thousand dollars divided by the total Mursi population of eight thousand souls comes to eighty-five cents per capita per year. The attached agreement also stipulated that a sum would be subtracted from the annual grant for every animal killed by the Mursi—$300 for a Zebra, much more for species of greater tourist vaue.

One of the problems facing Omo Park management and the tourist industry it seeks to encourage is a shortage of charismatic wildlife. With that in mind, funds have been sought to buy some baby rhinosaurus from Hluhluwe Umfolozi Park in South Africa. Hluhluwe has an active white and black rhino-breeding program. Whites go for 50,000 Rand ($7,000) and blacks for about triple that price.

As this book attests, the Mursi's fate is not unique. "Once the idea of pristine nature separate from people is accepted," according to conservation historian William Adams, "it is a small step to the idea that it needs to be protected from ordinary human activity, especially from direct use of land, water, plants or animals. This idea goes deep within the dominant modern model of conservation. It has made the extinction of occupancy rights and eviction or resettlement a common experience across the world, in both industrialized and developing countries."[3]

What is also not unique about the situation in Ethiopia is the privatization of sovereignty. That is occurring around the world, though particularly in Africa where quasi-private institutions like APF, profit-seeking investors, and ecotourism entrepreneurs are being handed tacit power over indigenous communities like the Mursi by state governments that have, by international agreement, been assumed to be the ultimate guarantors of human rights.

On December 7, 2007, APF announced it was pulling out of Ethiopia and terminating its five-year conract to manage both Nech Sar and Omo National Parks. The APF press release reads in part:

African Parks Network has decided to terminate its management activities in Nech Sar National Park and Omo National Park in Southern Ethiopia. Both parks face considerable challenges arising from the unsustainable use by one or more ethnic groups, often in competition and conflict with each other. In order for a sustainable solution to be achieved, formal agreements on the limits of resource utilization need to be discussed and agreed with the various ethnic groups, paving the way for a land use plan recognized and respected by all stakeholders. African Parks attempted to achieve such a situation in Nech Sar but the outcome was not sanctioned by the authorities. In the case of Omo the situation is more complicated and a similar result is inevitable. Compromises will be necessary and therefore such a process needs to be fully sanctioned by Government and supported by human rights organizations to ensure that the ethnic groups are properly consulted and represented. Such a process will pave the way for the formal gazetting of the protected areas and will form the foundation of a sustainable management solution for the benefit of both people and nature. Failure of the process will almost certainly result in the permanent loss of the parks and continued conflict amongst ethnic groups.

It would be unfair to speculate on the subtext of that statement, although given the short history of the relationship and the abruptness of APF's termination, there almost certainly is one. What is fair to point out, however, is some of the wording in the release, particularly the phrase "unsustainable use," coming, as it does, from a foundation whose wealth was built on the surplus of box-store retailing and oil exploration. How sustainable is that? And the repeated use of the term *ethnic groups* can only be seen as words carefully chosen to avoid granting indigeneity and long-term land tenure to the Mursi, Nyangatom, and other ancient tribes in the region.

Some version or another of what the Mursi experienced in Ethiopia has been repeated a thousand times or more in as many protected areas around the world. What is unusual about their story, however, is that with APF out of the picture they might actually win their battle to stay in the Omo National Park. And that will occur for a host of reasons, not the least of which is the realization among Euro-American conservation leaders that the exlcusionary, tourism-driven, recreational "Yosemite" model of conservation is failing to protect biological diversity. But when tribute for a positive outcome is paid, it should be largely to the Mursis themselves, who unlike many of their colleagues on other continents simply refused to be moved without an open public debate.

From the vast global movement for indigenous rights has arisen a new conservation paradigm. Tribal people on every occupied continent have come to realize that the best way to avoid displacement from new protected areas is to form their own. Imagine if Tenaya, rather than John Muir, had lobbied Theodore Roosevelt to turn his homeland into a national park. The chief might not have called it a park, preferring Indigenous Reserve or Community Conservation Area, two of several terms in modern use to describe protected areas that are mapped, managed, and in a growing number of places in the world, actually owned by indigenous peoples.

18
First Stewards

We were not given land, we gave you land.
—Byron Mallot, Tlingit elder

The world's traditional societies have come to some kind of terms with their environments, or they would not have lasted long enough to become "traditional."
—Eugene Anderson, University of California

We won't win this struggle by being there at the beginning, but by being there at the end.
—Patricia Cochran, attendee at Inuit Circumpolar Conference

In 1992, after a decade or more of intense protest and pressure from worldwide indigenous groups, Sir Shridath Ramphal,[1] president of IUCN, opened the fourth World Parks Congress in Caracas by observing that "quite simply, if local people do not support protected areas, then protected areas cannot last." That statement, from someone of Ramphal's stature, was among the first to indicate that transnational conservation was beginning to grasp the fact that the Yosemite model of biodiversity conservation was approaching a historical dead-end.

While this has been a sad transition for wilderness romantics like John Terborgh, David Foreman, John Oates, Clive Spinage, and Holmes Rolston, indigenous peoples around the world were elated by Ramphal's remark. However, they have since taken the process far beyond the concept of "support." The message they now bring to conservation conventions is that creating a protected area is merely a dedication to protection. It's a piece of paper, and too many protected areas remain that way forever: dedication on paper. But when native people initiate the creation of a reserve something very different happens: a lasting local commitment to preserving biological diversity in an ancient homeland—something a growing sector of the conservation establishment now embraces as "community conservation."

What are now officially called Community Conservation Areas (CCAs, also known as Biocultural Heritage Sites, Community Reserves, and Locally Managed Marine Areas) by IUCN and most of its members, have in fact existed, unnamed, for thousands of years. On every continent, biodiversity hot spot scouts are discovering human settlements that have been practicing scientifically sound conservation for generations without calling it "conservation," or anything for that matter.

Whether in shoreline communities with locally enforced no-catch zones (*tabus*), inland settlements rotating crops, community wildlife reserves, or in large grazing areas reserved for future use of pastoral nomads, traditional indigenous practices have been found, in many instances, to enhance biodiversity. Indigenous motivation is more likely to be food or water security than wildlife conservation, but the net effect is the same—biologically sustainable landscapes. And frequently there is a cultural or spiritual component as well. In most such cases the impulse to conserve arises spontaneously in a forest village or coastal community that notices a decline in a species vital to livelihood. Conservation is self-imposed.

If uncharted CCAs and Locally Managed Marine Areas (LMMAs) were included under the IUCN rubric of "Protected Area," they would come close to doubling the surface area of the planet under conservation. And conservation biologists are finding that the very existence of unintentional conservation offers an ideal laboratory for comparisons between official and unofficial protected area formation and management, between traditional and Western ecological knowledge, between community-driven and BINGO-driven conservation. These discoveries, many made by scientists employed by BINGOs, are gradually changing the practice of conservation biology, and hastening the demise of exclusionary conservation.

At the core of international efforts to preserve both biological diversity and indigenous cultures is a conflict between the agro-industrial market and indigenous natural resource management systems. The agro-industrial system tends to see conservation as something happening elsewhere, where agriculture is not being practiced. Conservation is pursued as preservation of biodiversity and the maintenance of ecosystems for aesthetic, recreational, or scientific purposes. For pastoralists, hunter-gatherers, and other indigenous managers of natural resources, conservation and sustainable agriculture simply mean landscape stewardship to sustain livelihood. And of course, behind that agro-industrial/ indigenous conflict are the eternally confounding questions of land tenure, title, communal ownership, property rights, and collective human rights.

A rights-based approach to conservation tends to gives practicing conservationists a headache. Compared to the rather simple equations that flow from attempts to find compensating livelihood for people displaced in the interest of conservation, a rights approach brings a troubling moral and ethical dimension to the situation, or as anthropologist Peter Brosius describes the dilemma: "Questions [are raised] as to who has the standing or legitimacy to displace people, under what conditions is displacement justified, whether rights can be extinguished against the will of those who possess them, and whether they can be extinguished through monetary transactions. The discourse of rights is fundamentally about human dignity, about the exercise of power, and about a prior context of histories of marginalization."[2]

Naturally, people who are facing eviction and seek to create an indigenous-owned and -operated conservation project will open their case for doing so with a rights-based argument.

"Caring for Country"

There is no one pathway to a sustainable future.
—David Bray, Florida International University

A unique and increasingly popular form of rights-based CCA is the Indigenous Protected Area (IPA), an invention of Australian Aboriginals, who shun the word *wilderness* and speak instead of *country*, by which they mean both land and sea. The Australian Homelands Movement (AHM) has for the past thirty years been resettling people back into the country that was theirs for millennia, with an agenda that restores all custodial rights to its original owners. The AHM phrasing for the initiative is "The Caring for Country Movement."

The first Australian IPA was formed in 1998 in Natawarrina in the Flinders Ranges of South Australia. Several more were formed in other parts of the country during the year that followed. The process of creating IPAs in Australia is entirely voluntary. The area is claimed, mapped, and rules are set and enforced by the Aboriginals involved. The only requirement set by the national government is that indigenous people develop a management plan committed to conserving biodiversity, or in their words to "caring for country."

Caring for country "involves a holistic relationship between people and country," according to AHM leader Joe Morrison. "Our aim is to get the country back, not to get rich. We walk the country with modern scientists and exchange traditional with nontraditional knowledge. We know that bad management of country leads to bad health."

At the heart of caring for country is the notion, slowly and reluctantly accepted by white Australians, that Aboriginals were in fact the first stewards of the continent, and by all indications did a pretty good job of preserving healthy, biodiverse landscapes. However, while the caring part is rarely debated any longer, territorial rights remain a point of contention. "IPAs are still facing adverse circumstances in Australia," says Morrison. "We are still debating land title." The national government's fear, as in so many countries, is that land title will lead to demands for self-determination, which will lead to a movement for secession.

New Models

All nature conservation and environmental management are inevitably projects in politics.
—Charles Zerner, Sarah Lawrence College

In 1930, Lakota Chief Iktomi Lila Sica proposed America's first native-owned and managed Community Conservation Area. It was to be a national park in South Dakota and would contain an "Indian University" that would teach Lakota ecological knowledge and culture. He proposed that similar projects be created in Yellowstone and Glacier National Parks. The idea was rejected by the National Parks Service until the 1970s, when the Blackfeet, Ogala Sioux, and Havasupi reservations each voluntarily established parks within or adjacent to their reservations.

Many indigenous communities throughout the world have regained ownership and territorial autonomy under new treaties with their national governments, and IPAs in various forms are appearing everywhere, from Lao fishing villages along the Mekong River to the Mataven Forest in northeastern Columbia, where six indigenous tribes,[3] living in sixteen indigenous *resgaurdos* along two rivers bordering a four-million-acre ecologically intact reserve, manage the conservation of a national park within the reserve, and collectively own considerable acreage around its border.

Before the Mataven conservation area was created, the indigenous communities mapped the boundaries of the land to be protected, requested title, created a "Council of Traditional Authorities," proposed their own operating rules and restrictions, and sought independent funding to pay for management of the reserve, which today is regarded worldwide as a model of indigenous conservation. Are the BINGOs there? Yes, but as scientists, rather than rulers or managers, as stakeholders not rights-holders—in short, as servants of the Mataven Forest. It's a good relationship. Everyone seems happy with it. There can be no question that the Mataven model of conservation is gradually displacing the Yosemite/Yellowstone model, although perhaps too slowly to satisfy the thousands of indigenous communities that still suffer under the yoke of imperial conservation. They do take heart in the creation of IPAs elsewhere. Some examples that give them hope:

• In February 2002, the Colombian government again recognized the rights of an indigenous tribe, the Inganos, to design and manage a national park. Located in the upper watershed of the Colombian Amazon, the Alto Fraqua-Indiwasi National Park protects a vast ecosystem in the Andes. The name, which means "House of the Sun" in the Ingano language, has been a sacred site of the tribe for many generations. It is now an integral part of their *Plan de Vida* (life plan).

• Coron Island at the northern tip of Palawan in the Philippines contains
a string of pristine freshwater lakes, all but one considered sacred by the
seafaring Tagbanwa people, who for centuries have regarded the island
as their ancestral domain. Until the mid-1980s, the territorial rights of
the Tagbanwa were not recognized. Itinerant fishermen, tourism operators, government officials, and erstwhile developers all used the island
at their pleasure. Marine resources and biodiversity were threatened. In
the mid-1980s the Tagbanwa tribe applied for and was granted a "Community Forest Stewardship Agreement." But that was not satisfactory to
tribal leaders, as it did not include marine areas. In 1998 the islanders
finally won a "Certificate of Ancestral Domain Claim," and with a high-
quality map and a management plan won collective rights to 22,284
hectares of land and marine waters. When the government proposed
adding Coron Island to the national protected area system, the Tagbanwa, fearing they would lose title and authority, protested the decision
and thus far have retained their autonomy.

News of the success of Coron Island's Tagbanwa has reached other
clans in the remote islands of the western Pacific. Elders and community
leaders throughout coastal Asia are exchanging information on the
process of securing tenure over ancestral domains by turning them into
CCAs. The initiative has put the Philippines on the world map of indigenous conservation as the first government to recognize "ancestral waters
claims." And the Tagbanwa have become an inspiration to indigenous
communities seeking similar claims in Maluku, Indonesia, and the Torres
Straits of Australia.

• Melanesia is well-suited to CCAs and IPAs given that conservation has
been part of island culture for millennia. It had to be so, for in coastal
communities reliant on the sea for protein there is no other way to
protect food security than to manage fisheries in a conscious and responsible manner. Locally Managed Marine Area (LMMA) is the name conservationists have given to a practice that is thousands of years old.

Almost every coastal village I visited in Fiji, Vanuatu, the Solomon
Islands, and Papua New Guinea had set aside about a third of their
waterfront and offshore reefs as *tabus*, defined earlier in this book as
strict no-catch zones off limits to local and visiting fishers alike. In some
locations scientists from the University of the Pacific in Fiji offer technical

assistance with fish surveys, and in others international NGOs like Sea-cology provide financial incentives to communities experiencing eco-nomic hardship as a consequence of limiting their catch. As chapter 16 attests, not all conservation organizations are as aware of the historical traditions of Melanesia.

• To stop the construction of a national highway through their land in Panama, the Kuna, an ancient Mesoamerican tribe that originated in what is today Colombia, established a biosphere reserve at the point where the road would have entered Kuna Yala, which they regard as their nation. Today the Kuna assume ownership of and management responsibility for the reserve, where ecologists and wildlife biologists are welcome to study.

Such alliances are more likely to succeed, according to anthropologist James Igoe, who has spent much of his career studying conservation initiatives, "where indigenous peoples have legal authority over natural resources and are allowed to live inside protected areas where they have themselves initiated the relationship with conservation."

Box 18.1

Nagas

The Nagas are a complex, ancient ethnicity of sixteen autonomous tribes straddling the border between the remote northeastern region of India and Western Myanmar (Burma). While tribes differ noticeably in dress, orna-ment, culture, and dialect, each Naga recognizes the tribes' common Sino-Tibetan ancestry and feels very much akin to other Nagas, with whom they share a ferocious desire for independence.

For over a century, India's one million Nagas have pursued the longest-lasting separatist insurrection in the world. Their early enemy was the British, whom they first confronted in the Angami Naga rebellion of 1878 and fought on and off until India's independence in 1947. However, the departure of the occupiers didn't end the insurrection, which continued sporadically against the Indian government until quite recently, when peace negotiations were opened.

The four Naga hill tribes of Myanmar, who reside mostly in the Chind-win Valley, share their Indian brethren's passion for self-determination, particularly in the face of a vicious Burmese military regime. And they resent the Indian-Burmese border, drawn as it was by British colonials, because it divides their true nation, which the Nagas of India and Myanmar call Nagalim. Similar in some respects to Kurdistan, Nagalim is a homeland, in name only, to a stateless diaspora.

One of the consequences of the interminable state of war in Nagaland is the growth of a well-armed militia of skilled riflemen, who when not doing battle against Indian troops were indiscriminately killing wildlife, of which they have traditionally been proud hunters. But when rifles replaced spears and arrows, hunting became a destructive process. Today almost every Naga family owns at least one firearm, and every Naga man is a sharpshooter. To the rest of India it seems as if "everything in the North East that flies, walks or crawls is hunted," according to Ashish Kothari and Neema Pathak, who have studied the area together. "That reputation is not entirely undeserved."*

However, sometime in the mid-1990s, a Khonoma village leader named Tsilie Sakhrie in the Kohima district of Nagaland noticed that many once-abundant species of hornbills, primates, and cats, as well as the officially threatened Blyth's Tragopan (a pheasant), had been driven to near extinction by Naga hunters. And since 1996, rampant timber extraction has led to serious deforestation.

After gaining support of his fellow villagers and a local forest official, himself a Naga residing in the same village, Sakhrie called a series of village meetings throughout the district to pursue the idea of instituting an outright hunting ban and the creation of community-managed wildlife reserves.

Eighty-eight percent of Nagaland's forests belong to communities or individuals, rather than the state, which is generally the case in the rest of India. The challenge Sakhrie faced, therefore, was to convince villagers and private landowners to join the ban and commit their land to wildlife recovery. That was no easy task, even in the relatively democratic environment of Nagaland. But with the support of India's Forest Department, the idea took hold and spread slowly through the region as tribal elders—who pined for the days when from their homes they could see their revered hornbills and monkeys—began to encourage and support the hunting ban.

The Khonoma hunting ban caught the attention of other villages in Kohima district and beyond. Slowly but surely, self-initiated conservation became a new cultural feature in Nagaland as people convinced themselves that on their own, without the assistance or control of outside conservation NGOs, they could sustain themselves and nature at once. Some villages passed their own "wildlife protection acts" with new local rules for land management. Others on river banks banned unsustainable fishing methods and created no-catch zones where edible fish could breed and restore their dwindling numbers.

While there have been few formal scientific studies made of Nagaland's ecosystems, empirical reports indicate that the Blyth's Tragopan, Grey Peacock, Mrs. Hume's Pheasant, and hornbills are all making impressive recoveries, while the Asiatic Black Bear and Clouded Leopard, once popular prey for hunters, are returning in real numbers to the Zanibu range. In Khonoma, twenty-five amphibian species are in recovery and the officially "threatened" Dark-rumped Swift is seen with growing frequency.

"Given its history, what Nagaland is witnessing is nothing short of revolutionary," say Kothari and Pathak. "For village after village to declare no-hunting and no-deforestation zones, and for people to show that they want to sustain nature conservation, is no mean feat." The Nagas, they say, are demonstrating "that wildlife has a future in the hands of those who live closest to it."[**]

Nagaland's community conservation efforts have by no means been a perfect success. Leadership rivalries, minor corruption, and the uncertainty created by insurrection have hampered progress in some communities. Yet government wildlife authorities seem impressed enough with the initiative that they wish to be involved. However, when they approached the village of Khonoma and asked its council to turn its Tragopan reserve over to the Forest Department in return for some funding, the villager counselors quite wisely rejected the offer.

When the state government considered declaring the villages "community reserves" as defined by the Wildlife Protection Act, again the villagers demurred. Why would communities surrender control over land use when they already have strong village councils operating as wildlife monitors? The Tragopan reserve was, it seems, destined to remain a community project and the Naga way of community conservation a model and exemplar for India and the world.

---

[*] Ashish Kothari and Neema Pathak, "Tragopans and Tribals: A Naga Transformation," (unpublished paper).
[**] Ibid.

Not only are IPAs spreading like wildfire, but a new relationship between native people and transnational conservation is clearly taking hold. Once an IPA is established, almost anywhere in the world, and territorial rights are assured, the founding community often follows the Mataven example and invites CI, TNC, WCS, or WWF to send their ecologists and wildlife biologists to share in the task of protecting biodiversity by combining Western scientific methodology with traditional ecological knowledge. And on occasion community members might ask for help negotiating with reluctant governments.

For instance, after asking the Bolivian government to declare part of their traditional homeland a national park, Guarani Izocenos Indians invited the Wildlife Conservation Society, one of the slowest of all BINGOs to accept the potential value of indigenous stewardship, to mediate a co-management agreement with the government, which today allows the tribe to manage and own part of the new Kaa-Iya National Park.

Kaa-Iya is worth a closer look. Kaa-Iya del Gran Chaco National Park and Integrated Management Area was established in September 1995. At 8.5 million acres (3.44 million hectares), it is the largest dry tropical forest reserve in the world and one of the largest protected areas in South America. It is situated in the northern reaches of a huge neotropical dry forest known as the Gran Chaco, a million-square-kilometer bioregion that reaches into Bolivia, Paraguay, Brazil, and northern Argentina. The Chaco is a biologically rich expanse, with sixty-nine species of mammals recorded in the Kaa-Iya alone, five of them endemic to the Chaco.

Prior to creation of Kaa-Iya there were twelve other small protected areas in the Chaco, nine in Argentina, and three in Paraguay. Together they covered just over one percent of the entire Chaco. And they were all experiencing management challenges that derived partly from strained relationships between indigenous peoples and their national governments.

Thus when the Capitania del Alto y Bajo Azozog (CABI), the local Izoceno-Guarani Indian organization, representing nearly ten thousand Izocenos living in twenty-five villages along the Parapeti River, stepped forward in 1991, and in the face of powerful external economic interests offered to manage a proposed new protected area, the Bolivian government listened. And so did Andrew Taber, a dedicated wildlife biologist who at the time was working for WCS in Bolivia. Both Taber and the government knew that the Izoceno-Guarani were a strong, wise, and self-confident people with a long tradition of agitating for land rights. The Izocenos also possessed sophisticated ecological knowledge and had proven themselves over generations to be exemplary land stewards.

Previous to the creation of Kaa-Iya, Bolivia had serious problems with other protected areas, most notably with Amboro National Park, a top-down conservation initiative established without adequate local support or involvement. It was time to try something new and different. Enter Andrew Taber.

Taber describes his role in the creation of Kaa-Iya as "behind the scenes." The project, he says, "had many mothers and fathers." Taber arrived in Bolivia in 1991 to survey the Gran Chaco for the Giant Peccary and other endangered species. Like so many biologists before him, he proposed and began to lobby for a protected area in the Bolivian Chaco. And as most of the others either knew or soon discovered, Taber found indigenous people living in the very area he sought to protect. But there the similarity ceases.

In 1991 Taber met with Don Bonifacio Barrientos, chief of the Izoceno people. "I told him that it seemed likely that some kind of protected area would be established in that area and that they needed to be sure that they did not get marginalized in the process. My job was wildlife conservation, and community-based conservation ideas were less developed at that time, yet this seemed the right thing to say as I had developed an affinity for the people of this tough environment—with so much land and so few people, there had to be room for both the critters and the most marginalized people's needs."

In 1993 Taber proposed that USAID fund a CCA inside Gran Chaco. When the agency dragged its feet, Taber advanced WCS funds to the project, all the while insisting that the Izoceno-Guarani play a seminal and equal role in the creation and eventual management of the park. Two years later the park was signed into law, a generous USAID grant came through, and Izoceno park rangers and parabiologists began their training.

As they respond to such invitations for assistance, more and more Western conservation scientists realize that most of the areas they have sought to protect are rich in biodiversity precisely because the people who were living there, like the Izocenos, have come to understand the value and mechanisms of biological diversity without formal schooling in ecology, botany, or zoology.

Conservationists have also learned from bitter experience that national parks and protected areas surrounded by angry, hungry people, who describe themselves as "enemies of conservation," are generally doomed to fail. As Cristina Eghenter of WWF observed after working with communities surrounding the Kayan Mentarang National Park in Borneo, "It is becoming increasingly evident that conservation objectives can rarely be obtained or sustained by imposing policies that produce negative impacts on indigenous peoples." And perhaps the most heartening news came in a recent note from Taber, reporting that WCS now has "many projects in their portfolio that work extremely equitably with native peoples."

But too much hope should not be placed on belated epiphanies, or in a handful of successful co-management models. Running counter to those small triumphs is an unrestrained global lust for energy, hardwood, medicines, and strategic metals, which threatens the aims of both conservation and cultural survival.

In an era of unrestrained profiteering, as megacorporations plunder the planet's resources with reckless abandon, it's hard to fault the forces of modern conservation for anything they do. But the random displacement of people for a good purpose is as heartless and culturally destructive as it is for a bad one. In a sense it is worse, because it turns the refugee against the good purpose.

Nevertheless, the abuse of tribal people continues, and for the moment at least some international conservation organizations, particularly Conservation International and WWF, remain comfortable working in close quarters with some of the most ambitious corporate prospectors for global resources. Their rationale for doing so is to assure that extractive companies do their work in an environmentally responsible manner. That explanation would have much more credibility if the conservation groups declined to accept generous donations from their corporate "partners." Of course if CI and other BINGOs divorced those companies they would forfeit millions of dollars of revenue, and an access to global power without which they sincerely believe they could not be as effective. That debate is for another book. But the cozy relationship between big conservation and transnational corporations remains a troubling curiosity to indigenous leaders worldwide, who often mistrust their BINGO counterparts simply because of such partnerships.

Perhaps the only remaining solution is for the true and first stewards of nature, who still reside in the last remaining biodiverse regions of the planet, to move beyond their justifiable rage at transnational conservation, refuse to be regarded as "stakeholders," assume protective responsibility for the ecological health of their homeland then press for the authority to manage it, solicit funding if necessary, and eventually retake control of the global conservation agenda. There are people and organizations in the developed world with access to power and money that are committed to helping these stewards.

If there is one place on Earth where transnational conservation has an opportunity to do things right by indigenous peoples, it's in Gabon, a remote but prosperous West African nation that has just created thirteen new national parks and received over $50 million from the U.S. government to manage them. The whole world is watching as almost every major conservation organization claims a foothold there. And observers wonder whether or not they will blow their golden opportunity.

19

Gabon: An Irresistible Opportunity

When legendary American conservationist Michael Fay completed his remarkable 1,200-mile, 455-day megatransect of the Congo Basin in 2002 and arrived in west Gabon, he called President El Hadj Omar Bongo Ondimba and asked for a meeting. Because Fay, an employee of the Wildlife Conservation Society (WCS), had drawn worldwide attention to his amazing feat, Bongo, the longest-serving national leader in all of Africa, agreed to see him, and asked if he could bring his entire cabinet along. Of course, said Fay.

The meeting, called without agenda by Bongo, was scheduled for August 1, 2002, in Gabon's long and stately cabinet room furnished in fine mahogany and equipped with plasma screens visible from every chair. It was a perfect venue for Mike Fay's now legendary Power Point presentation—an hour of dramatic wildlife photos interspersed with vignettes from a grueling rainforest trek.

As Fay had crossed the last of six countries in the vast Congo Basin, finding pristine forests the size of Oregon side by side with massive logging concessions, he saw an opportunity to create wildlife reserves and other protected areas in places that remained as they had been before humankind evolved, and, in the process, save a lot of biological diversity.

At the meeting, Fay showed Bongo and his cabinet forestry maps of Gabon with logging concessions shown in red. Almost the entire nation was red. Gabon was facing a nationwide clear-cut that would leave the country bereft of forests and wildlife. Then Fay showed Bongo an imaginary "virtual" map with thirteen emerald-green patches scattered around the country. These, he said, could be national parks. Combined, they would cover about 7.5 million acres, 10 percent of Gabon's surface. They would protect hundreds of species of flora and fauna from extinction and create a nationwide magnet for ecotourism, the fastest-growing sector of the fastest-growing industry in the world (see box 19.1). Fay emphasized the proposed parks represented a crucial and fleeting opportunity for Gabon to diversify an economy that relied heavily on oil and other dwindling extractive resources.

When Bongo's minister of forest economy, Emile Doumba, expressed an interest in one of Fay's proposed parks, Bongo overruled him, and shocked both Fay and his cabinet by saying he wanted all the proposed parks gazetted and opened immediately. He ordered Doumba to produce thirteen separate decrees, one for each park, which he agreed to sign that very day. An ecstatic Fay promised to find the money to manage the new parks. He stressed that Gabon was about to become the most ecologically significant nation in Africa, and a world-class experiment in biodiversity preservation.

But there was another, more historically significant opportunity facing Gabon, one that Fay merely hinted at in his presentation. It was the opportunity Fay's own industry, transnational conservation, had in Gabon to do right by the thousands of tribal people living inside those emerald patches, by allowing them to remain in their homelands and participate directly in the stewardship and management of the new parks, not as stakeholders, the usual fate of indigenous peoples, which this book has addressed in detail, but as rights-holders and equal players in the complex and challenging process of defending biodiversity. (For a sense of what might be in store for the tribal people of Gabon's new parks under WCS management, review chapter 5.)

Keeping his promise to Bongo, Fay returned to the United States and began the arduous process of raising the millions of dollars that would be needed to turn paper parks into real parks, and keep them safe from poachers and resource prospectors. As an inveterate and well-known conservation lobbyist, with connections to powerful fixers like Gabon's registered foreign agent, David Barron,[1] and high officials in the U.S. State Department, Fay managed to get the attention of key congressmen, most notably Ed Royce, chairman of the House International Relations Subcommittee on Africa. On March 11, 2003, Royce called on Fay to testify about his amazing voyage and seek support for protected areas in the Congo Basin, which Fay would emphasize hosts a tropical forest territory second in size only to the Amazon Basin.

"We have an historic opportunity here," Fay told the subcommittee, "to create what will be one of the world's most important national park systems covering over twenty-five million acres in one of the richest areas for biodiversity on the planet, but we have an opportunity to do much more really. We have an opportunity to shift how entire landscapes are developed and to assure that future generations can sustain and enhance their lives."

Those were encouraging words to Gabon's indigenous people and their supporters, nervous as any African tribe would be at the mere mention of parks or protected areas. Fay went on to speak of "maximizing benefits for local people"—more music to the ears of Gabon's poorest and most forsaken people, the Bakas, Babongo, Akula, Bakoya, and Fang, all of whom are painfully aware of how their counterparts have been treated elsewhere in Africa, in the interest of wildlife conservation.

Aid as Obstacle

American foreign aid is rarely provided for conservation alone. Conservation may be an aspect, intention, or side effect of an aid package, but the driving motivation of almost all aid grants, particularly from USAID, is economic, and the economic advantage is likely to be greater than the ecological benefits, and more likely to favor American over foreign business interests. The same applies to NGOs. And the $53 million commitment Michael Fay wrangled out of the Central African Regional Program for the Environment (CARPE) would be no exception. What was funded by CARPE with that appropriation was a vast international entity called the Congo Basin Forest Partnership (CBFP), which describes itself as "a United States-led initiative to promote the conservation and responsible management of the Basin's tropical forests."

In partnership with the governments of the United States, Cameroon, Central African Republic, Democratic Republic of Congo, Equatorial Guinea, Gabon, United Kingdom, Japan, Germany, France, Canada,

South Africa, the European Commission, and civil society NGOs like the Jane Goodall Institute, the IUCN, Conservation International, Wildlife Conservation Society, World Wildlife Fund, World Resources Institute and Forest Trends, is the World Bank, the International Tropical Timber Organization, the Society of American Foresters, the American Forest & Paper Association, Association Technique Internationale des Bois Tropicaux, and the Center for International Forestry Research. That mix suggests that conservation will not be the only force driving the CBFP. In fact, it may not be the primary force.

On September 4, 2002, U.S. Secretary of State Colin Powell launched the CBFP at the World Summit on Sustainable Development in Johannesburg, reiterating the $53 million USAID commitment. The following day he traveled to Gabon for the official inauguration of the new park system. In both venues he emphasized the economic opportunities offered by the partnership, no doubt the factor that stimulated enthusiastic support for the partnership from the administration of President George W. Bush. It would be up to the international conservation NGOs, which had agreed to match federal funds and participate fully in the partnership, to protect the biodiversity of the forest. And they would clearly confront powerful extractive industries with which many indigenous peoples around the world have found international conservationists to be far too cozy.

Gabon is the only country outside the United States that hosts offices of four of the five BINGOs. All but The Nature Conservancy are there in force, and TNC would almost certainly open an office were it invited to manage a park, as the Worldwide Fund for Nature was in 2002. WWF has a $10 million, seven-year contract with the Global Environment Facility (GEF) to manage the Tri-national Dja-Odzala-Minkebe (Tridom) Park, a huge, biologically rich ecoregion spanning vast sections of Gabon, Cameroon, and Congo Brazzaville. The park hosts large and vibrant populations of lowland gorillas, chimpanzees, bonobos, and forest elephants. The area also provides food, material, and shelter for over twenty million people, and is a vital sink for global emissions of carbon dioxide.

The checkered social history and enormous influence of transnational conservation naturally makes indigenous people and their representatives uneasy about the Gabon initiative. Perhaps they shouldn't be, as there are signs that big conservation may take a more progressive approach in Gabon than it has elsewhere on the continent. WCS and WWF have in fact conducted thorough social-economic surveys of human settlements where access and use rights might be impacted by the new parks, and have tried to assess the welfare impacts of the entire CBFP. WCS is also teaching basic ecological knowledge (Western and traditional) in village schools in and near the parks and WWF is training sixty-five ecoguards and ecoguides. And participatory mapping is being conducted in all affected areas.

A convenient truth about Gabon, appreciated by Michael Fay and his associates, is that the rural sectors of the heavily urbanized country are sparsely populated. There are fewer than two hundred thousand people living outside the nation's few cities, most of them in isolated communities, completely cut off from the modern world. This not only means less human impact on what Fay insists on calling "wilderness," but also a sparse and stable population reduces the likelihood that conservationists will be able to claim human impact as a justification for displacement.

As elsewhere in Africa, bush meat hunting and consumption is a major concern of conservationists. In other countries governments have been persuaded to issue outright bans on the killing of all wildlife, depriving entire communities of their sole source of protein. WCS appears to have learned some painful lessons from those bans. In a recent communiqué found on its website, the organization acknowledges that "bush meat is an important source of protein for villagers, as meat from domesticated animals is prohibitively expensive. Though it is not possible or even desirable to completely stop hunting by villagers for their own consumption, commercial hunting done by outsiders must be better controlled."

Those are all heartening signs of sensitivity to indigenous cultures, but they do not necessarily assure a good outcome. Similar projects and studies have been performed elsewhere in the Congo Basin, and similar observations made in protected areas that have since been cleared of human inhabitants, as previous chapters attest. And some of the scientists who conducted those studies question the methodology of the WCS/WWF surveys in Gabon. Kai Schmidt-Soltau, who has conducted similar research for the World Bank elsewhere in the Congo Basin, and is now stationed with the African Development Bank in Cameroon, found "the methodology inappropriate for social research and tailored to produce results biased to document that there are no adverse social impacts."

However, some painful lessons have been learned from the evictions that followed previous research, even with better methodology, particularly in cases of parks that became regarded as negative institutions, so that popular support for them eroded and their very survival was jeopardized. Thus a new conservation paradigm might still be tested in Gabon, its success or failure depending very much on the compassion and understanding of global conservationists, and a willingness on the part of the Gabonese government to treat tribal folk as full citizens and participants in the Congo Basin Forest Partnership, equal in power and status with national governments, conservation NGOs, and extractive corporations. And of course the true test of all parties' commitment to conservation will come when the USAID grant runs out and there is no visible means of support for national parks and their contracted managers.

Box 19.1

Nature as Merchandise

Given his record, it seems certain that a notorious kleptocrat like Omar Bongo would not have agreed to create thirteen new national parks in his country were there not an extraordinary economic payoff. Something had to offset the enormous losses that would occur from the denial of logging and mining concessions in those huge tracts of land. Forest products alone accounted for 7 percent of Gabon's GDP. Add manganese mining and oil extraction and Gabon has an industrial base that makes it one of the wealthiest of all African economies.

So tourism became the selling point, and to conservationist organizations like Michael Fay's Wildlife Conservation Society (WCS), the only acceptable tourism for national parks and wildlife reserves is environmentally friendly and thoroughly green tourism, known in the travel marketplace as "nature tourism" or by that term's more recent offspring: "ecotourism."

So what is ecotourism? And which of its many forms and manifestations is truly eco-friendly? Is it really different in impact from ordinary tourism, or is *eco* simply a convenient prefix for a new, slightly greener form of travel? And either way, does ecotourism assure a continued livelihood to people displaced or inconvenienced by its business practices and infrastructure?

The common standard set for ecotourism by conservationists is that a project's "distinguishing feature should be that it benefits biodiversity."* However, there are many in the field—people like John Terborgh and John Oates, who tend to believe that any human disturbance has a negative effect on biodiversity—who wonder whether that goal is possible to meet through any form of tourism.

There is no question that ecotourism is booming. It is in fact the fastest-growing sector of the fastest-growing industry in the world. Of the 842 international tourist arrivals in 2006, about 20 percent or 168 million described themselves as "ecotourists." By the turn of the millennium this new travel sector was so large and influential that the United Nations declared 2002 to be the International Year of Ecotourism; while the World Bank, Asia Development Bank, and a host of other international lending agencies added ecotourism to their lists of development strategies, and the Overseas Private Investment Corporation (OPIC) launched a global curriculum for ecotourism entrepreneurs.

But the economic advantages of ecotourism are not what they seem or purport to be. Take Nepal for example, a country where virtually all tourism is "eco." Sixty-nine percent of the money spent by tourists traveling to Nepal never reaches the country. It is spent on airline tickets, travel planners, and foreign outfitters based outside Nepal who arrange treks and climbs for adventurous travelers. Of the 31 percent of the money that does reach Nepal, most is paid to domestic outfitters, transportation companies, and porters and guides stationed in Katmandu. A mere 1.2 percent finds its way into the villages and communities through which tourists pass on their way to Chitwan National Park, Mount Everest, and the Annapurna Sanctuary.

A similar situation exists around Kenya's Maasai Mara Reserve, the most popular wildlife-viewing area in East Africa. There are about four thousand tourist beds in the immediate vicinity of the reserve, in which cattle grazing is allowed, but on an extremely limited, emergency basis because tour operators insist that tourists do not want to see anything that spoils the idea of "pristine wilderness." Throughout the Mara reserve's 90-day high season, about 75 percent or three thousand of those beds are occupied by people, almost all of them paying $40 per day to enter the reserve. That's $120,000 in revenue per day, or close to $11 million for the three peak months of business. Twenty percent of that money is supposed to go directly to the Maasai villages and communities in the immediate area; virtually none of it ever arrives. Again, anonymous ecotourism entrepreneurs get rich, while people who were on the land long before the

Maasai Mara Reserve was created, and whose livelihoods are ruined by restricted grazing and scarce water, are the ones who suffer.

Furthermore, despite claims to the contrary, the overall environmental impact of ecotourism is little better than that of ordinary tourism. Yes, ecotourism saves some water and energy if sheets and towels aren't laundered every day (it also saves costs), but flying to Nepal for a trek leaves the same monstrous carbon footprint as flying to Greece to board a Mediterranean cruise ship. And barreling around the Serengeti in a four-wheel-drive Land Rover to photograph elephants is about as earth friendly as taking a stretch limo from JFK International Airport into Manhattan.

As ecotourism has gained a major foothold on every continent, conservationists and cultural survivalists alike have begun to raise serious questions about individual ecotourism projects and about the industry itself. Ecotourism for whom, they ask? For tourists? Investors? Outfitters? Lodge managers? Locals? Or: for wildlife? For biodiversity?

Ecotourism entrepreneurs would likely say "all of the above." And they would do what they could to meet the standards put forth by a growing number of rating services that travel the world inspecting ecotourism facilities and granting green stars, green leaves or green points to each venture based on its environmental rectitude, energy consumption, and labor practices. Unfortunately, the treatment of indigenous communities absorbed or overwhelmed by ecotourism projects is rarely a factor in the rating process. As a consequence, tourists seeking socially just resorts and treks rarely are made aware when local people have been displaced to make room for their lodge or tour. For example:

• In Prainha do Canto Verde village, near the Brazilian city of Fortaleza, 1,100 fishermen and subsistence farmers in twelve coastal communities are in conflict with a massive ecotourism project funded by the Inter-American Bank that will overrun their villages and end their traditional lifeways. Not far from Canto Verde, in Tatajuba village, the massive Conadado Ecologico hotel complex, which when finished will cater to fifteen thousand guests, threatens the residence and livelihood of 150 more nomadic fishing and farming families. Ironically, both Prainha do Canto Verde and Tatjuba have long been regarded as "unspoilt" tourist destinations.

• Tanzania's national government is threatening to evict more Maasai from the Ngorongoro Crater to promote luxury safari ecotourism. Local Maasai who were evicted from the crater in the 1950s to make a park are calling for a shift to community-based and culturally oriented ecotourism.

• Although Bedouins in the desert-based mountain Wadi Rum region of Jordan hold prior land rights in the area, conservationists and ecotour developers are calling for their removal to establish a "special regulations area" (ecotour park), with financial support from the World Bank.

• In India, another World Bank "eco-development plan" calls for the eventual eviction of Adivasis from forest homeland. While awaiting eviction they are forbidden to plant fruit trees or restrict the trespass of destructive elephants on their farmland. The India government is offering resettlement and financial assistance, but is harassing and intimidating those who decline the offers.

• In Thailand, Padaung hill tribe people are being forced from their homelands into fake villages (human zoos) for tourists to visit. A $1.2 billion economic development scheme funded by a massive Asia Development Bank development program, with a strong ecotourism component, threatens the homelands and livelihoods of other ethnic highlanders throughout the Greater Mekong Region.

• In the Philippines, where there is widespread conversion of public to private lands, there is a plan to convert the entire Taal Lake area into an ecotourist haven. On March 14, 2003, 250 people were violently evicted. In the action dozens of homes were demolished and seventeen people injured, four seriously.

• In Bangladesh, the Madhupar Eco Park in Tangail was inaugurated in April 2001 with plans to cut fifteen hundred acres of forest, build a concrete boundary wall twenty-two thousand feet long, and remove seven villages (a thousand families). When the indigenous people of Madhupar protested, police fired on the gathering, killing twenty-year-old Piren Slan and injuring twenty-five others, women and children among them. A massive hunger strike and a recent change of government may reduce the threat of outright eviction. However, armed forest guards continue to provide full-time security for the wall construction crew. And to keep conservationists happy, the government reiterated that its primary goal for the project was to "save the forest and its biodiversity." **

To be sure, some indigenous communities have welcomed ecotourism into their homelands, particularly when comparing it to the almost inevitable alternatives: logging, cattle ranching, mining, or fossil fuel extraction. One example is the Kainamaro people of Guyana, a small community happy to share its culture and handicrafts with a strictly limited number of visitors who are briefed beforehand on the cultural sensitivities of the tribe.

In 2004, OPIC, in cooperation with the U.S. State Department and various NGOs, sponsored a conference on ecotourism investment in Gabon and the Congo Basin.

---

* Katrina Brandon and Richard Margoulis, "The Bottom Line: Getting Conservation Back into Ecotourism," *Yale Forestry and Environmental Science Bulletin* 99 (1996): pp. 28–38.
** I am grateful for research provided by TourismConcern in London, which provided these examples.

In his testimony before Congress to the African subcommittee, Michael Fay made an interesting and revealing comparison.

I often hear that protected areas work in the United States because we have wealth and health and peace and democracy and all of those things. In Africa, the logic goes where poverty, disease, and war are more the norm, national parks really have no place in development. We hear that very often.

I believe that Teddy Roosevelt had it right. In 1907, when the United States was at the stage in its development not dissimilar to the Congo Basin today, he said: "In utilizing and conserving natural resources of the nation, the one characteristic more essential than any other is foresight. The conservation of our natural resources and their proper use constitute the fundamental problem which underlies almost every other problem of our national life."

President Roosevelt, with Congress, made the creation of 230 million acres of protected areas the cornerstone of that foresight. I was just up there last weekend. One hundred years the Sespe has been there. It is still there, and it is still an intact ecosystem.

Obviously there has been a lot of debate over the years, but that is what is good about conservation. It creates a debate. It also creates a national ethos on land use and its management. I think that when you look at what Roosevelt did, that is what he did. He brought that debate to the United States, and it has been very important in every land use decision made in this country for over a century.

My work in the Congo Basin has been basically to try to bring this U.S. model to Africa. People think well, you know, that is this, that is that, but I do not see that there is any great difference in the United States' development over the last 150 years and what is currently happening in Africa almost throughout—resource exploitation, people occupying the landscape. That is what is happening everywhere.

The model starts with the identification of large landscapes where land use management systems can be put in place before the arrival of industrial resource use and human expansion. This model does not call for the curtailment of resource use, only for well-reasoned land use and resource management.

It requires, I think, a ground-up plan that includes the creation and management of core national parks to protect the biodiversity mother lode, integrated with land use management in exploitation zones in the surrounding landscapes that maximizes benefits for local people.

We find that parks quickly become national treasures, but they also become the cornerstones in a process where logging companies and other resource users change wasteful practices, local people change land use practices, and governments change policies. Other development objectives that help people like poverty alleviation, health, education, and private investment are also facilitated in these landscapes. It goes right up to the national level. That debate begins when this model is applied.

There are currently many organizations, American and European, working with national governments on projects in various stages of this landscape model.

These initiatives have strong national support, and many U.S. and international organizations are working very hard with national governments to make them happen.

It is worth noting, first, that Fay's erstwhile hero, Teddy Roosevelt, signed off on the creation of Yosemite National Park, which became a fifty-year social catastrophe and a highly questionable ecological initiative. He also inspired a resource management regime in the United States that created a Forest Service that has sanctioned the harvest of over 95 percent of the old-growth timber in the country, a Bureau of Land Management that offers virtual free range to western cattle barons, and a Bureau of Mines that has allowed the tops of innumerable mountains to be removed in search of coal and left millions of strip-mined acres of federal landscape too toxic for any other use. And while he was singing the praises of "wise use," T. R. also proclaimed that "the rude, fierce settler who drives the savage from the land lays all civilized mankind under a debt to him. It is of incalculable importance that America, Australia, and Siberia should pass out of the hands of the red, black, and yellow aboriginal owners and become the heritage of the dominant world races."

Is this really the legacy American conservationists want spread about the world? And is the U.S. method of protecting biological diversity, with its paternalistic view of nature, appropriate to the rest of the planet? Does it even work? The epilogue, which follows, grapples with that final question.

As this book went to press there was still no certainty that the various tribes occupying the new parks in Gabon would get a fair shake. There were proposals in place for eight of the parks requiring the resettlement of an estimated fifteen thousand people from the Babongo, Bakoya, Baka, Barimba, Bagama, Kouyi, and Akoa tribes. Between seven and ten thousand of those peoples are citizens of Gabon, but with fewer rights and much less political influence than one might expect for a citizen. It remains an open question at the moment whether or not the two agencies formed to implement the resettlement plan—the Forest and Environmental Sector Program (FESP) and the Indigenous Peoples Development Plan (IPDP)—will provide adequate compensation, equally productive new land, and new housing for the resettled citizens. The World

Bank that funds the GEF is unable to provide cash compensation. That will have to come from the government of Gabon through the IPDP, which currently has about $450,000 to work with, less than 4 percent of the FESP budget for relocation.

Following the current situation in Gabon closely is Martijn ter Heegde, program coordinator for Africa for the U.K.-based Rainforest Foundation UK. Ter Heegde, who spent four years with the IUCN in Central Africa, believes that "Gabon is just more of the same old nonsense" he saw happening elsewhere in the region. In fact "it's already well on the way to becoming an utter disaster for forest peoples." The only reason people have not yet been displaced from new protected areas in Gabon, he says, is that "the interior of the country is so devoid of people." He worries that because all the resources for running the parks come from overseas, "the parks are effectively outside of government authority," to be managed by BINGOs under contract with the U.S. State Department. Ter Heegde worries too that "there has been no effort whatsoever to ensure popular participation in conservation policies or the creation of parks; instead it's the same old same old story—buying off authorities with gifts and money and putting ecoguards in place to stop poaching." Gabon, he predicts, will not become a model of progressive conservation. Instead it "is more likely to become another case of 'conservation colonization.' "[2]

Whether or not ter Heegde's prediction proves right, Gabon seems certain to become the newest playing field in the age-old conflict between science-based and rights-based conservation. While the park sites were carefully selected by Fay and his colleagues at the Wildlife Conservation Society to minimize social impact, there remains a strong bias within the conservation establishment against human communities in national parks and wildlife reserves. And ecotourism entrepreneurs continue to seem bent upon offering their customers a human-free environment (except for resort servants). While previous chapters attest that community-based conservation is a tried and proven method, not everyone at WCS, or any of the other conservation NGOs in Gabon, has completely accepted the model. Gabon is nonetheless worth watching.

If you go far enough back into the history of almost any injustice, current events begin to look better. Such is the nature of progress. And if you project yourself far enough into the future, you can sometimes imagine a happy ending. Such is the nature of hope. And such may be the case with the slowly improving, 100-year relationship between organized conservation and indigenous peoples.

Epilogue

Vital Diversities: Balancing the Protection of Nature and Culture

We are living today only because the generations before us—our ancestors—provided for us by the manner of their responsible living.
—Simon Ortiz, Native American poet

One day, while studying population distribution and migration, Arizona geographer David Hancocks made an astonishing observation. When he overlaid a map of the United States showing the duration of residency of each county with another map displaying counties with the most threatened or endangered species, he found an almost perfect correlation between unstable populations and high species loss. Very interesting, he thought, and wondered: Could this be related to studies by anthropologists and ethnobiologists in rainforests, montane regions, savannahs, and coastal communities that found a strong association between cultural and biological diversity?

Anthropologist Mac Chapin had a similar experience in 1991, when he perused a map entitled "Indians of Central America" next to a map of the region's vegetation. What was immediately evident was that Central America's lowland indigenous peoples all lived under the continent's richest forest cover. Chapin combined the two maps into one. The result was not only a statement about the "right livelihood" of people whose existence was barely recognized, it also "helped to strengthen what soon became a widespread campaign for protecting and legalizing their territories," recalls Chapin.

Hancocks's and Chapin's correlations were confirmed again in 1998, when the Worldwide Fund for Nature (WFF) completed its long-awaited Global 200 project in which 233 of the Earth's biologically richest ecoregions were identified and mapped. Examination of the human populations in these landscapes revealed that about 80 percent of the ecoregions were occupied by an estimated three thousand separate indigenous communities, most of which had thrived there for hundreds if not thousands of years.[3] One might deduce from these discoveries that stable communities, even without formal knowledge or understanding of conservation biology, had developed ways to protect native plants and animals from external threats.

But conservation has a recorded history and a literary tradition. Evicted aboriginals have only memory and the bitter oral narrative I have heard over the past four years while visiting their makeshift villages and refugee camps. Their pre-eviction experience is rarely recorded outside the annals of anthropology. So the perspective of "fortress conservation" and the preference for "virgin" wilderness have lingered on in a movement that has tended to value all nature but human nature, and refused to recognize the positive wildness in human beings. Thus the well-written and widely read memoirs of early American eco-heroes like John Muir, Lafayette Burnell, Samuel Bowles, George Perkins Marsh, and Aldo Leopold inform a conservation mythology that until quite recently separated nature from culture and portrayed natives and early settlers of frontier areas as reckless, irresponsible abusers of nature, with no sense or tradition of stewardship, no understanding of wildlife biology, and no appreciation of biodiversity. It was the "manifest destiny" of conservation leaders, then, to tame what Michael Wigglesworth had earlier described poetically as:

A waste and howling wilderness
Where none inhabited
But hellish fiends and brutish men
That devils worshipped.

Countering that view, in an essay titled "Ecologies of the Heart," cultural ecologist Gene Anderson observes that the world's traditional societies long ago came to "some kind of terms with their environment, or they would not have lasted long enough to become 'traditional.'" "Encoded in the moral teachings of most people who have spent generations on the same land, Anderson believes, "is a practical wisdom about the environment and the individual's duty to treat it with respect."

Perhaps that explains the correlation Hancocks found in his maps; and the professional transformation English zoologist Marcus Colchester made after living for a while in an indigenous community in the Amazon Basin. Now a practicing anthropologist, Colchester observes, "it is exactly because the areas that indigenous people inhabit have not been degraded by their traditional resource use practices that they are now coveted by conservationists who seek to limit their activities or expel them altogether from their customary lands."

It has taken big conservation a long and painful century to see the folly of some of its heroes, like Richard Leakey for example, who recently denied the existence of indigenous peoples in his home country, Kenya, and called for the removal of all "settlers" from game reserves and other protected areas. Today all but the most stubborn and entrenched enclose-and-exclude conservationists, who are fortunately dying off faster than the species they yearn to protect, are willing to admit that conflating nature with wilderness and occupants with "first visitors" is specious reasoning. And they have come to realize, from simple empiricism, that even if they don't own it, indigenous peoples manage immense areas of biologically rich land. And most are managing it well.

Some conservationists will even opine that regarding the impoverishment of indigenous people as tolerable, in the face of destructive development, a policy that has wrecked the lives of ten million or so poor, powerless, but eco-wise people, has been an enormous mistake; not only a moral, social, philosophical, and economic mistake, but an ecological one as well. Enlightened conservationists are asking themselves: "If in the course of saving biological diversity we destroy cultural diversity, what have we accomplished?" And they are beginning to accept the biocultural axiom that says: Only by preserving cultural diversity can biological diversity be protected, and vice versa.

Even Steven Sanderson, president of the Wildlife Conservation Society and outspoken challenger of melding social and conservation initiatives, has come to admit that "wildlife biology has been very confused historically about people. Protected areas have been demarked without regard to local people. Indigenous peoples and frontier folk alike have been demeaned by some protectionist strategies or dislocated by well-meaning conservationists. In the United States and in preindependence Africa wilderness and preservation were concepts that were developed without regard to people."[4] And Richard Leakey confesses that he might not be so conservation-minded if he were "cold and hungry."[5]

It is heartening to see credentialed conservation scientists challenging the scientific basis of their central strategy, which has failed to contend with newer, fast-moving threats like global climate change, invasive species, shifting disease vectors, and "spatially dynamic marine systems" that defy the utility of fixed protected areas.[6]

When, after setting aside a "protected" land mass the size of Africa, global biodiversity continues to decline and the rate of species extinction approaches one-thousand times background levels, the message seems clear that there might be something terribly wrong with this plan, particularly after the Convention on Biological Diversity has documented the astounding fact that in Africa, where so many parks and reserves have been created and where indigenous evictions still run highest, 90 percent of biodiversity lies outside of protected areas, most of it in places occupied by human beings.[7] If we really want people to live in harmony with nature, history is showing us that the dumbest thing we can do is kick them out of it.

And while encouraging good stewards to remain good stewards, conservationists might also reconsider the entire protected-area strategy. As the numbers just stated suggest, protected areas may not be the best way to conserve biodiversity. A better strategy might be simply to turn more human beings into true conservationists by teaching the value of natural capital at every level of education, and creating incentives in every society to conserve natural resources. This strategy would reward people who are already conservationists in practice by protecting them from poverty, rather than driving them into it as we do. Of course, it would help if human population growth were somehow stemmed.

The next step would be to find ways to produce economic wellbeing without compromising vast ecosystems, or to put it in more spiritual terms, without assaulting creation. Of course, eventually that would mean regarding the entire planet as a protected area, a sacred site if you will, worthy of equal protection—no more "sacrifice zones" anywhere on Mother Earth.

If that's too radical a concept, why not simply stop creating protected areas for a while, compare the ones that exist to biologically rich areas that haven't been "protected" but are managed under strict rules imposed by surrounding communities (undeclared but de facto protected areas), and evaluate what has been accomplished by creating parks and wildlife reserves to protect biodiversity. Such studies are showing that "parks and protected areas may not be the optimal governance structure for promoting local conservation," at least as they are currently designed and managed.[8]

Surely of the 108,000 registered protected areas in place, some are unnecessary, even counterproductive to wildlife conservation. Why not de-protect them, give the land back to their rightful owners, and find more ecologically vulnerable and socially suitable places to protect? And why not consider a new and different social contract with people living in or near protected areas, a contract designed to advance conservation?

Most of the evicted people I have interviewed over the past four years told me that if they could return to their land they would be willing to accept a contract with the conservation establishment and, if need be, with their national government. Such an agreement, similar to the sort of covenant that accompanies a standard conservation easement, might restrict forest harvesting of flora and fauna to the indigenous people's own (noncommercial) use.[9] Most also agreed to do nothing to compromise downstream water supply or quality, to control the growth of their own population, and never again to cultivate coca or opium for the illicit drug market (reserving the right to grow either for their own medicinal use). The only thing they were unwilling to accept is poverty, a state most found themselves in shortly after being evicted from homelands where they had thrived in relative wealth and security for generations. Why not sign that contract and let these native people return to the place in the world they love best and are ready to steward in partnership with modern science? Strangely enough, many of the social activists and cultural survivalists I spoke with while researching this book were opposed to such contracts, regarding them as unwarranted violations of sovereignty and self-determination, despite the fact that at least some of those conditions were written into the design of Community Conservation Area projects they helped develop.

And why not perform more social audits on protected areas where the impact on human communities has been severe? Surely there are some protected areas that have caused so much misery by evicting and excluding local peoples that whatever conservation goals they may have accomplished simply aren't worth it. Close down these parks and reserves too. Then take the ones that are working for conservation and make them work for people as well. As Martin Saning'o reminds us, if local people aren't for conservation, it simply won't work. The dozens of successful models in place on every continent prove that community-initiated and -managed conservation can work. Try it with the Batwa in Uganda and they might coin a word for *future*.

A Leaked Document

The natural and social calamities pass away.
—Peter Kropotkin

I have a copy of an internal Conservation International memorandum in my files. It's about a tribe that has lived for centuries in an area slated for protection. The memo's author laments the possibility of "these people ever coming into possession of shotguns and chain saws." The clause was redacted before the next draft of the memo was circulated, perhaps at the suggestion of someone in CI who perceived its implicit prejudice, or better still recalled that the white man has not always made responsible use of the shotgun and chain saw. I hope that was the reason.

I have no doubt that there are similar memos in the files of every major conservation organization. Someone just happened to leak one to me from CI. It in fact expresses a very old sentiment in international conservation. Early colonial governments in Africa passed laws forbidding natives to own guns for fear they would hunt game to extinction. Even farmers whose fields were routinely destroyed by rogue elephants and buffalo were forbidden to own firearms. When sympathetic colonials in 1928 suggested that each farmer be allowed one muzzle-loading rifle to protect his fields, conservationist T. H. Henfrey wrote: "Pray God it will never be allowed."[10]

As I read the revised draft of the CI memo, I hoped there had also been a discussion at headquarters about the rank unfairness of "enforced

primitivism"—requiring indigenous people who wished to stay in protected areas to remain "native," to not adopt modern practices or technologies, and in worse cases urging them to turn their community into
a human zoo, where proud adults are paid by lodge owners to dress up
in ceremonial garb and perform fertility dances for visiting ecotourists.
The modern transformation of societies from primitive to technological
cultures has proved to be disastrous for ecological health and biodiversity. It needn't be that way. The Kayapo and thousands of other tribal
communities have demonstrated that they can enter the twenty-first
century as equal players in the modern world, without repeating the
destructive patterns of the people who have tried to restrain them.

"The central irony of the twentieth century for conservationists,"
according to conservation historian William Adams, "is that the remarkable growth in size and influence of their movement has been accompanied by accelerating destruction of nature." I believe that is so because
the whole concept of land and resource stewardship came to Western
civilization very late in its history, perhaps too late, whereas stewardship
has for centuries, even millennia been the primary impulse of people who
have too often been pushed off their land.

From the very moment two families decided somewhere on the planet,
thousands of generations ago, to live and forage side by side, they realized, probably without even saying so, that the health and future of the
social construct we now call community could not survive without concerted care for land, air, water, and the life-giving services they provide.
That was, and remains, the original settlers' first impulse. They were and
still are the first stewards. We have so much more to learn from them
than we realize.

Appendix A

Indigenous Peoples and Conservation: WWF Statement of Principles

A WWF International Position Paper

Contents

Foreword

Preamble

I. Rights and Interests of Indigenous Peoples

II. Conservation Objectives

III. Principles of Partnership

Foreword

Indigenous peoples inhabit nearly 20 percent of the planet, mainly in areas where they have lived for thousands of years. Compared with protected area managers, who control about 6 percent of the world's land mass, indigenous peoples are the earth's most important stewards.

During more than three decades of conservation work, WWF has been approached by many indigenous and rural communities seeking collaboration on issues like protected area management and the conservation of natural resources. Notable amongst them are the Hupa Indians of northern California, the Inuit of Isabella Bay in Canada, the Zoque Indians of Mexico, the Karen of Thailand, the Shona people in Zimbabwe, the Kuna of Panama, the Shimshali of Pakistan, the Phoka people of northern Malawi, the Imagruen of Mauritania, the Ewenk of Siberia, and many others scattered all over the globe. WWF is, or has recently been, working with indigenous peoples in all regions of the world: in Europe, Latin America, North America, Asia, the Pacific, and Africa.

WWF's views on the relationship between indigenous peoples and modern conservation have been touched upon in several of our recent publications. As a result of its central role in discussing indigenous peoples' issues at the IV World Congress on National Parks and Protected Areas, WWF published the book *The Law of the Mother*, edited by Elizabeth Kemf, which collects and analyses experiences at the interface between indigenous peoples and conservation, including several project sites where WWF has been involved. In publications like Conservation with People and Forests For Life, WWF has expressed its conviction that indigenous peoples are crucial actors in conservation. Together with IUCN and UNEP, in Caring for the Earth WWF acknowledged the need for recognition "of the aboriginal rights of indigenous peoples to their lands and resources . . . and to participate effectively in decisions affecting their lands and resources."

Despite this history, the statement which follows represents WWF's first attempt to enunciate a broad policy to guide its work. It has been prepared following extensive consultation throughout the WWF network, which has an institutional presence in more than 50 countries. Building consensus on an emotive and politically sensitive topic is far from easy; moreover, there is a great diversity of national and regional situations in countries where WWF is active. The statement is our current best effort, but there may remain certain issues on which full consensus has still to be built. The interpretation and application of the statement may thus need to be adapted according to each national context. These variations must be interpreted as an expression of the diversity of circumstances within and outside the organization. From time to time, as WWF learns more about the topic, the statement may be updated to incorporate new views or perspectives.

Over the coming months, WWF will be preparing guidelines to assist its Programme staff in their work as it relates to the statement. As always, the implementation of such guidelines will be determined by the twin constraints of personnel and funds.

We believe the statement is a far-sighted step for an international organization whose mission is the conservation of nature, but we also recognize it may not be perfect to all eyes. Therefore, we would be pleased to receive comment and criticism from readers of this statement, to enable us to continue to improve our approach and contribution in this field.

Dr Claude Martin
Director General

Dr Chris Hails
Programme Director

Gland, Switzerland
22 May 1996

Indigenous Peoples[1] and Conservation: WWF Statement of Principles

Principles for partnership between WWF and indigenous peoples' organizations in conserving biodiversity within indigenous peoples' lands and territories, and in promoting sustainable use of natural resources

Preamble

1. Most of the remaining significant areas of high natural value on earth are inhabited by indigenous peoples. This testifies to the efficacy of indigenous resource management systems. Indigenous peoples and conservation organizations should be natural allies in the struggle to conserve both a healthy natural world and healthy human societies. Regrettably, the goals of conserving biodiversity and protecting and securing indigenous cultures and livelihoods have sometimes been perceived as contradictory rather than mutually reinforcing.

2. The principles for partnership outlined in this statement arise from WWF's mission to conserve biodiversity, combined with a recognition that indigenous peoples have been often stewards and protectors of nature. Their knowledge, social, and livelihood systems—their cultures—are closely attuned to the natural laws operating in local ecosystems. Unfortunately, such nature-attuned cultures have become highly

vulnerable to destructive forces related to unsustainable use of resources, population expansion, and the global economy.

3. WWF recognizes that industrialized societies bear a heavy responsibility for the creation of these destructive forces. WWF believes that environmental and other non-governmental organizations, together with other institutions worldwide, should adopt strategies with indigenous peoples, both to correct the national and international political, economic, social, and legal imbalances giving rise to these destructive forces, and to address their local effects. The following principles aim to provide guidance in formulating and implementing such strategies.

I.   Rights and Interests of Indigenous Peoples

4. WWF acknowledges that, without recognition of the rights of indigenous peoples, no constructive agreements can be drawn up between conservation organizations and indigenous peoples groups.

5. Since indigenous peoples are often discriminated against and politically marginalized, WWF is committed to make special efforts to respect, protect, and comply with their basic human rights and customary as well as resource rights, in the context of conservation initiatives. This includes, but is not limited to, those set out in national and international law, and in other international instruments.

In particular, WWF fully endorses the provisions about indigenous peoples contained in the following international instruments:

• Agenda 21

• Convention on Biological Diversity

• ILO Convention 169 (Convention Concerning Indigenous and Tribal Peoples in Independent Countries)[2]

• Draft UN Declaration on the Rights of Indigenous Peoples[3]

6. WWF appreciates the enormous contributions indigenous peoples have made to the maintenance of many of the earth's most fragile ecosystems. It recognizes the importance of indigenous resource rights and knowledge for the conservation of these areas in the future.

7. WWF recognizes indigenous peoples as rightful architects of and partners for conservation and development strategies that affect their territories.

8. WWF recognizes that indigenous peoples have the rights to the lands, territories, and resources that they have traditionally owned or otherwise occupied or used, and that those rights must be recognized and effectively protected, as laid out in the ILO Convention 169.

9. WWF recognizes the right of indigenous peoples to exert control over their lands, territories, and resources, and establish on them the management and governance systems that best suit their cultures and social needs, whilst respecting national sovereignty and conforming to national conservation and development objectives.

10. WWF recognizes, respects, and promotes the collective rights of indigenous peoples to maintain and enjoy their cultural and intellectual heritage.

11. Consistent with Article 7 of the ILO Convention 169, WWF recognizes indigenous peoples' right to decide on issues such as technologies and management systems to be used on their lands, and supports their application insofar as they are environmentally sustainable and contribute to the conservation of nature.

12. WWF recognizes that indigenous peoples have the right to determine priorities and strategies for the development or use of their lands, territories, and other resources, including the right to require that States obtain their free and informed consent prior to the approval of any project affecting those lands, territories, and resources.

13. WWF recognizes and supports the rights of indigenous peoples to improve the quality of their lives, and to benefit directly and equitably from the conservation and sustainable use of natural resources within their territories.

14. In instances where multiple local groups claim rights to resources in indigenous territories, WWF recognizes the primary rights of indigenous peoples based on historical claims and long-term presence, with due regard for the rights and welfare of other legitimate stakeholders.

15. WWF respects the rights of indigenous peoples to enjoy an equitable share in any economic or other benefits realized from their intellectual property and traditional knowledge, building on the provisions of the Convention on Biological Diversity.

16. In conformity with the provisions of the ILO Convention 169, WWF recognizes the right of indigenous peoples not to be removed from the territories they occupy. Where their relocation is considered necessary as an exceptional measure, it shall take place only with their free, prior informed consent.

II.   Conservation Objectives

17. At the heart of WWF's work is the belief that the earth's natural systems, resources, and life forms should be conserved for their intrinsic value and for the benefit of future generations.

WWF bases all of its conservation work on the principles contained in its Mission statement.

In addition, WWF fully endorses the provisions about biodiversity conservation and sustainable development contained in the following documents:

• Agenda 21

• Convention on Biological Diversity

• Convention on Trade in Endangered Species of Flora and Fauna (CITES)

• Convention on Wetlands of International Importance (Ramsar Convention)

• Caring for the Earth

18. WWF encourages and supports ecologically sound development activities, particularly those that link conservation and human needs. WWF may choose not to support, and may actively oppose, activities it judges unsustainable from the standpoint of species or ecosystems, or which are inconsistent with WWF policies on endangered or threatened species or with international agreements protecting wildlife and other natural resources, even if those activities are carried out by indigenous communities.

19. WWF seeks out partnerships with local communities, grass roots groups, non-governmental organizations, governments, corporations, international funding institutions, and other groups, including indigenous communities and indigenous peoples' organizations, who share WWF's commitment to the following conservation objectives:

i) Conservation of biodiversity: to conserve biological diversity at the genetic, species, and ecosystem levels; to improve knowledge and understanding of species and ecosystems; to protect endangered species of animals and plants; to maintain ecosystem functions; to maintain protected areas and improve their management.

ii) Sustainable use of resources: to ensure that any harvest of natural resources is sustainable; to support community management of renewable resources according to subsistence and cultural needs; to use recycling methods where appropriate; to use resource-efficient methods and technologies; and to substitute non-renewable with renewable resources wherever possible.

iii) Pollution prevention: to prevent, wherever possible, discharges of environmentally damaging substances, and ensure that products and processes are non-polluting.

III.   Principles of Partnership

20. The following principles will govern: (i) WWF conservation activities within indigenous peoples' lands and territories; (ii) WWF partnerships with indigenous peoples' organizations; (iii) WWF partnerships with other organizations whose activities may impact upon indigenous peoples.

21. Whenever it promotes conservation objectives, and in the context of its involvement in conservation activities affecting indigenous peoples' lands and territories, WWF will encourage governments to "take steps as necessary . . . to guarantee effective protection of [indigenous peoples'] rights of ownership and possession" of those lands and territories, as determined by the ILO Convention 169 (Art. 14).

22. Prior to initiating conservation activities in an area, WWF will exercise due diligence to:

• seek out information about the historic claims and current exercise of customary rights of indigenous peoples in that area; and

• inform itself about relevant constitutional provisions, legislation, and administrative practices affecting such rights and claims in the national context.

23. When WWF conservation activities impinge on areas where historic claims and/or current exercise of customary resource rights of indigenous peoples are present, WWF will assume an obligation to:

• identify, seek out, and consult with legitimate representatives of relevant indigenous peoples' organizations at the earliest stages of programme development; and

• provide fora for consultation between WWF and affected peoples, so that information can be shared on an ongoing basis, and problems, grievances, and disputes related to the partnership can be resolved in a timely manner.

In addition, consistent with the relevance and significance of the proposed activities to the achievement of conservation objectives, WWF will be ready to:

• assist indigenous peoples' organizations in the design, implementation, monitoring, and evaluation of conservation activities, and to invest in strengthening such organizations and in developing relevant human resources in the respective indigenous communities;

• assist them in gaining access to other sources of technical and financial support to advance those development objectives that fall outside WWF's mission.

24. In instances where states or other stakeholders, including long-term residents, contest the rights of indigenous peoples, WWF will be ready to assist indigenous peoples to protect, through legally accepted mechanisms, their natural resource base, consistent with the achievement of WWF's Mission and subject to availability of resources.

25. Where the resource rights of indigenous peoples are challenged by national governments, private corporations, and/or other groups, and the defence of those rights are deemed relevant and significant to the achievement of its Mission, WWF will, in coordination and consultation with indigenous peoples' organizations and subject to availability of resources:

• seek out and/or invest in the development of legitimate and transparent mechanisms to resolve conflicts at local, regional, national, and international levels, as appropriate;

• seek to ensure that the primary rights and interests of indigenous peoples are well represented in such fora, including investment to inform and prepare indigenous peoples' representatives to take part in negotiations.

26. Consistent with WWF conservation priorities, WWF will promote and advocate for the implementation of Article 7 of the ILO Convention 169:

"Governments shall take measures, in co-operation with the peoples concerned, to protect and preserve the environment of the territories they inhabit."

27. WWF will not promote or support, and may actively oppose, interventions which have not received the prior free and informed consent of affected indigenous communities, and/or would adversely impact—directly or indirectly—on the environment of indigenous peoples' territories, and/or would affect their rights. This includes activities such as:

• economic or other development activities;

• natural resources exploitation;

• commercially oriented or academic research;

• resettlement of indigenous communities;

• creation of protected areas or imposition of restrictions on subsistence resource use;

• colonization within indigenous territories.

28. With respect to the existing knowledge of indigenous communities, prior to starting work in a particular area, WWF will establish agreements with the indigenous organizations representing local communities, to ensure that they are able to fully participate in decisions about the use of knowledge acquired in or about the area they inhabit, and equitably benefit from it. These agreements will explicitly determine the ways and conditions under which WWF will be allowed to use such knowledge.

29. In the context of its partnerships with organizations other than those specifically representing the interests of indigenous peoples (including national governments, donor agencies, private corporations, and non-governmental organizations), WWF will:

• ensure that such partnerships do not undermine, and if possible serve to actively promote, the basic human rights and customary resource rights of indigenous peoples;

• ensure that all relevant information developed through such partnerships and accessible to WWF, is shared with the appropriate representatives of indigenous peoples;

• ensure that any national or international advocacy or fundraising activity related to indigenous peoples will be undertaken in consultation with representatives of relevant indigenous peoples' organizations.

30. WWF recognizes that the resolution of problems related to indigenous peoples may require action in international fora, in addition to national interventions. In pursuit of the foregoing principles, and in order to enhance its own understanding of indigenous peoples' issues, and when consistent and relevant to its conservation objectives, WWF will:

• actively seek inclusion and engagement in relevant international, as well as national fora.

• initiate an ongoing process of dialogue with indigenous peoples' groups on the principles for partnership proposed herein.

31. WWF commits itself to promoting nationally and internationally, whenever possible and appropriate, the implementation of all of these principles in the context of conservation actions within indigenous peoples' lands and territories.

32. WWF is committed to upholding the above principles, and the spirit that informs them, to the best of its abilities.

Notes

1. In this position statement, as well as in other institutional documents, WWF refers to indigenous and tribal peoples using the definition of the ILO Convention 169. Unless explicitly said otherwise, the term "indigenous peoples" includes both concepts, "indigenous" and "tribal."

2. Adopted by the General Conference of the International Labour Organization on 27 June 1989.

3. As adopted by the Working Group on Indigenous Populations of the Sub-Commission on Prevention of Discrimination and Protection of Minorities of the UN Commission on Human Rights, at its eleventh session (UN document E/CN.4/Sub.2/1993/29, Annex I).

Appendix B

United Nations Declaration on the Rights of Indigenous Peoples

The General Assembly,

Guided by the purposes and principles of the Charter of the United Nations, and good faith in the fulfillment of the obligations assumed by States in accordance with the Charter,

Affirming that indigenous peoples are equal to all other peoples, while recognizing the right of all peoples to be different, to consider themselves different, and to be respected as such,

Affirming also that all peoples contribute to the diversity and richness of civilizations and cultures, which constitute the common heritage of humankind,

Affirming further that all doctrines, policies and practices based on or advocating superiority of peoples or individuals on the basis of national origin or racial, religious, ethnic or cultural differences are racist, scientifically false, legally invalid, morally condemnable and socially unjust,

Reaffirming that indigenous peoples, in the exercise of their rights, should be free from discrimination of any kind,

Concerned that indigenous peoples have suffered from historic injustices as a result of, inter alia, their colonization and dispossession of their lands, territories and resources, thus preventing them from exercising, in particular, their right to development in accordance with their own needs and interests,

Recognizing the urgent need to respect and promote the inherent rights of indigenous peoples which derive from their political, economic and social structures and from their cultures, spiritual traditions, histories and philosophies, especially their rights to their lands, territories and resources,

Recognizing also the urgent need to respect and promote the rights of indigenous peoples affirmed in treaties, agreements and other constructive arrangements with States,

Welcoming the fact that indigenous peoples are organizing themselves for political, economic, social and cultural enhancement and in order to bring to an end all forms of discrimination and oppression wherever they occur,

Convinced that control by indigenous peoples over developments affecting them and their lands, territories and resources will enable them to maintain and strengthen their institutions, cultures and traditions, and to promote their development in accordance with their aspirations and needs,

Recognizing that respect for indigenous knowledge, cultures and traditional practices contributes to sustainable and equitable development and proper management of the environment,

Emphasizing the contribution of the demilitarization of the lands and territories of indigenous peoples to peace, economic and social progress and development, understanding and friendly relations among nations and peoples of the world,

Recognizing in particular the right of indigenous families and communities to retain shared responsibility for the upbringing, training, education and well-being of their children, consistent with the rights of the child,

Considering that the rights affirmed in treaties, agreements and other constructive arrangements between States and indigenous peoples are, in some situations, matters of international concern, interest, responsibility and character,

Considering also that treaties, agreements and other constructive arrangements, and the relationship they represent, are the basis for a strengthened partnership between indigenous peoples and States,

Acknowledging that the Charter of the United Nations, the International Covenant on Economic, Social and Cultural Rights and the International Covenant on Civil and Political Rights as well as the Vienna Declaration and Programme of Action, affirm the fundamental importance of the right to self-determination of all peoples, by virtue of which they freely determine their political status and freely pursue their economic, social and cultural development,

Bearing in mind that nothing in this Declaration may be used to deny any peoples their right to self-determination, exercised in conformity with international law,

Convinced that the recognition of the rights of indigenous peoples in this Declaration will enhance harmonious and cooperative relations between the State and indigenous peoples, based on principles of justice, democracy, respect for human rights, non-discrimination and good faith,

Encouraging States to comply with and effectively implement all their obligations as they apply to indigenous peoples under international instruments, in particular those related to human rights, in consultation and cooperation with the peoples concerned,

Emphasizing that the United Nations has an important and continuing role to play in promoting and protecting the rights of indigenous peoples,

Believing that this Declaration is a further important step forward for the recognition, promotion and protection of the rights and freedoms of indigenous peoples and in the development of relevant activities of the United Nations system in this field,

Recognizing and reaffirming that indigenous individuals are entitled without discrimination to all human rights recognized in international law, and that indigenous peoples possess collective rights which are indispensable for their existence, well-being and integral development as peoples,

Recognizing also that the situation of indigenous peoples varies from region to region and from country to country and that the significance of national and regional particularities and various historical and cultural backgrounds should be taken into consideration,

Solemnly proclaims the following United Nations Declaration on the Rights of Indigenous Peoples as a standard of achievement to be pursued in a spirit of partnership and mutual respect:

Article 1
Indigenous peoples have the right to the full enjoyment, as a collective or as individuals, of all human rights and fundamental freedoms as recognized in the Charter of the United Nations, the Universal Declaration of Human Rights and international human rights law.

Article 2
Indigenous peoples and individuals are free and equal to all other peoples and individuals and have the right to be free from any kind of discrimination, in the exercise of their rights, in particular that based on their indigenous origin or identity.

Article 3
Indigenous peoples have the right to self-determination. By virtue of that right they freely determine their political status and freely pursue their economic, social and cultural development.

Article 4
Indigenous peoples, in exercising their right to self-determination, have the right to autonomy or self-government in matters relating to their internal and local affairs, as well as ways and means for financing their autonomous functions.

Article 5
Indigenous peoples have the right to maintain and strengthen their distinct political, legal, economic, social and cultural institutions, while retaining their right to participate fully, if they so choose, in the political, economic, social and cultural life of the State.

Article 6
Every indigenous individual has the right to a nationality.

Article 7
1. Indigenous individuals have the rights to life, physical and mental integrity, liberty and security of person.

2. Indigenous peoples have the collective right to live in freedom, peace and security as distinct peoples and shall not be subjected to any act of genocide or any other act of violence, including forcibly removing children of the group to another group.

Article 8

1. Indigenous peoples and individuals have the right not to be subjected to forced assimilation or destruction of their culture.

2. States shall provide effective mechanisms for prevention of, and redress for:

(a) Any action which has the aim or effect of depriving them of their integrity as distinct peoples, or of their cultural values or ethnic identities;

(b) Any action which has the aim or effect of dispossessing them of their lands, territories or resources;

(c) Any form of forced population transfer which has the aim or effect of violating or undermining any of their rights;

(d) Any form of forced assimilation or integration;

(e) Any form of propaganda designed to promote or incite racial or ethnic discrimination directed against them.

Article 9

Indigenous peoples and individuals have the right to belong to an indigenous community or nation, in accordance with the traditions and customs of the community or nation concerned. No discrimination of any kind may arise from the exercise of such a right.

Article 10

Indigenous peoples shall not be forcibly removed from their lands or territories. No relocation shall take place without the free, prior and informed consent of the indigenous peoples concerned and after agreement on just and fair compensation and, where possible, with the option of return.

Article 11

1. Indigenous peoples have the right to practise and revitalize their cultural traditions and customs. This includes the right to maintain, protect and develop the past, present and future manifestations of their cultures, such as archaeological and historical sites, artefacts, designs, ceremonies, technologies and visual and performing arts and literature.

2. States shall provide redress through effective mechanisms, which may include restitution, developed in conjunction with indigenous peoples, with respect to their cultural, intellectual, religious and spiritual property taken without their free, prior and informed consent or in violation of their laws, traditions and customs.

Article 12

1. Indigenous peoples have the right to manifest, practice, develop and teach their spiritual and religious traditions, customs and ceremonies; the right to maintain, protect, and have access in privacy to their religious and cultural sites; the right to the use and control of their ceremonial objects; and the right to the repatriation of their human remains.

2. States shall seek to enable the access and/or repatriation of ceremonial objects and human remains in their possession through fair, transparent and effective mechanisms developed in conjunction with indigenous peoples concerned.

Article 13

1. Indigenous peoples have the right to revitalize, use, develop and transmit to future generations their histories, languages, oral traditions, philosophies, writing systems and literatures, and to designate and retain their own names for communities, places and persons.

2. States shall take effective measures to ensure that this right is protected and also to ensure that indigenous peoples can understand and be understood in political, legal and administrative proceedings, where necessary through the provision of interpretation or by other appropriate means.

Article 14

1. Indigenous peoples have the right to establish and control their educational systems and institutions providing education in their own languages, in a manner appropriate to their cultural methods of teaching and learning.

2. Indigenous individuals, particularly children, have the right to all levels and forms of education of the State without discrimination.

3. States shall, in conjunction with indigenous peoples, take effective measures, in order for indigenous individuals, particularly children, including those living outside their communities, to have access, when possible, to an education in their own culture and provided in their own language.

Article 15

1. Indigenous peoples have the right to the dignity and diversity of their cultures, traditions, histories and aspirations which shall be appropriately reflected in education and public information.

2. States shall take effective measures, in consultation and cooperation with the indigenous peoples concerned, to combat prejudice and eliminate discrimination and to promote tolerance, understanding and good relations among indigenous peoples and all other segments of society.

Article 16

1. Indigenous peoples have the right to establish their own media in their own languages and to have access to all forms of non-indigenous media without discrimination.

2. States shall take effective measures to ensure that State-owned media duly reflect indigenous cultural diversity. States, without prejudice to ensuring full freedom of expression, should encourage privately owned media to adequately reflect indigenous cultural diversity.

Article 17

1. Indigenous individuals and peoples have the right to enjoy fully all rights established under applicable international and domestic labour law.

2. States shall in consultation and cooperation with indigenous peoples take specific measures to protect indigenous children from economic exploitation and from performing any work that is likely to be hazardous or to interfere with the child's education, or to be harmful to the child's health or physical, mental, spiritual, moral or social development, taking into account their special vulnerability and the importance of education for their empowerment.

3. Indigenous individuals have the right not to be subjected to any discriminatory conditions of labour and, inter alia, employment or salary.

Article 18
Indigenous peoples have the right to participate in decision-making in matters which would affect their rights, through representatives chosen by themselves in accordance with their own procedures, as well as to maintain and develop their own indigenous decision-making institutions.

Article 19
States shall consult and cooperate in good faith with the indigenous peoples concerned through their own representative institutions in order to obtain their free, prior and informed consent before adopting and implementing legislative or administrative measures that may affect them.

Article 20
1. Indigenous peoples have the right to maintain and develop their political, economic and social systems or institutions, to be secure in the enjoyment of their own means of subsistence and development, and to engage freely in all their traditional and other economic activities.

2. Indigenous peoples deprived of their means of subsistence and development are entitled to just and fair redress.

Article 21
1. Indigenous peoples have the right, without discrimination, to the improvement of their economic and social conditions, including, inter

alia, in the areas of education, employment, vocational training and retraining, housing, sanitation, health and social security.

2. States shall take effective measures and, where appropriate, special measures to ensure continuing improvement of their economic and social conditions. Particular attention shall be paid to the rights and special needs of indigenous elders, women, youth, children and persons with disabilities.

Article 22

1. Particular attention shall be paid to the rights and special needs of indigenous elders, women, youth, children and persons with disabilities in the implementation of this Declaration.

2. States shall take measures, in conjunction with indigenous peoples, to ensure that indigenous women and children enjoy the full protection and guarantees against all forms of violence and discrimination.

Article 23

Indigenous peoples have the right to determine and develop priorities and strategies for exercising their right to development. In particular, indigenous peoples have the right to be actively involved in developing and determining health, housing and other economic and social programmes affecting them and, as far as possible, to administer such programmes through their own institutions.

Article 24

1. Indigenous peoples have the right to their traditional medicines and to maintain their health practices, including the conservation of their vital medicinal plants, animals and minerals. Indigenous individuals also have the right to access, without any discrimination, to all social and health services.

2. Indigenous individuals have an equal right to the enjoyment of the highest attainable standard of physical and mental health. States shall take the necessary steps with a view to achieving progressively the full realization of this right.

Article 25

Indigenous peoples have the right to maintain and strengthen their distinctive spiritual relationship with their traditionally owned or otherwise occupied and used lands, territories, waters and coastal seas and other resources and to uphold their responsibilities to future generations in this regard.

Article 26

1. Indigenous peoples have the right to the lands, territories and resources which they have traditionally owned, occupied or otherwise used or acquired.

2. Indigenous peoples have the right to own, use, develop and control the lands, territories and resources that they possess by reason of traditional ownership or other traditional occupation or use, as well as those which they have otherwise acquired.

3. States shall give legal recognition and protection to these lands, territories and resources. Such recognition shall be conducted with due respect to the customs, traditions and land tenure systems of the indigenous peoples concerned.

Article 27

States shall establish and implement, in conjunction with indigenous peoples concerned, a fair, independent, impartial, open and transparent process, giving due recognition to indigenous peoples' laws, traditions, customs and land tenure systems, to recognize and adjudicate the rights of indigenous peoples pertaining to their lands, territories and resources, including those which were traditionally owned or otherwise occupied or used. Indigenous peoples shall have the right to participate in this process.

Article 28

1. Indigenous peoples have the right to redress, by means that can include restitution or, when this is not possible, just, fair and equitable compensation, for the lands, territories and resources which they have traditionally owned or otherwise occupied or used, and which have been

confiscated, taken, occupied, used or damaged without their free, prior and informed consent.

2. Unless otherwise freely agreed upon by the peoples concerned, compensation shall take the form of lands, territories and resources equal in quality, size and legal status or of monetary compensation or other appropriate redress.

Article 29

1. Indigenous peoples have the right to the conservation and protection of the environment and the productive capacity of their lands or territories and resources. States shall establish and implement assistance programmes for indigenous peoples for such conservation and protection, without discrimination.

2. States shall take effective measures to ensure that no storage or disposal of hazardous materials shall take place in the lands or territories of indigenous peoples without their free, prior and informed consent.

3. States shall also take effective measures to ensure, as needed, that programmes for monitoring, maintaining and restoring the health of indigenous peoples, as developed and implemented by the peoples affected by such materials, are duly implemented.

Article 30

1. Military activities shall not take place in the lands or territories of indigenous peoples, unless justified by a significant threat to relevant public interest or otherwise freely agreed with or requested by the indigenous peoples concerned.

2. States shall undertake effective consultations with the indigenous peoples concerned, through appropriate procedures and in particular through their representative institutions, prior to using their lands or territories for military activities.

Article 31

1. Indigenous peoples have the right to maintain, control, protect and develop their cultural heritage, traditional knowledge and traditional cultural expressions, as well as the manifestations of their sciences,

technologies and cultures, including human and genetic resources, seeds, medicines, knowledge of the properties of fauna and flora, oral traditions, literatures, designs, sports and traditional games and visual and performing arts. They also have the right to maintain, control, protect and develop their intellectual property over such cultural heritage, traditional knowledge, and traditional cultural expressions.

2. In conjunction with indigenous peoples, States shall take effective measures to recognize and protect the exercise of these rights.

Article 32

1. Indigenous peoples have the right to determine and develop priorities and strategies for the development or use of their lands or territories and other resources.

2. States shall consult and cooperate in good faith with the indigenous peoples concerned through their own representative institutions in order to obtain their free and informed consent prior to the approval of any project affecting their lands or territories and other resources, particularly in connection with the development, utilization or exploitation of mineral, water or other resources.

3. States shall provide effective mechanisms for just and fair redress for any such activities, and appropriate measures shall be taken to mitigate adverse environmental, economic, social, cultural or spiritual impact.

Article 33

1. Indigenous peoples have the right to determine their own identity or membership in accordance with their customs and traditions. This does not impair the right of indigenous individuals to obtain citizenship of the States in which they live.

2. Indigenous peoples have the right to determine the structures and to select the membership of their institutions in accordance with their own procedures.

Article 34

Indigenous peoples have the right to promote, develop and maintain their institutional structures and their distinctive customs, spirituality, traditions, procedures, practices and, in the cases where they exist, juridical systems or customs, in accordance with international human rights standards.

Article 35
Indigenous peoples have the right to determine the responsibilities of individuals to their communities.

Article 36
1. Indigenous peoples, in particular those divided by international borders, have the right to maintain and develop contacts, relations and cooperation, including activities for spiritual, cultural, political, economic and social purposes, with their own members as well as other peoples across borders.

2. States, in consultation and cooperation with indigenous peoples, shall take effective measures to facilitate the exercise and ensure the implementation of this right.

Article 37
1. Indigenous peoples have the right to the recognition, observance and enforcement of treaties, agreements and other constructive arrangements concluded with States or their successors and to have States honour and respect such treaties, agreements and other constructive arrangements.

2. Nothing in this Declaration may be interpreted as diminishing or eliminating the rights of indigenous peoples contained in treaties, agreements and other constructive arrangements.

Article 38
States in consultation and cooperation with indigenous peoples, shall take the appropriate measures, including legislative measures, to achieve the ends of this Declaration.

Article 39
Indigenous peoples have the right to have access to financial and technical assistance from States and through international cooperation, for the enjoyment of the rights contained in this Declaration.

Article 40

Indigenous peoples have the right to access to and prompt decision through just and fair procedures for the resolution of conflicts and disputes with States or other parties, as well as to effective remedies for all infringements of their individual and collective rights. Such a decision shall give due consideration to the customs, traditions, rules and legal systems of the indigenous peoples concerned and international human rights.

Article 41

The organs and specialized agencies of the United Nations system and other intergovernmental organizations shall contribute to the full realization of the provisions of this Declaration through the mobilization, inter alia, of financial cooperation and technical assistance. Ways and means of ensuring participation of indigenous peoples on issues affecting them shall be established.

Article 42

The United Nations, its bodies, including the Permanent Forum on Indigenous Issues, and specialized agencies, including at the country level, and States shall promote respect for and full application of the provisions of this Declaration and follow up the effectiveness of this Declaration.

Article 43

The rights recognized herein constitute the minimum standards for the survival, dignity and well-being of the indigenous peoples of the world.

Article 44

All the rights and freedoms recognized herein are equally guaranteed to male and female indigenous individuals.

Article 45

Nothing in this Declaration may be construed as diminishing or extinguishing the rights indigenous peoples have now or may acquire in the future.

Article 46

1. Nothing in this Declaration may be interpreted as implying for any State, people, group or person any right to engage in any activity or to perform any act contrary to the Charter of the United Nations or construed as authorizing or encouraging any action which would dismember or impair, totally or in part, the territorial integrity or political unity of sovereign and independent States.

2. In the exercise of the rights enunciated in the present Declaration, human rights and fundamental freedoms of all shall be respected. The exercise of the rights set forth in this Declaration shall be subject only to such limitations as are determined by law, and in accordance with international human rights obligations. Any such limitations shall be non-discriminatory and strictly necessary solely for the purpose of securing due recognition and respect for the rights and freedoms of others and for meeting the just and most compelling requirements of a democratic society.

3. The provisions set forth in this Declaration shall be interpreted in accordance with the principles of justice, democracy, respect for human rights, equality, non-discrimination, good governance and good faith.

Notes

Preface

1. Convention on Biological Diversity, *Sustaining Life on Earth,* p. 5. Thirty-four thousand plant species and 5,200 animal species, including one in eight of the world's bird species, face extinction, as do 30 percent of farm animal species. About 10 percent of coral reefs—among the planet's richest ecosystems—are completely destroyed, and a third more face collapse within the next ten to twenty years.

2. *Millennium Ecosystem Assessment Synthesis Report,* initiated in 2001 at the behest of UN Secretary Kofi Annan, It was completed in 2005 by 1,300 experts from ninety-five countries.

A Word About Terms

1. *Encarta® World English Dictionary* © 1999 Microsoft Corporation. All rights reserved. Developed for Microsoft by Bloomsbury Publishing Plc.

2. There is a lot of literature on the subject of indigeneity. For those interested in pursuing the topic, I recommend the following: Ronald Niezen, *The Origins of Indigenism: Human Rights and the Politics of Identity* (University of California Press, 2003); S. James Anaya, *Indigenous Peoples and International Law* (Oxford University Press, 2004); Tania Li, "Articulating Indigenous Identity in Indonesia: Resource Politics and the Tribal Slot," *Comparative Studies in Society and History* 42, no. 1: 149–179 (January 2000); Michael R. Dove, "Indigenous People and Environmental Politics," *Annual Review of Anthropology* 35 (October 2006): 191–208; James Igoe, "Becoming Indigenous Peoples: Difference, Inequality, and the Globalization of East African Identity Politics," *African Affairs 2006* 105: 399–420.

Introduction

1. "Biodiversity," a neologism derived from "biological diversity," replaced its predecessor rationale for conservation—preservation of individual charismatic

species—in the mid-1980s. The term was coined in 1986 at a joint conference of the U.S. National Academy of Sciences and the Smithsonian Institution by Walter G. Rosen, senior program officer in the Board on Basic Biology, a unit of the Commission on Life Sciences in the National Research Council of the National Academy of Sciences. E. O. Wilson cochaired the conference and coedited the proceedings, which he titled *Biodiversity*.

2. IIFB statement presented to the CBD plenary session on February 14, 2008, and signed by representatives of the Global Forest Coalition, Pojoaju (The Association of Paraguayan NGOs), Kalpavriksh (India), Equations (India), the Timberwatch Coalition (South Africa), O'le Siosiomaga Society (Samoa), Censat/ Amigos De la Tierra (Colombia), CDO (Nepal), Global Justice Ecology Project (United States), Forest Peoples Programme (U.K.), Friends of the Earth International, And COECO-CEIBA/Friends of the Earth-Costa Rica.

3. Roderick Neumann, *Imposing Wilderness: Struggles over Livelihood and Nature Preservation in Africa* (University of California, 1998), 2.

4. Kent Redford, J. G. Robinson, and William Adams, "Parks as Shibboleths," *Conservation Biology* 20:1–2; Kent Redford and Steven Sanderson, "No Roads Only Directions," *Conservation and Society* 4, no. 3 (Sept. 2006): 379–382.

5. Conservation literature has been virtually silent on the issue of displacements. Most of the few existing studies on indigenous evictions have been performed and published by geographers, anthropologists, and other social scientists.

6. The "hot spot" approach to conservation, favored by Conservation International, is the invention of a British ecologist named Norman Meyers. Myers believes that about 45 percent of plant species and 35 percent of vertebrates are concentrated in less than 2 percent of the Earth's land surface. Only by demarcating and enclosing this land area into twenty-five protected areas ("hot spots") does CI believe that nature can be preserved. The problem with the hot spot approach, of course, is that it pretty much ignores the other 98 percent of the planet and the clearly endangered species living outside protected areas, and it leaves most of the world wide open to extractive industries.

7. Richard Leakey, addressing the World Congress on Protected Areas in Durban, South Africa, on September 8, 2003.

Chapter 1

1. Governor Burnett's full quote was "A war of extermination would continue to be waged until the Indian race should become extinct." In Rebecca Solnit, *Savage Dreams*, (Sierra Club Books, 1994), p. 271.

2. Years later, Tenaya was killed by some Mono Paiutes who believed he had stolen their horses.

3. George Catlin, *The Manners and Customs of the North American Indians* (1844).

4. Ibid.

5. Samuel Bowles, *Parks and Mountains of Colorado: A Summer Vacation in the Switzerland of America* (1868), (Universityof Oklahoma Press, 1991), 145–147.

6. Donald Worster, *The Wealth of Nature: Environmental History and the Ecological Imagination* (Oxford University Press 1993).

Chapter 2

1. P. West and D. Brockington, "An Anthropological Perspective on Some Unexpected Consequences of Protected Areas," *Conservation Biology* 20, no. 3 (2006): 609–616.

2. Gary Nabhan, *Cultures of Habitat* (Counterpoint Press, 1997).

3. World Rainforest Movement, *Protected Areas, Protected Against Whom?*, p. 14.

4. John Roach, "Indigenous Group Keeps Ecology All in the Family," *National Geographic*, June 29, 2006.

5. Ibid.

6. World Rainforest Movement, *Protected Areas, Protected Against Whom?*, p. 14.

7. Ibid.

8. Ibid.

Chapter 3

1. Raymond Bonner, *At the Hand of Man* (Knopf, 1993), p. 137.

2. "Serengeti" is the Maasai word meaning endless plains.

3. Bernhard Grzimek, *Serengeti Shall Not Die* (Ballantine Books, 1974).

4. Ibid.

5. Louis Leakey, "Memorandum on the Serengeti National Park Problem," 1959.

6. Now called Fauna and Flora International.

7. Roderick Neuman, *Imposing Wilderness* (University Of California, 1998), pp. 146–147.

8. Adamson and Fitzjohn earned their fame from the popular feature film *Born Free*, the classic tale of a lion pride that Adamson befriended. The Fitzjohn/Adamson trust is supported by Hollywood celebrities like Sylvester Stallone and Clint Eastwood, who with financial assistance from Cartier, Tiffany's, and British Petroleum made *To Walk With Lions*, the sequel to *Born Free*.

9. From Fitzjohn/Adamson Trust fundraising material.

10. Dan Brockington, *Fortress Conservation* (Indiana University Press, 2002), p. 3.

11. Ibid., p. 132.

12. Letter from the trust to *World Watch* journal. No date.

13. David Lovatt Smith, "Maasai Hopes and Fears," *People and the Planet* 6, no. 4 (1997).

14. One, named Gertie, who possessed a particularly long horn, became the poster child of the World Wildlife Foundation's first fundraising appeal.

Chapter 4

1. The source of that story now works for a competitive environmental organization and asked me not to reveal his identity.

2. Another 40 percent of the same USAID total was shared by five other American-based conservation NGOs. Fourteen percent went to The Nature Conservancy, 8 percent to the African Wildlife Foundation, 7 percent to the World Resources Institute, 6 percent to Conservation International, and 4 percent to the Wildlife Conservation Society.

3. Critical Ecosystems Partnership Fund Annual Reports.

4. WWF communiqué, "How We Work: Using 200 Priority Ecoregions," Washington, DC, 2004.

5. Thomas McShane, "The Devil in the Detail of Biodiversity Conservation." *Conservation Biology* 17, no. 1 (2003): 1–3.

6. Arvind Khare and David Bray, *Study of Critical New Forest Conservation Issues in the Global South,* unpublished report.

7. Ibid.

8. Ibid.

9. Conservation International letter to *World Watch* journal.

10. Ibid.

11. The Nature Conservancy letter to *World Watch* journal.

12. Sally Jeanrenaud, *People-oriented Approaches in Global Conservation: Is the Leopard Changing its Spots?* IUCN, 2002.

Chapter 5

1. Paradoxically, when naturalists and wildlife biographers regarded Pygmies as "part of the fauna," a complimentary observation with racist overtones, they were safe from eviction and other colonial abuses. It was not until Pygmies were welcomed into the human race (albeit not as equals) that life became dangerous for them.

2. When challenged on her claim that the Batwa were killing gorillas, Dian Fossey allowed that she may have exaggerated, but insisted that the wire snares

the Batwa used to trap small game had at times entrapped and injured young apes.

3. This unattributed quote is from an unsigned government press release.

4. She's right, of course. In fact, the entire indigenous people's story has been stolen and commodified by adventurers, cultural romantics, ecotour guides, anthropologists, and yes, journalists.

Chapter 6

1. John Terborgh, *Requiem for Nature* (Island Press, 1999).

2. Kent Redford and Steven Sanderson, "Extracting Humans From Nature," *Conservation Biology* 14, no. 5 (2000): 1362–1364.

3. Ibid., 1364.

4. Quoted in S. Schwartzman et al., "Rethinking Tropical Forest Conservation: Perils in Parks," *Conservation Biology* 14, no. 5: 1355.

5. Terborgh, "Reflections of a Scientist on the World Park's Congress," *Conservation Biology* 18 (2004): 619–620.

6. Terborgh, *Requiem for Nature,* see note 1, p. 7.

7. Robert Collier, "Can Gordon Moore Save the Amazon?" *San Francisco Chronicle*, Nov. 19, 2006.

8. Julia Ohl-Schacherer et al., "The Sustainability of Subsistence Hunting by Matsigenka Native Communities in Manu National Park, Peru," *Conservation Biology* 21, no. 5 (October 2007): 1174–1185.

9. Ibid., 170.

10. Ibid., 56.

11. Ibid.

12. Ibid., 156.

13. Ibid., 140.

14. Ibid.

15. Katrina Brandon, Kent H. Redford, and Steven E. Sanderson, *Parks in Peril, People, Politics and Protected Areas* (Island Press, 1998).

16. Kent Redford and Steven Sanderson, "Biodiversity Politics and the Contest for Ownership of the World's Biota," chapter 6, in *Last Stand: Protected Areas and the Defense of Tropical Biodiversity,* ed. Randal Kramer Carel van Shaik and Julie Johnson. (Oxford University Press, 1997).

17. John F. Oates, *Myth and Reality in the Rain Forest* (University of California Press, 1999), xiii.

18. Ibid.

19. Ibid.

20. Terborgh, *Requiem for Nature*, see note 1, p. 188.

21. Ibid., p. 9.

22. Holmes Rolston III, "Feeding People vs Saving Nature," in *World Hunger and Morality*, 2nd ed., ed. William Aiken and Hugh LaFollette (Englewood Cliffs, NJ: Prentice-Hall, 1996), pp. 248–267.

23. Holmes Rolston III, "Saving Nature, Feeding People and the Foundations of Ethics," *Environmental Values* 7 (1998): 349–357.

24. Ibid.

25. Ibid.

26. Ibid.

27. Ibid.

28. C. Spinage, "Social Change and Conservation Misrepresentation in Africa," *Oryx* 32, no. 4: 265–276.

29. M. Colchester, "Self-Determination or Environmental Determinism for Indigenous Peoples in Tropical Forest Conservation," *Conservation Biology* 14, no. 5 (2000): 1365–1367.

30. Terborgh, "The Fate of Tropical Forests, a Matter of Stewardship," *Conservation Biology* 14, no. 5 (2000): 1358.

31. Ibid., 1365.

32. Ibid.

33. *Wild Earth* journal (Winter 1992), unattributed editorial.

34. Shefa Seigel, *Conservation at All Costs*, Special Report to Corp-Watch, December 2003.

Chapter 8

1. Ethnobiology and ethnoecology are closely related late-twentieth-century interdisciplinary fields that combine the intuitions, skills, and research of anthropologists, botanists, zoologists, geographers, sociologists, and linguists to study the relationship of human societies and the plant and animal environments.

2. From an FDCC report to the secretariat of the Convention on Biological Diversity (1996).

3. Fikret Berkes, *Sacred Ecology: Traditional Ecological Knowledge* (Taylor and Francis, 1999).

4. M. M. R. Freeman, "The Nature and Utility of Traditional Ecological Knowledge," *Journal of the Canadian Arctic Research Committee*. 20, no. 1.

5. Joseph Grinnell's classic treatise "Fauna of the National Parks of the United States" invoked the Organic Act's stipulation that "scenery, natural objects and wildlife should remain unimpaired" in national parks.

6. John Sallenave, "Giving Traditional Ecological Knowledge Its Rightful
Place in Environmental Impact Assessment," *Northern Perspective* 22, no. 1
(Spring 1994).

Chapter 9

1. Ian Mackinnon, *The Scotsman*, May 24, 2003, 13.

2. The Soligas people have an intimate link with the forest. They have named
107 species of trees, 11 grasses, 13 types of fiber, 55 species of birds, 15 snakes,
97 insects, and 41 other animal species. The forest classification scheme of the
Soligas divides their environs into *kanu kadu* (thick forest where animals live),
mala kadu (thin forest where animals and Soligas live), *nadu kadu* (open thorn
forests), and *bole* (where tall grasses grow and animals like bear are found).
Water sources also are included in their classification of forests. The forest is a
place for them to live and celebrate their festivals. It provides them with honey,
fruits, tubers, and roots to eat. They have their own medicinal system known as
naru-beru oushadi (roots and tuber medicine). Traditional healers effectively
treat common ailments, set fractured bones, and even manage mental health
problems. The Soligas use more than three hundred herbs for treatment. Thus
nature has been the single largest factor of their culture and their concern for
the environment is a product of their necessity, intuition, and knowledge (Antoine
Lasgorceix and Ashish Knotari of Kalpavriksh).

3. "India: End of Forest Evictions? New Forest Bill," *World Rainforest Movement Bulletin 106* (June 2006).

4. Ramachandra Guha, "Ecology for the People," *India Together*, May 16,
2006.

5. Ashish Kothari, "Forest Rights Act: Stormy Start, Uncertain Future," unpublished paper, p. 8.

Chapter 10

1. K. M. Homewood and W. A. Rodgers, "Pastoralism and Conservation,"
Human Ecology 12, no. 4 (1987): 431–441.

2. F. Berkes and C. Folke, "Back to the Future: Ecosystems Dynamics and Local
Knowledge," in *Understanding Transformations in Human and Natural Systems*,
ed. H.Gunderson and C. S.Hollings (Island Press, 2002), pp. 121–146.

3. Allan Savory, personal communication.

4. Homewood and Rogers, see note 1.

5. Sarah DeWeerdt and Chuck Striplen, "Old Science, New Science: Incorporat-
ing Tranditional Ecological Knowledge into Contemporary Management," *Conservation in Practice* (Summer 2002): 21–27.

6. David Barton Bray et al. "The Drivers of Sustainable Landscapes: A Case Study of the 'Mayan Zone' in Quintana Roo, Mexico," *Land Use Policy* 21 (2004): 333–346.

7. Paul Robbins, Kendra McSweeney, ThomasWaite, and Jennifer Rice, "Even Conservation Rules Are Made to Be Broken: Implications for Biodiversity," *Environmental Management* 37, no. 2: 162–169.

Chapter 11

1. Basildon Peta, *The Independent,* January 3, 2004.

Chapter 12

1. World Bank OMS 4.20 lists the following five characteristics of indigenous peoples: "Close attachment to ancestral land, self-identification and identification of others, an indigenous language different from the national one, presence of customary and social institutions, and primarily subsistence oriented production."

2. Sir Sridath Ramphal, *Report of the IVth World Congress on National Parks and Protected Areas* (IUCN, 1993) p. 57.

3. Michael Cernea and Kai Schmidt-Soltau, "Poverty Risks and National Parks," *World Development* 34, no. 10 (2006): 1808–1830.

4. CEESP's mission is "to contribute to the IUCN Mission by providing insights and expertise on ways to harmonize biodiversity conservation and cultural concerns of human communities, such as livelihoods, poverty eradication, development, equity, human rights, cultural identity, security and the fair and effective governance of natural resources."

5. An IUCN-drafted treaty, the Convention on Biological Diversity was signed in Rio de Janeiro in June 1992 by 156 states and the European Community at the United Nations Conference on Environment and Development (UNCED). By 2001 the treaty had 181 signatories. Conservation was global.

6. Ronald Niezen, *The Origins of Indigenism: Human Rights and the Politics of Identity* (University of California Press, 2003) p. 24.

7. Ibid.

8. Coordinador a de las organizaciones Indílgenas de la Cuenca Amazonica (COICA), *Two Agendas for Amazon Development,* undated report.

9. Brandon, Kent Redford, and Steven Sanderson, eds. *Parks in Peril: People Politics and Protected Areas* (The Nature Conservancy and Island Press, 1998).

10. The Nature Conservancy, *How We Work, Supporting People and Places.*

11. UN press release, September 13, 2007.

Chapter 13

1. G. H. Yeoman, "High Altitude Forest Conservation in Relation to Dorobo People," *Kenya Past and Present* (1993).

2. Ibid.

Chapter 14

1. It was a conversation with Poole, a direct and intense Englishman married to a Cherokee-American woman, that started me on the long course of inquiry that led to this book.

2. P. Poole, "Geomatics, Who Needs It?" *Cultural Survival* 18, no. 4.

3. J. B. Harley, *Maps, Knowledge and Power* (The Johns Hopkins University Press, 2001).

4. N. L. Peluso, "Whose Woods Are These? Counter-mapping Forest Territories in Kalimantan, Indonesia," *Aantipod* 27: 383.

5. Mac Chapin, "Identifying Obstacles and Finding Solutions," a speech given June 2005 in Nairobi, Kenya.

Chapter 15

1. Janet Chernela, letter to *WorldWatch* journal in response to Mac Chapin's article.

Chapter 17

1. David Turton, "The Mursi and the Elephant," in *Conservation and Mobile Indigenous Peoples*, ed. Dawn Chatty and Marcus Colchester. (Berghahn Books, 2002).

2. David Turton, *The Mursi and National Park Development* (1987), (World Bank, 1994) p. 179.

3. William M. Adams, *Against Extinction,* (Earthscan 2004) p. 114.

Chapter 18

1. Sir Shridath "Sonny" Ramphal served as foreign minister of Guyana from 1972 to 1975. He was the chancellor of the University of Warwick from 1989 to 2002 and the University of the West Indies until 2003 and also served as chancellor of the University of Guyana. He studied at the London School of Economics. He was made an Honorary Fellow of the Royal Society of Arts in May 2006.

2. J. Peter Brosius, "Reflections on Conservation, Displacement and Exclusion," WCS Working Paper 29, p. 110.

3. The Sikuani, Piapoco, Piaroa, Puinave, Cuuipaco, and Cubeo.

Chapter 19

1. David Barron's Washington-based firm, Barron-Birrell, has also been a registered lobbyist for the Republic of Congo and the rebel group Rassemblement Congolais Pout La Democratie in the Democratic Republic of Congo. In the late 1990s, Barron-Birrell also provided PR services for President Charles Taylor of Liberia while Taylor was using revenues from illegal logging to finance arms purchases and promote regional destabilization. Barron is also a board member of the Boulder, Colorado-based Wilderness Leadership Foundation (WILD) of which Michael Fay is also a trustee.

2. Conversation with ter Heegde.

Epilogue

1. Victor M. Toledo, "Indigenous Peoples and Biodiversity," in *Encyclopedia of Biodiversity*, ed. S. Levin et al. (Academic Press 1999).

2. Steven Sanderson, keynote address to Conservation Biology convention, October 7, 2003.

3. Ibid.

4. J. P. Roderiguez et al., "Globalization of Conservation: A View from the South," *Science* 317, no. 5839 (August 2007): 755–756.

5. Over 70 percent of the wildlife in the Maasai Mara region of Kenya exist outside the Maasai Mara reserve, on land that is grazed by Maasai pastorals and spotted with their traditional villages.

6. Tanya Hayes, "Parks People and Forest Protection: An Institutional Assessment of the Effectiveness of Protected Areas," *World Development* 34, no. 12 (2006): 2064–2075.

7. Such a covenant might say in effect: "The land where you have lived for generations has high biodiversity because you have been good stewards. Remain good stewards and the land is yours."

8. T. H. Henfrey, *Is Game Preservation Compatible with Agricultural Development?* (1928), p. 118.

Index

Abedi, Agha Hasan, 50
Aborigines. *See also* Indigenous
  peoples
  Adivasi and, 118–132
  Australian, 116–117, 171–172,
  237–238
  Australian Homelands Movement
  (AHM) and, 237–238
  *Eddie Mabo and Others v. The
  State of Queensland* and, 151
Ache, 111
Adams, Ansel, 8, 15–16
Adams, Bill, ix, 16, 45
Adams, Jonathan, xxiv
Adams, J. S., 30
Adams, William, 139, 231, 269
Adamson, George, 31, 41, 299n8
Adamson, Joy, 41
Adamson, Rebecca, xxii, 46, 147
Adivasi, xix, 118
  agriculture and, 119
  British rule and, 128
  Buddhism and, 121
  compensation claims and, 125–126
  Conventional on Biological Diversity
  and, 125
  cultural contributions of, 121–122
  equality and, 121
  evictions of, 119–132
  Hinduism and, 121–122
  hunting and, 119–120
  legal issues and, 124–127
  lions and, 119

Nagarhole National Park and, 120,
  123
  as scapegoats, 119–120
  The Scheduled Tribes and Other
  Traditional Forest Dwellers Bill
  and, 127
  slavery and, 125
  social structure of, 121–122
  tiger crisis and, 127–132
  tribes composing, 121
  Wildlife Protection Act and,
  123–124
AES Energy Corp, 55
Africa, xii. *See also* Specific country
  British colonialists and, 23–26
  conflicts in, xix
  European colonialism and, 194
  Grzimek and, 23–26, 30
  gun ownership and, 268
  hunting restrictions and, 23–24
  tribal blending and, 28
African Development Bank, 254
African Parks Foundation (APF),
  222–223
  Community Fund of, 231
  Dutch backing of, 226
  evictions and, 226–233
  food aid and, 229–231
  Mursi and, 226–233
  Omo National Park and, 226–233
  shifting blame by, 227–228
African Wildlife Foundation (AWF),
  xxii, 51–52, 97, 221

Convention on Biological Diversity
and, 118
exclusionary policies and, 79–99
first stewards and, 235–247
flagship species and, xi, xxvii, 66
Indigenous Protected Areas (IPAs)
and, 237–247
merchandising nature and,
254–257
Milne Bay and, 209–221
neologism of, 297n1
protected areas (PAs) and, 236 (*see
also* Protected areas (PAs))
protest and, 157–158
rotational clearings and, 135–139
semantics of, 19
technology and, 81
traditional ecological knowledge
(TEK) and, 107–118
Uganda and, 66–67
utilitarianism and, 86
WWF Statement of Principles and,
273–280
Biological Armageddon, 79
Biological corridors, xxii
Biomes, 136, 153
Bioprospecting, xxv, 218–220
Bird Life International, 12
Birds, 120, 223, 243–245
Blackfeet, 11, 239
Blyth's Tragopan, 243
Bodi, 223
Body Shop, The, xxv
Boise Cascade, 55
Boling, John, 3
Bolivia, 97–98, 164, 177, 244–245
Bongo, 71
Bongo Ondimba, El Hadj Omar,
249–250, 254
Bonner, Raymond, 176
Bonobos, 252
Born Free (film), 299n8
Boston Evening Transcript, 4
Botswana, xii, xix, xxvi, 123, 140
Basarwa and, 141–152
cattle grazing and, 230–231

Central Kalahari Game Reserve
(CKGR) and, 42, 142, 144–147
diamonds and, 141, 146
First People of the Kalahari (FPK),
146–147, 149
Khama and, 142, 144, 210
Mogae and, 143
nonrecognition of First People,
142–146
protests and, 156
Remote Area Dwellers and,
142–143
Restitution of Land Rights Act and,
148
Wildlife Management Areas and,
142
Botswana Department of Wildlife and
National Parks, 147
Boumba National Park, 197
Bowles, Samuel, 5–6, 264
Brandon, Katrina, 80–84, 98, 169
Bray, David, 59, 137, 153, 237
Brazil, xviii, 138, 164, 176 244
Altamira-Xingu River Complex and,
203–204
Central Plateau of, 201
Declaration of Belem and, 114–115
deforestation and, 201–207
Kayapo and, xx, 199, 201–207
merchandising nature and, 256
Sarney and, 204
Brazil nuts, xxv
Bribri, 195
Bridal Veil Falls, 4
Bridgeport Tom, 14
Bristol Myers Squibb, 219
British Columbia, xvii–xviii
Brockington, Dan, 7, 17, 21, 32
Brody, Hugh, 89
Bronx Zoo, 51, 72
Buddhism, 103, 121
Buenos Aires Biodiversity
Convention, 70
Buffalo, 39, 67, 223
Bunderra, Allambie, 117
Bunnell, Lafayette, 2–4, 8, 264

evictions of, 26, 29–33, 256
Grzimek and, 23–26, 30, 41
human-wildlife conflict and, 40
hygiene and, 25
Kenya Land Commission and,
   185–186
laibon and, 28
Leakey on, 25–26
marriage customs of, 27–28
Mau Forest and, 184
Mkomazi and, 30–34, 42
Ngorongoro and, 26, 29–30
power structure of, 28
religion and, 28
Saning'o and, xv–xvi, xxvi, 40–41,
   47, 268
social structure of, 27–28
Soltani and, 35–36
symbiosis and, 40
territorial rights and, 26
tourism and, 27
Maasailand, xv, 27
Maasai Mara Reserve, 11, 26,
   255–256
Maasai Park, 38
Maathai, Wangari, 186
McArthur Foundation, xxiii, 217
McCormick, Stephen, 60, 62
McDonald's, 55
McKay, Peter, 216–217
MacNamara, Robert, 50
McShane, Thomas, xxiv, 30, 57
Madhupar Eco Park, 257
Madhya Pradesh, 119, 125–126
Madre de Dios, 79
Madrigal, Liliana, 48
Mago National Park, 224
Mahogany trees, 136–137
Malas, Jakob, 19, 148
Malawi, 226
Malaysia, 137, 151, 156, 171, 175
Mallot, Byron, 235
Man and Nature (Marsh), 16, 133
Mandela, Nelson, xviii–xix
Manifest destiny, 5, 264
Manu National Park, 79–82

Mapping, xxix, 26
Batwa and, 67
bias and, 193, 198–199
credibility and, 198–199
culture and, 194–195
currents and, 193
data correlations in, 263–265
deforestation and, 193
erosion and, 193
European colonialism and, 194
forest density and, 193
Geographic Information Systems
   (GIS) technologies and, 194–197
Global 200 project and, 263–264
global positioning satellite (GPS)
   receivers and, 192, 205
Kayapo and, 204
legal issues and, 194
logging and, 196–199
migratory routes and, 193
mining and, 194–199
Native Lands and, 196
negative consequences of, 198
Ogiek and, 188–189
participatory, 196–197
pollution and, 193
Poole and, 191–195, 199
power from, 191–198
protest and, 157, 166–167
as science of princes, 193
South American shorelines and, 195
species distribution and, 193
tenure, 194–195
Maribe, Clifford, 146–147
Marine Protected Areas (MPA), 216
Mariposa County, 2–3
Mariposa Grove, 5, 8–9
Mariposa Battalion, 2
Market solutions, xxv–xxviii
culinary, 214
merchandising nature and, 254–257
Marriage customs, 27–28
Marsh, George Perkins, 16, 133, 264
Martin, Claude, 273
Martin, Vance, 177–179
Marxism, 88

Salmon, Enrique, 20–21
Sambaa, 31
San, 140, 196–197. *See also* Basarwa
Sanderson, Steven, xix, 80–84,
   265–266
Saning'o, Martin, xv–xvi, xxvi, 40–
   41, 47, 268
Santal, Kanhu, 128
Santals, 121
Sarah Lawrence College, 238
Sarawak, 137
Sariska, 129–130
Sarney, 204
Sarstoon River, 191
Sarstoon-Temash National Park, 136,
   192, 199
Satan, 3
Savage, James, 2, 8
Savannahs, xv, 263
   Amboseli, 37–41
   disturbances and, 135
   Maasai and, 26–27, 37, 39
   protests and, 153
   Pygmies and, 65
Savory, Allan, 135
Schaller, George, 41
Scheduled Tribes and Other
   Traditional Forest
   Dwellers Bill, The, 127
Schindler, Paul, 141
Schmidt-Soltau, Kai, 253–254
S. C. Johnson Co., 210
Scoones, Ian, 134–135
Scott, Colin, 116
Scott Polar Research Institute, 89
Seacology, 241
Sea cucumbers, 214–215, 218
Second Continental Summit of
   Indigenous Peoples and
   Nationalities, 177
Seligmann, Peter, 48, 55, 178
   anthropologists' warnings and,
      214–215
   cargo mentality and, 213–214, 218,
      220
   exclusionary policies and, 95

fundraising and, 210
leaked field reports and, 60–61
luxury lifestyle of, 209–212, 214
Milne Bay and, 209–213
public relations fight by, 213
yacht trip of, 209–212, 214
Semantics, xi, xxi–xxiii
   Ba (people), 65
   biodiversity, 19
   collaboration buzzwords and,
      167–168
   Community Conservation Areas
      (CCAs), 236
   defining national park, 13
   evictions, 74
   First People, 142
   indigenous stewardship area, 192
   nature, 15–22
   nonrecognition of First People,
      142–146
   place names, 12
   protected areas (PAs), 236
   Pygmy, 65
   tabula rasa, 18
   traditional ecological knowledge
      (TEK), 108
   wilderness, xxviii, 15–16, 19–20,
      253
Senama, 89
Senate Appropriations Committee,
   204
Sengwer, 197
Serengeti, xv, 11–13
   debate over use of, 26
   disturbances and, 134
   evictions and, 26
   Grzimek and, 23–26, 30, 41
   inhabitation of, 24–25
   Mkomazi and, 30–34, 42
   Ngorongoro and, 26, 29–30
Serengeti Shall not Die (Grzimek), 25
Sesana, Roy, 142–143, 146–151
Sex, 28, 71
Shamba, 27
Shark fins, 214–215
Sheep, 5–8, 35, 37, 113, 185